UNIX
Programming
Tools

UNIX Programming Tools

Eric Foster-Johnson

 **M&T Books**
A Division of MIS:Press, Inc.
A Subsidiary of Henry Holt and Company, Inc.
115 West 18th Street
New York, New York 10011
http://www.mispress.com

Limits of Liability and Disclaimer of Warranty

First Edition—1997

```
Johnson, Eric F.
   UNIX programming tools / by Eric Foster-Johnson.
      p.   cm.
   ISBN 1-55851-482-1
   1. UNIX (Computer file)  2. Operating systems (Computers)
 I. Title
 QA76.76.063J627  1997
 005.2'82--dc21                                      96-30089
                                                          CIP
```

10 9 8 7 6 5 4 3 2 1

Associate Publisher: *Paul Farrell*

Executive Editor: *Cary Sullivan*   **Editor:** *Laura Lewin*

Technical Editor: *Kevin Reichard*   **Copy Edit Manager:** *Shari Chappell*

Production Editor: *Maya Riddick*

Dedication

To Norma, and many years together

CONTENTS-IN-BRIEF

CONTENTS

SECTION 1 • BUILDING PROGRAMS

Contents

x

Contents

Contents

SECTION 2 • MAINTAINING YOUR PROGRAMS

Contents

SECTION 3 • DOCUMENTING YOUR WORK

Contents

INTRODUCTION

UNIX Programming Tools

Welcome to *UNIX Programming Tools*. Whether you're new to UNIX or are a hard-core UNIX developer, I think you'll find a lot of useful tips and techniques in this book. Within this book, you'll find out how to create software on UNIX and discover the many tools available to help speed your work.

Most programming books cover just the semantics of the C and C++ programming languages, leaving it to the developer—you—to figure out the UNIX environment. You're left trying to get your programs to compile, starting the debugger, and building libraries, all of which are quite different on UNIX from on other operating systems, such as Windows or Macintosh.

This book covers everything *but* programming. It covers how to compile, link, install, debug, maintain, and document your programs on UNIX. There are plenty of programming books devoted to showing the ins and outs of C, C++, Java, Perl, Tcl, and every other programming language. The problem with most programming books, however, is that they don't show how to actually make things run on your system. Few C or C++ programming books, for example, show how to compile or build a library on UNIX. If these books do show how to compile, chances are the discussion sticks to one vendor's compiler on Windows 95.

This book focuses on how to get things done on UNIX. It aids software developers by covering all the nitty-gritty details for creating—and maintaining—working programs in the UNIX environment.

One of the first things you'll notice is that most UNIX systems don't provide integrated development environments like Microsoft's or Borland's offerings. (Actually, you can purchase such environments, usually tied to a specific architecture, such as Sun's Solaris on SPARC workstations, but few developers seem to have these integrated development environments in daily use.)

2

Instead, the UNIX philosophy favors small tools that, when put together, present a whole environment. Thus, UNIX systems tend to contain many small, separate software tools, such as compilers, linkers, debuggers, and source formatters. Among these small utilities, you'll find some gems that will prove essential for your day-to-day programming tasks.

I like this philosophy, because I can pick and choose which tools will help me get the job done. There's no one right way to do things under UNIX, and you have a far-ranging toolbox to help you. Due to the wide variety of tools, though, newcomers tend to find UNIX daunting. Don't worry. In short order, you'll be wondering why Microsoft implemented its operating systems the way it did, after the many years of experience already available in the UNIX community. This is not to say that UNIX is perfect—in fact, it suffers from severe problems.

Throughout this book, I take a very practical approach. If something works in a brain-dead fashion, I won't hesitate to say so. And, with the varied history of many UNIX tools, you'll find a number of brain-dead tools and systems. You'll also find some of the most elegant systems for developing software.

To cover programming tools on UNIX, I divided this book into three sections to tackle the tasks of building programs, maintaining software, and finally documenting your work. For each step, UNIX provides a huge number of useful tools—some as a standard part of UNIX distributions and some as freeware available on the CD-ROM that accompanies this book. I've tried to include a wide variety of tools. From the text, you should be able to determine whether or not a particular tool will help your work. After all, these tools are intended to make your work easier and quicker and to provide higher quality. Talk about buzzwords!

Conventions Used In This Book

To help you get more out of this book, I've followed some formatting conventions to make it easier to find what you need, including the following icons:

CROSS-PLATFORM

One of the banes of the UNIX world is that there are far too many flavors of UNIX, each of which differs slightly. These versions are close enough to fool you into thinking they are the same, but different enough to cause problems. This icon identifies areas that help with differences in UNIX flavors, as well as differences between major platforms like Windows and Macintosh systems.

The Note icon indicates something that demands special attention.

The Warning icon warns about actions that could be hazardous to your software.

The CD-ROM icon refers to items found on the CD-ROM that accompanies this book.

Within the text, the following special formatting conventions should help you decode what are commands and what aren't:

- **Bold** type refers to a file on disk, a directory, or a UNIX command (commands are files in UNIX).
- *Italic* type refers to new concepts and provides special emphasis.
- Monospaced type refers to commands you'll type at the keyboard, program output directly from the screen, and program source code. Many of the keyboard examples list the UNIX command-line prompt, by default a dollar sign, $. For example:

```
$ rcsmerge -r1.7 -r1.7.1.5 -p filename.c > combined_file
```

In this example, you should not type in the $ prompt.

Contacting the Author

The best way to contact me is through my Web page on the Internet, at *http://ourworld.compuserve.com/homepages/efjohnson*, where you'll also find more information on my favorite UNIX applications, especially tools that help in creating applications.

SECTION 1

Building Programs

This section introduces the UNIX environment from the point of view of programmers. It shows how to make effective use of UNIX tools for building programs, making them run, and delivering them to the end users.

Chapter 1 introduces many of the concepts of UNIX and explains how these concepts apply to the task of building programs. If you're already familiar with UNIX, you can skip ahead to Chapter 2.

Chapter 2 starts the main topic of this book: how to compile, link, and run programs using a variety of programming and scripting languages. Chapter 2 covers UNIX tools for compiling, linking, and running C and C++ programs; building libraries of functions with **ar**; compiling and executing Java programs with the Java Developer's Kit; and executing Perl and Tcl scripts.

Chapter 3 shows how to automate the software building process using a handy program called **make**. This chapter delves into some **make** extensions provided by GNU **make**—which is included on the CD-ROM—and what to watch out for when creating portable Makefiles.

Because all programs on UNIX start out as source code in text files, Chapter 4 introduces the most common text editors on UNIX: **vi** and **emacs**. In addition to these workhorse editors, Chapter 4 discusses a number of alternatives, including **nedit**, one of the best graphical text editors, and **xcoral**, which provides built-in support for browsing C and C++ programs.

Chapter 5 covers even more UNIX tools for working with text files, including **grep**, the strangely named program that becomes part of every UNIX developer's arsenal. Other tools discussed include **find**, **ctags**, and **etags** for calling up text editors where a given function is defined, using strings on binary files, and even the lowly **wc** program.

Chapter 6 shows how to install your software. There are a number of UNIX utilities that help pack, unpack, and install your programs into the proper locations. Chapter 6 covers a host of these tools, including **tar**, **shar**, **compress**, **gzip** and **install**.

CHAPTER 1

Getting Used to UNIX

This chapter covers:

- A brief run-down on UNIX
- The UNIX environment
- The UNIX command shell
- Getting help on UNIX
- Working with the shell
- The UNIX file system and how to find things on disk
- Working with files
- Multitasking on UNIX
- UNIX graphics: the X Window System
- The Common Desktop Environment

UNIX—Argh!

8

If you're new to UNIX, you'll find this operating system takes a lot of getting used to before you feel productive. Especially if you're coming over to UNIX from the Macintosh or Windows world, you'll soon discover that UNIX is a lot more command-driven and a lot less graphical than those systems. What you'll also discover is the rich programming history that led to the creation of UNIX. UNIX has always been—first and foremost—a system for programmers.

This chapter introduces the UNIX environment for programmers, delving into many handy UNIX commands. You'll find a lot about what UNIX is like and how to get it to do what you want, from navigating the file system to where to find files.

If you already feel comfortable with UNIX, skip ahead to Chapter 2. If you're not used to UNIX, then this chapter should help a lot.

The UNIX Environment

From the user's perspective, UNIX environments tend to share some characteristics that differ from Windows and Macintosh systems, including:

- UNIX is command-driven.
- Multiple command windows dominate the screen.
- Many applications run at the same time.
- The X Window System provides graphics.

UNIX is Command-Driven

Most of the time you spend on UNIX will be using a shell, or command line, often in a shell window, such as **xterm**, **dtterm**, or **winterm**, all of which mimic old DEC VT102 terminals. The most common of these shell windows, **xterm**, appears in Figure 1.1.

Figure 1.1 The **xterm** command shell window.

When using any shell, from a window like that shown in Figure 1.1 or from the UNIX console, you'll see a shell prompt.

The Shell

A *shell* in UNIX parlance is a command-line interpreter. Unlike Windows though, UNIX frees you to choose the shell program you want to run (instead of **command.com**). The most common shells are **sh**, the Bourne shell, **csh**, the C shell (popular with many programmers), **ksh**, the newer Korn shell, and **bash**, the Born Again shell, a freeware enhancement to **sh**. Each shell provides a different means to customize the shell environment and each shell includes slightly different commands, mostly for writing *shell scripts*—files of shell and UNIX commands that you can execute from a UNIX shell.

Even so, the differences between the UNIX shells are minor. All shells support the full range of UNIX commands.

Compared with MS-DOS, most UNIX commands tend to be terse. Some of the more common commands, and their DOS equivalents, are listed in Table 1.1.

Table 1.1 UNIX and DOS Commands Side by Side

DOS Command	UNIX Command	Usage
CD	cd	Change current directory
CHDIR	cd	Change current directory
CLS	clear	Clear terminal window
COPY	cp	Copy files
DATE	date	Get and set date
DEL	rm	Delete files
DIR	ls	List files in a directory
DOSKEY	history	List and select previous commands
ECHO	echo	Print message to screen
EXIT	exit	Quit command shell
MKDIR	mkdir	Create directory
MODE	stty	Change terminal settings
MORE	more, less	Display file one page at a time
MOVE	mv	Move, or rename files
REM	#	Comment in batch file
RENAME	mv	Rename files
RMDIR	rmdir	Remove directory
TIME	date	Get and set time
TYPE	cat	Display file
UNDELETE	None	Watch out!

NOTE MS-DOS is not case-sensitive, so *COPY*, *cOpY*, and *Copy* are all the same command. UNIX, however, is rigid about case; the UNIX command is **cp**, *not CP or Cp.*

Each shell presents a command prompt, where you can enter your UNIX commands. The default prompt for **sh** is $ and for **csh**, it is %, but each shell offers a way to change the default prompt.

Getting Help

One of the most useful UNIX commands, **man**, displays entries from the extensive array of UNIX online documentation. You'll find the format somewhat terse, but the **man** command is essential for all UNIX programming. Each entry lists the command or function call, the command-line parameters, or options, and a brief description. Here's the first screenful of the manual entry on the **man** command itself:

```
man(1)                          man(1)


NAME
     man - format and display the on-line manual pages
     manpath - determine user's search path for man pages

SYNOPSIS
     man   [-adfhktwW]      [-m system] [-p string]
          [-C config_file] [-M path] [-P pager]
          [-S section_list] [section] name  ...

DESCRIPTION
   man   formats  and displays the on-line manual pages. This
   version knows about the MANPATH and  PAGER  environment
   variables, so you can have your own set(s) of personal man
   pages and choose whatever program you like to display the
   formatted  pages.  If section is specified, man only looks
   in that section of the manual.  You may also  specify the
   order to search the sections for entries and which prepro-
```

The descriptions for some commands tend to be more terse than others.

You'll also find copious online documentation on just about every programming API, as shown here in the (highly edited) manual entry for the C fopen function:

```
FOPEN(3)


NAME
  fopen, fdopen, freopen - stream open functions


SYNOPSIS
  #include <stdio.h>


  FILE *fopen( char *path, char *mode);
  FILE *fdopen( int fildes, char *mode);
  FILE *freopen( char *path, char *mode, FILE *stream);


DESCRIPTION
  The fopen function opens the file whose name is the string
  pointed to by path and associates a stream with it.


  The argument mode points to a string beginning with one of
  the  following sequences (Additional characters may follow
  these sequences.):


  r   Open text file for reading. The stream      is
      positioned at the beginning of the file.


RETURN VALUES
  Upon successful completion fopen, fdopen and freopen
  return a FILE pointer. Otherwise, NULL is returned and
  the global variable errno is set to indicate the error.


ERRORS
  EINVAL The  mode provided to fopen, fdopen, or freopen was
  invalid.
```

```
The fopen, fdopen and freopen functions may also fail  and
set  errno for any of the errors specified for the routine
malloc(3).

The fopen function may also fail and set errno for any  of
the errors specified for the routine open(2).
```

```
SEE ALSO
  open(2), fclose(3)
```

One of the trickiest parts of using the **man** command is finding out what command to call up in the first place. The SEE ALSO section is very useful for this task.

The SEE ALSO entries for the fopen function list numbers in parenthesis, such as open(2), fclose(3). These numbers refer to the major sections (originally chapters) of the UNIX manual. There is often more than one entry for the same name, especially common names like open (there is also a Tcl command called open, for example). To get the entry you really want, you can pass the section number to **man** like this:
```
$ man 2 open
```

Some UNIX systems require a slightly different syntax to reference other sections of the online manual. See the manual entry for the **man** command for more information. (Yes, this is a not-so-subtle attempt to convince you to use the **man** command.)

Finding the Proper Manual Entry

Each UNIX command and API call is documented in the online manuals, but there's no table of contents and no index. This remains one of the main problems with finding information from UNIX. While there's a huge amount of online material, it's nearly impossible to sort it all out. To help with this, many UNIX systems (unfortunately, not all) provide two handy commands: **apropos** and **whatis**.

The **apropos** command returns information about a keyword you provide. For example, to get information about the keyword *shell* (a very important concept in UNIX), you'd use a command like the following:

```
$ apropos shell
```

The **apropos** command, if set up on your system, returns data like the following:

```
ash (1)                          - a shell
bash (1)                         - GNU Bourne-Again SHell
chsh (1)                         - change your login shell
dialog (1)                       - display dialog boxes from shell scripts
getusershell, setusershell, endusershell (3)
                                 - get legal user shells
mc (1)                           - Visual shell for UNIX-like systems.
mkmanifest (1)                   - create a shell script to restore
                                   UNIX filenames
rsh remote shell (1) -
shar (1)                         - create shell archives
shells (5)                       - pathnames of valid login shells
shlock (1)                       - create lock files for use in
                                   shell scripts
splitvt (1)                      - run two shells in a split window
su (1)                           - run a shell with substitute user
                                   and group IDs
system (3)                       - execute a shell command
tclsh (1)                        - Simple shell containing
                                   Tcl interpreter
tcsh (1)                         - C shell with file name completion
                                   and command line editing
wildmat (3)                      - perform shell-style wildcard matching
wish (1)                         - Simple windowing shell
zsh (1)                          - the Z shell
shelltool (1x)                   - run a shell (or other program) in
                                   an OpenWindows terminal window
```

As you can see, **apropos** provides a valuable tool for finding the right manual entry to call up.

The **whatis** command presents a one-line summary for the manual entries for a given command. For example:

```
$ whatis man
man (1)          - format and display the on-line
                   manual pages
manpath          - determine user's search path for
                   man pages
man (7)          - macros to format man pages
man.config (5) - configuration data for man
```

xman—Not a Comic Superhero

In addition to **apropos** and **whatis**, two commands that are unfortunately not available on all UNIX systems, you'll find the **xman** command very useful. **xman** is an X Window (hence graphical) viewer for online manual entries, as shown in Figure 1.2.

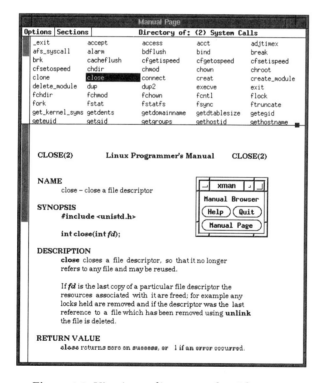

Figure 1.2 Viewing online manuals with **xman**.

The **doc_tool/man** directory on the CD-ROM contains the source code for **xman**.

With the advent of Web browsers and handy Internet Web pages, the old UNIX problem of lots of information and poor organization is getting better. You can find many helpful hints and information on UNIX on the Internet. See Appendix A for some of the most useful sites.

Working with the Shell

UNIX shells provide a lot more capability than the MS-DOS prompt under Windows. To start with, you can redirect the input and output of most commands. For example, the following command redirects the output of the **man** command with the entry on fopen to the file **info.txt**:

```
$ man fopen > info.txt
```

The greater-than sign redirects the output of a command into a file. If the file **info.txt** already exists, its previous contents will be wiped out and replaced by the output of the man fopen command.

If you don't want the previous contents of the file to be wiped out, you can use two greater-than signs (>>) instead of one:

```
$ man fopen >> info.txt
```

This says to append the data onto the end of the file **info.txt**.

The less-than sign, <, similarly redirects the input for a command to come from a file:

```
$ cat < input.data
```

This command redirects all the input for the **cat** command to come from the file **input.data**. (The **cat** command concatenates files to the screen.)

NOTE UNIX generally allows you to create very long file names. You can have as many periods as you like, but no spaces. Certain other characters should also be avoided, such as: ! ` $<>/?" | ' ~*. You also do not want to name any file ., .., or start the file name with a hyphen (-).

You can combine the two forms and redirect both input and output:

```
$ cat < input.data > ouput.data
```

Pipes

You can extend input and output redirection with the concept of pipes. A *pipe* is a data channel, maintained by the shell, that sends the output of one command to be the input of another command. For example, the following command sends the output of **cat** to be the input of **sort**, and the output of the **sort** command is then sent as the input to the **more** command:

```
$ cat input.data | sort | more
```

This command copies the file **input.data** (normally to the screen, but in this case redirected into the pipeline) to the **sort** command, which sorts the data. Finally, the sorted data is sent to the **more** command, so that you can view the data one screenful at a time.

Wildcards

While DOS shells support some form of wildcards, like ***.txt**, UNIX shells perform much better. The basic wild card, ***.txt**, matches all files in the current directory that end in **.txt**. For example:

```
$ ls *.txt
a.txt        betty.txt   f.txt       fritz.txt
albert.txt   eric.txt    fred.txt    kevin.txt
```

You can extend this to **f*.txt** to match only those files that start with a lowercase *f* and then end in **.txt**:

```
$ ls f*.txt
f.txt        fred.txt     fritz.txt
```

You can further extend this to see all files that start with the letter *f* and then have any number of characters (*), and end with **z.txt**:

```
$ ls f*z.txt
fritz.txt
```

While wildcards work on DOS, too, this kind of wildcard works only on UNIX; DOS fails at this wildcard.

A question mark character, ?, matches any one character. For example, the following command matches any file that has any character—but only one character—and then **.txt**:

```
$ ls ?.txt
a.txt   f.txt
```

There's even more you can do with wildcards, which you can find out from the online manual entries for the shell you use, such as **csh** or **ksh**.

The most common UNIX shells—**bash**, **csh**, and **ksh**—also provide a history of previous commands, which you can recall and execute without typing the whole command. These shells provide *aliases*, which allow you to create new commands that are aliases for other commands.

This means you can type in **dir**, but your shell converts your command into ls -l, which produces output similar to the DOS **dir** command. For example, you may want to alias **dir** to be the same as ls -l.

bash already supports **dir** as a built-in command.

In the C shell, **csh**, the following command aliases **dir** to ls -l:

```
% alias dir  ls -l
```

The File System

Files are the basic building blocks on UNIX. More than any other operating system, UNIX uses files for virtually all configuration data, and it even goes so far as to represent devices, such as tape drives, serial ports, and printers, as files.

The first basic rule to remember is that UNIX uses a forward slash (/) to separate directory names, rather than the DOS backslash (\) or the Macintosh colon (:).

In addition, there are no drive letters, like **A:** or **C:**. All UNIX disk drives are mounted under the root directory hierarchy, represented by /. The idea is to present a single directory hierarchy of all files accessible by the UNIX system, blurring the distinction between different disk drives and logical partitions. (To better see what drives are available on your system, use the **df** command.)

Where Things Are

While there are some variations, most UNIX systems place files in standard locations, making it easy for you to work on any UNIX variant. Starting from the root directory, /, UNIX follows the conventions shown in Table 1.2.

Table 1.2 UNIX File System Conventions

Directory	Usage
/bin	UNIX commands (read as binary)
/dev	Files that represent physical devices
/etc	Configuration files, especially for networking
/lib	Libraries of software modules for C programmers
/tmp	Temporary files
/usr	Programming files and user information

Originally, **/usr** was for all user accounts and information. But over the years, **/usr** has become the main repository for programming tools, files, and libraries.

Table 1.3 lists some of the common locations important to software developers.

Table 1.3 Where UNIX Stores Important Files

Directory	Usage
/usr/include	Include files for C and C++ programming
/lib, /usr/lib	Libraries for C and C++ programming
/usr/man	Online manual files
/bin, /usr/bin	UNIX commands.

To separate UNIX system files from files you (or your system administrator) place on the system, **/usr/local** exists for locally produced files, as shown in Table 1.4.

Table 1.4 Locations of Locally Produced Files

Directory	Usage
/usr/local/bin	Local commands
/usr/local/include	Local include files for C programming
/usr/local/lib	Local C libraries
/usr/local/man	Local online manuals

Many popular UNIX commands, such as the **emacs** text editor covered in Chapter 4, exist only as freeware and are not shipped with the UNIX system. Most such programs, which you can get over the Internet or on the CD-ROM that accompanies this book, get installed in **/usr/local**. The main reason for this is that it provides a safe area to prevent UNIX upgrades from messing with your programs.

As always, however, your system administrator decides where everything goes.

Home Directories

When you log on to a UNIX system, UNIX makes your home directory the starting location from which you work. This is the place in the complex UNIX directory hierarchy that you can call your own. You can place your files here and create your programs here. On UNIX, most home directories for users start with the user name as the directory name. Usually, these home directories get placed under **/home**, **/users**, or **/usr**. For example, with a user name of *erc*, my home directory is **/home/erc** on Linux.

Listing Files

The **ls** command (short for *list*) forms the primary way to list file names on UNIX. In its basic format, **ls** merely lists the files—in sorted order—in the current directory. But, you can use options to **ls** to list files in different orders—very useful for finding old code files—or with extra information.

The **ls** command with the **-l** option, mentioned earlier, provides a long list of files, with file owners, last modification date, and size among the information presented:

```
$ ls -l /usr/doc/vim

drwxr-xr-x  2 root root    1024 Aug 14 19:03 ./
drwxr-xr-x 79 root root    2048 Aug 14 19:16 ../
-rw-r-r-  1 root root    2187 Aug 14  1994 README
-rw-r-r-  1 root root    1866 Aug  9  1994 archie.doc
-rw-r-r-  1 root root   20566 Aug 10  1994 difference.doc
-rw-r-r-  1 root root    2230 Aug  9  1994 digraph.doc
-rw-r-r-  1 root root   12449 Aug 10  1994 index
-rw-r-r-  1 root root  210836 Aug 14  1994 reference.doc
-rw-r-r-  1 root root    3078 Apr 15  1994 uganda.txt
-rw-r-r-  1 root root     796 Aug 10  1994 unix.doc
-rw-r-r-  1 root root     238 Apr 15  1994 vim132
-rw-r-r-  1 root root   15407 Aug 12  1994 windows.doc
```

The **ls -t** command lists files by the time saved:

```
$ ls -t /usr/doc/vim
README          windows.doc    unix.doc        digraph.doc    uganda.txt
reference.doc   index          difference.doc  archie.doc     vim132
```

The wide list, though, may not make it apparent the order of the files. The **-1** (that's one, not ell) option to **ls** specifies only one column of output data, as shown here with the **-t** option:

```
$ ls -t1 /usr/doc/vim
README
reference.doc
windows.doc
index
unix.doc
difference.doc
digraph.doc
archie.doc
uganda.txt
vim132
```

The **ls -u** command lists files in order of most recent access:

```
$ ls -u1 /usr/doc/vim
README
archie.doc
difference.doc
digraph.doc
index
reference.doc
uganda.txt
unix.doc
vim132
windows.doc
```

The **-r** option reverses the order. You can combine this with other options to list files in reverse access times, for example:

```
$ ls -url /usr/doc/vim
windows.doc
vim132
unix.doc
uganda.txt
reference.doc
index
digraph.doc
difference.doc
archie.doc
README
```

Removing Files

The **rm** command deletes files—permanently. The syntax is as follows:

```
$ rm filename
```

WARNING

The **rm** command really deletes the file. And there's no undelete, so watch out.

You can run **rm** in interactive mode with the **-i** option. This forces you to confirm each file to be deleted; this is such a handy thing that I alias (see the earlier section on shells) the **rm** command to be the same as **rm -i**, so I always have to confirm file deletion.

Similar to **rm**, the **rmdir** command deletes a directory:

```
$ rmdir directoryname
```

Multitasking on UNIX

In addition to being able to select your own command shells, UNIX differs from Windows and Macintosh systems in the sheer number of processes running at the same time. Most modern operating systems provide the ability to run more than one task at a time, but UNIX takes far more advantage of this than most systems.

With UNIX, the entire operating system is broken down into many concurrent processes. There's still a large central process—called the *kernel*—that controls the whole system, but most services run as separate processes.

With the **ps** command, you can see all the processes running on your system. Depending on your version of UNIX, try either **ps -ef** or **ps -aux** (one or the other will likely error out). This should give you an idea of the large number of processes a normal UNIX system runs, just when idling.

Combined with this model of running many processes at the same time, UNIX was built on the idea of having many small tools, each of which performs a single task. You can then use the shell and pipes (described earlier) to combine the various small tools to get your job done.

This means fewer tools are integrated. Most UNIX software comes in the building block variety. In contrast, on most Windows or Macintosh systems, integrated software dominates. While you can purchase integrated software development environments, few environments span the various flavors of UNIX. This means that no matter what, you need to know some of the basic UNIX commands necessary for software development.

Processes

With the **ps** command, you can see the many processes UNIX executes, even in a workstation at rest. You can use the **kill** command to kill the process:

```
$ kill -9 process_id
```

The process ID is the ID number of the process you want to kill. You can get this ID number from the output of the **ps** command, which lists processes and includes both the ID number and command line that launched the process. With this information, you can usually figure out which process you want to kill.

What the **kill** command actually does is send a signal to the process. In the preceding example, the signal sent is 9 (called *SIGKILL*). When a process receives a signal, the signal handler function for that particular signal is invoked. If no signal handler was registered, then the default process signal handler makes the process commit suicide. This is a round-about way of allowing **kill** to kill processes.

Running Processes in the Background

To run a process in the background so that it no longer takes up your shell prompt, use an ampersand character, **&**, at the end of the command line. For example, to run the **xman** process in the background (with graphical programs, you normally want to do this), you can use the following command:

```
$ xman &
```

 NOTE Some versions of UNIX kill any process that you run in the background that prints data to the screen. If your UNIX version does this (HP-UX on Hewlett-Packard systems is one of the most common systems that do this), then you'll often see a cryptic error message like the following:

```
stopped (tty output)
```

This means that UNIX killed your background process, whether or not you like it.

cron and Batch Processes

cron, combined with **tar** (see Chapter 6), is very useful for making daily tape backups. **cron** executes programs at a particular time or times, such as 3:00 A.M. every day. What you do is store the instructions for **cron** in what is called a *crontab* file. These instructions then tell **cron** what to execute and when to do it, such as every day at 2:00 A.M., the first of the month, every Wednesday at noon, and so on.

To work with **cron**, you need to create a crontab file and then use the **crontab** command to copy this file into the system **cron** directory, usually **/usr/lib/crontab** or **/usr/spool/cron/crontabs** (see the online manual entries for **cron** and **crontab** for more on this).

A crontab file is simply a specially formatted text file, which you can create with any text editor. Each line describes a command to invoke at a particular time. To do this, each line has six fields, separated by spaces. The first five fields control the time, the last is the command.

Let's say that we wanted to run a command every day at 3:15 a.m. The structure of the crontab line looks something like this:

```
15 3 * * * command
```

The command is any command you want executed. Normally, this is some form of command for backing up files.

The asterisks mean that anything in a given field matches. The exact values associated with the five fields are listed in Table 1.5.

Table 1.5 Fields in a crontab Line

Field	Meaning
1	Minutes after the hour
2	Hour, in 24-hour format
3	Day of the month
4	Month
5	Day of the week

Days of the week start at 0 (Sunday) and go to 6 (Saturday). C programmers are already familiar with this method of counting from 0. The time of day is specified in 24-hour time.

After creating our crontab file (which must be saved under a file name of anything but crontab; we'll call it **daily.backup**), we can then install it, using the **crontab** command:

```
$ crontab daily.backup
```

This copies your file **daily.backup** into the proper **cron** directory. See the manual pages on **cron** and **crontab** for more on this.

On some systems, only administrators with super user privileges are allowed to use **cron**.

NOTE

UNIX Graphics: The X Window System

The X Window System is a network-transparent windowing system. That means X provides the neat ability to run an application on one machine and display the windows on another. This is very handy for testing your applications on a variety of UNIX workstations, without getting up from your seat.

A very strange part about this is the terminology. In X, the *server* is the program that owns the desktop. The X server draws the dots on the screen, reads the mouse, and handles keyboard input. A *client* is simply a graphical application. The client connects to the server to create windows and draw data to the screen. When you create X programs, what you're really creating is X client applications.

Because X can run over a network, a client can compute on any system on your network. The server is the machine in front of you at your desk. This usage is reversed from standard database terminology, where the server is the big machine somewhere on the network and the client resides on your desktop.

Programming Graphical Applications

Unlike most other windowing systems, such as Windows and Macintosh, X itself provides no inherent look and feel. Instead, each application provides its own look and feel. Because creating a programming toolkit with any sort of decent look and feel tends to be difficult, most X applications use the Motif look and feel, supported by the Motif programming API.

X layers programming APIs on top of each other. Each layer builds on the layers beneath it. At the bottom layer lies a set of low-level programming APIs, called the *X library* or *Xlib*. Above Xlib comes a higher-level abstraction layer called the *X Toolkit Intrinsics*, or *Xt* for short. On top of Xt comes particular look and feel libraries, such as Motif, the de facto standard toolkit for graphical applications on UNIX. In virtually all cases, Motif programs need to call functions in the Motif, X Toolkit, and X libraries.

NOTE

Motif is more than a set of programming APIs, which tends to confuse matters. First, there's the Motif window manager, a program that creates the title bars you see on the windows on your display. Yes, UNIX and the X Window System free you up to allow any window manager you desire, although most create title bars that look like those shown in Figure 1.3 (in a moment). If you're used to Windows or Macintosh systems, you know that the windowing system controls all the window title bars and presents a common look and feel. X separates the windowing system (X) from the window manager, a completely separate program. This allows you a lot of flexibility, but it also adds confusion.

In addition to the Motif window manager and programming API, Motif provides a style guide for applications. This style guide is very similar to the Windows and OS/2 Presentation Manager guidelines.

The best thing about X has always been that it was the first standard windowing system for UNIX workstations. While not limited to UNIX, X has been most popular on that operating system. X also runs on a variety of other platforms, including DOS, Windows, and the Macintosh. For UNIX programmers, it's important to note that if you create any sort of graphic interface on UNIX, chances are very high that you're using one of the X Window System programming APIs discussed in the next chapter.

Surprisingly, X is free, and the source code is available over the Internet from the X Consortium. (See Appendix A for more on this.)

The Common Desktop Environment

Most commercial UNIX systems from Sun, Hewlett-Packard, IBM, and others now sport what is called the *Common Desktop Environment*, or CDE.

This environment, built with the Motif programming APIs, provides a set of productivity applications, including a calendar, text editor, and file manager (the type of thing you'd take for granted on Windows and Macintosh systems). A typical CDE screen appears in Figure 1.3.

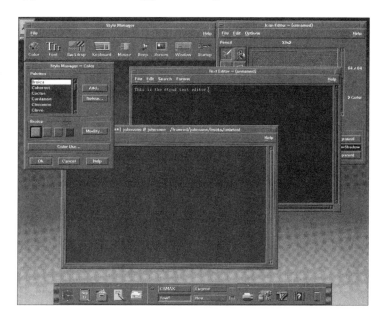

Figure 1.3 A typical UNIX screen under CDE.

If your UNIX vendor doesn't provide the CDE, your screen can still include a number of useful applications, as shown in the Linux screen in Figure 1.4. Linux is the most popular freeware version of UNIX, and it runs mainly on Intel-compatible machines.

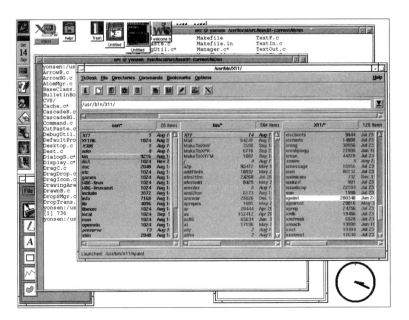

Figure 1.4 A typical screen under Linux.

Note how on both typical UNIX screens, the main application running is a command, or shell window—very similar to the MS-DOS prompt under Windows. That's because UNIX is a lot more command-driven than most other desktop operating systems.

xterm

Wrapped around the shell, in a graphical environment, lies **xterm**, which manages the interface to the X Window System, so that all the old UNIX text-based programs (UNIX has been around since before 1970), including the **vi** text editor or the **elm** mailer, work fine inside an **xterm** window.

Unlike a DEC VT102 terminal, though, you can customize the fonts, colors, and number of lines displayed in any **xterm** window. This is very handy for displaying large amounts of source code on a 19-inch monitor. Furthermore, **xterm** provides a form of mouse-driven copy and paste—even if the underlying text-based application doesn't support a mouse—so you can exchange data between **xterm** windows.

Summary

This chapter introduced a number of UNIX concepts and commands that are important for the software developer.

The **man** command displays entries from the online manuals. Thus, **man** is one of the most useful UNIX commands you'll ever need. In addition to **man**, **apropos** and **whatis** both provide some context information to help you decide which commands to look up with **man**.

The **xman** program presents a graphical interface to man, making it easier to look up entries from the online manuals.

The **ls** command lists files in a directory. The **rm** command removes—deletes—files. Watch out, there is no undelete that comes standard with UNIX.

The X Window System provides graphics on UNIX and allows you to view more than one program at the same time.

UNIX Commands Introduced in This Chapter

apropos

cron

crontab

ls

man

ps

rm

rmdir

whatis

CHAPTER 2

Creating Programs:
Compiling, Linking, and Running

This chapter covers:

- Creating programs
- Programs as text files
- Compiling and linking C and C++ programs
- How the compiler really works
- System libraries
- Linking with system libraries
- Creating your own libraries with **ar**
- Shared libraries
- Graphical applications with C
- Linking with the Motif library
- Compiling and running Java programs
- Interpreters
- Perl
- Tcl

Creating Programs

34

Programs start out as text files. That's true for C, C++, Java, Perl, Tcl, and just about every other programming language. This remains true on UNIX, which makes heavy use of text files, and on Windows and Macintosh systems.

So, creating program files forms the first step for programming on UNIX.

You can use any text editor you'd like; UNIX seems to include more text editors than you can imagine. If you like graphical text editors, you can choose from **dtpad** (on systems supporting the Common Desktop Environment, or CDE), **jot** (on Silicon Graphics workstations), **nedit**, **tkedit**, and **textedit**. The latter three are freeware and appear on the CD-ROM that comes with this book. Figure 2.1 shows **nedit**, one of the best windowed text editors.

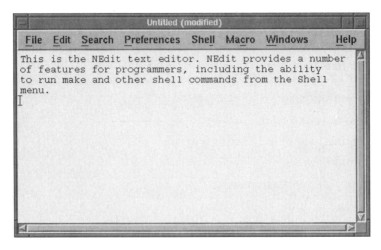

Figure 2.1 The **nedit** text editor.

For text editors originally created for ANSI terminals, the main choices are **emacs** and **vi**, which are also on the CD-ROM. **emacs** comes in both X (graphical) and text-based versions. Along with its built-in LISP interpreter and huge number of modules, **emacs** forms one of the most powerful, albeit complicated, software development systems.

But, no matter what editor you prefer, if you can create text files, you can create programs.

Once you've created a program, the next step is to get it to run. In the following sections, you'll see the UNIX tools for making C, C++, Java, Perl, and Tcl programs run. We'll start with C and C++.

Compiling and Linking C and C++ Programs

The C and C++ programming languages form the most-used languages on UNIX systems. In fact, UNIX was originally written in C. While Java offers some neat ideas, for the time being at least, C and C++ dominate; that's why most of this book focuses on C and C++ programming.

As on all other platforms, C and C++ programs (they are virtually the same because C++ is a superset of C) start as text files and then get compiled into the machine instructions for your system architecture. Most C programs are stored in one or more files that end with **.c**, for example, **gui.c** and **main.c**.

Table 2.1 lists the more common file name extensions for UNIX.

Table 2.1 UNIX File Name Extensions

File Suffix	Meaning
.a	Library
.c	C source file
.C	C++ source file (note the uppercase *C*)
.cc	C++ source file
.cpp	C++ source file
.cxx	C++ source file
.c++	C++ source file
.class	Java file compiled into byte codes
.e	Elffel source file
.el	**emacs** LISP source code
.f	FORTRAN source (no preprocessing with GNU FORTRAN)
.for	FORTRAN source (no preprocessing with GNU FORTRAN)

Table 2.1 UNIX File Name Extensions (continued)

File Suffix	Meaning
.F	FORTRAN source (preprocessed by **cpp** if GNU FORTRAN)
.fpp	FORTRAN source (preprocessed by **cpp** if GNU FORTRAN)
.h	C or C++ include file
.hxx	C++ include file
.java	Java source code
.o	Object module (compiled from a .c file)
.ob2	Oberon-2 source
.pl	Perl script
.pm	Perl module script
.s	Assembly code
.sa	Shared library stubs linked with your program
.sl	Shared library (on HP-UX)
.so.n	Run-time shared library, version number is n
.tcl	Tcl script
.tk	Tcl script

As you can see in Table 2.1, for many programming languages, you can pick from several alternative file extensions.

If you program on Silicon Graphics systems, don't name your C++ files with a **.cpp** extension. The Silicon Graphics C++ compiler names temporary files with the **.cpp** extension, messing up your files and generally reporting many inexplicable errors.

Compiling C Programs

When you compile a C file, the C compiler, **cc**, creates an object code file, usually ending with **.o**. The object file (or object module) contains unlinked machine code. The *linker* (called *linkage editor* in UNIX parlance), **ld**, then links the **.o** files to make an executable program. The default name for this program is **a.out**, although no one uses **a.out** as the program name. Instead, programs have names like **mycad**, **wunderword**, or **xman**. All of this is controlled by the **cc** command. (You don't usually have to execute **ld** directly; **cc** takes care of this for you.)

On Windows and Macintosh systems, which command you use to compile C and C++ programs depends on which compiler you've purchased. On UNIX, virtually all C compilers—free and commercial—use the name **cc**, short for *C compiler*. The C++ compiler, **CC**, follows the same conventions as **cc**.

To compile and link a C program, use the following command:

```
$ cc -o executable filename.c
```

This command compiles **filename.c** and creates the executable program executable, assuming there are no errors in **filename.c**. You now have a new UNIX program. You can type the name of the program at the command line and watch it run:

```
$ executable
```

Of course, you can use any name you want for **executable** and **filename.c**. These names are arbitrary. Watch out, though, for the name *test*; many UNIX shells have a built-in command named **test**.

NOTE

Compiling C++ Programs

For C++ programs, use the **CC** command for compiling:

```
$ CC -o executable filename.c
```

Most of the options for **CC** act like those of **cc**

Of course, virtually all C or C++ programs are divided into a number of source code files. One of the main reasons for separating C programs into multiple files is simply sanity: reading a 1-megabyte program in one file is ludicrous. And C programs do get to this size—and even bigger than 1 megabyte. Most of the C programs I work on take more than five hours to compile and link in their entirety. (Usually such long-running activity takes place at night.)

Compiling and linking multiple files together makes for a more complicated set of **cc** or **CC** commands.

Compiling and Linking for Complicated Programs

In this case, you need to compile each source code (**.c**) file separately into an object code (**.o**) file and then link the object code files into an executable program.

To compile a C file into an object file, use a command like the following:

```
$ cc -c filename.c
```

This command compiles **filename.c** into **filename.o**. You'll need to run a command like this for each C program file you have. When that's done, link all the object (**.o**) files into one executable program using the –o option (or parameter) to **cc**. This time, however, we pass a **.o** file at the end of the command line, rather than the **.c** file we used earlier:

```
$ cc -o executable filename.o
```

Note that **filename.o**, not **filename.c**, gets passed on the command line.

For example, enter the following C program and name the file **hi_unix.c**:

```
/*
 * hi_unix.c
 * Example C program.
 */
#include <stdio.h>

int main(int argc, char** argv)
```

```
{
    int i;

    if (argc > 1) {
        printf("Command-line parameters: ");

        for (i = 1; i < argc; i++) {
            printf("[%s] ", argv[i] );
        }

        printf("\n"); /* Output newline */
    } else {
        printf("Hi, UNIX.\n");
    }

}

/* end of file hi_unix.c */
```

If you're a Windows programmer, remember there's no WinMain on UNIX. UNIX programs use main as the entry point.

NOTE

To compile the **hi_unix.c** file to an object file, use the following command:

```
$ cc -c hi_unix.c
```

This creates the object file **hi_unix.o**. To then link this to make an executable program, use the following command:

```
$ cc -o hi_unix hi_unix.o
```

For one-file programs like **hi unix.c**, you can use the one-step method for compiling and linking:

NOTE

```
$ cc -o hi_unix hi_unix.c
```

The separate method works best when you have multiple **.c** files to compile and link.

Now, you can run the new program **hi_unix**:

```
$ hi_unix
Hi, UNIX.
```

The **hi_unix** program prints the simple message Hi, UNIX. unless you pass command-line parameters. *Command-line parameters* are extra data passed on the command line. While Macintosh and, to a lesser extent, Windows programs don't make much use of command-line parameters, UNIX tends to use the command line to control how a program should work.

If you pass command-line parameters to the **hi_unix** program, it will print them, one at a time, as shown here:

```
$ hi_unix 1 2 Three "Four 4" 5 6
Command-line parameters: [1] [2] [Three] [Four 4] [5] [6]
```

Note how the fourth parameter has a space in it.

Using the cc Command

In normal operation, the **cc** command executes a number of other commands under the hood. One such command is **cpp**, the C preprocessor. This reads a C program file, a **.c** file, and expands any # directives. In the short program given earlier, the #include directive means to include the file **stdio.h**. That is, **cpp** reads in **stdio.h** and inserts the contents right at the #include directive. Most C programs use one or more include files.

Include files are normally stored in **/usr/include**. If you use the angle brackets (<, >) around an include filename, like <stdio.h>, this means that **cpp** looks for a file named **stdio.h** in the standard places, of which **/usr/include** is the default. Chances are your C programs will require include files from directories other than **/usr/include**. To tell **cc** about these other directories, use the -I command-line parameter. With a directory name, the -I parameter can add more directories to the include file search path. For example, if some of the necessary include files are located in

/usr/openwin/include (used by OLIT and XView libraries), you can use the following **cc** command:

```
$ cc -I /usr/openwin/include filename.c
```

The **cc** command uses a number of command-line parameters to tell it what to do and to allow you to fine-tune the process of building executable programs from C language text files. Table 2.2 lists commonly used **cc** command-line parameters.

Table 2.2 cc Command-Line Parameters

Parameter	Meaning
-I*directory*	Searches the given directory for include files, as well as **/usr/include**.
-c *filename.c*	Compiles the file **filename.c** and builds the object module **filename.o**. This does not create an executable command.
-o *progname*	Names the executable program *progname*. The default name is **a.out**.
-g	Compiles with debugging information.
-O	Optimizes the program for best performance.
-l*Library*	Links the named library.

Most UNIX compilers don't allow you to mix the -g (include debugging information) and -O (optimize) options, but the freeware GNU C compiler does.

There are many **cc** command-line options; use **man cc** to see them all.

Building Libraries

When you've built up a stable set of routines that you want to re-use again and again, it's time to create a library. C and C++ libraries provide one of the easiest way to collect your routines together and then re-use them in other projects.

This section shows how to create software libraries on UNIX. The process is very much like on Windows, with the **LIB.EXE** command. You can collect your code into handy libraries, which makes it much easier to re-use your code and simplifies your Makefiles (see Chapter 3).

But before you build libraries, you should know which libraries already exist on your system. Most UNIX systems provide hundreds of libraries of prebuilt code.

System Libraries

Most UNIX systems include the libraries found in Table 2.3, although your system may not have some of the freeware libraries like Xpm.

Table 2.3 System Libraries

Library	Purpose
C	C++ base library
c	C base library
curses	Text-based windowing for ANSI terminals
dbm	Database/data management/hashing routines
g++	GNU C++ library
gen	Has regex and regcmp on Solaris
inet	Internet networking
m	Math
malloc	Alternative memory allocation functions
olgx	Low-level library used by **xview** library
PEX5	PEX 3D routines (X)
PW	Contains regex and regcmp on HP-UX
X11	Low-level X Window API
Xaw	Athena widget library (used by **xterm**)
Xext	X extension code, includes Shape functions for round windows

Xm	Motif toolkit (X)
Xmu	X miscellaneous utilities
Xol	Open Look OLIT library (mostly on Sun Solaris)
Xpm	X pixmap library for color bitmaps
Xt	X Toolkit Intrinsics
xview	XView toolkit

Each library is stored in the **/usr/lib** directory (or a few other directories as specified on your system). The full form of each library name includes *lib* (short for *library*), the library name, and a *.a* (for *archive file*; see the section on linking with system libraries for more on this). For example, the *inet* library should have a name of **libinet.a** in the **/usr/lib** or **/lib** directory.

Sometimes, you'll see a **.so** or **.sl** extension instead of **.a**. Normally, this means the library is a **shared library**. While each flavor of UNIX differs slightly, a shared library has code that gets loaded once and is re-used in memory for all applications that use the same library. (This is very much like Windows dynamic link libraries, or DLLs.)

For example, UNIX systems often provide the huge X11 library, used in virtually all graphical applications, as a shared library. This means that your version of UNIX loads only one copy of this large library, instead of one copy per application, as is the case with nonshared or static libraries. All X applications then share this same code on the memory required for the library.

Problems with Shared Libraries

Normally, you want to use as many shared libraries as possible, to keep your executable program size down to a reasonable size. However, using shared libraries creates two potential problems that you must be aware of.

First, your end users may not have the necessary shared library on their systems. If your program requires a certain shared library that isn't available, your program won't run. The C++ library, libC (note the uppercase *C*), often ships only with the C++ compiler. If your end users haven't purchased a C++ compiler, they may not have the necessary shared library, and they won't be able to run your programs. This is a common problem on Hewlett-Packard systems, where the default libC is shared.

Second, the user may have the shared library, but the library may be at an incompatible revision level. I've been hit by this mostly on IBM AIX systems; IBM is famous for having thousands of *patches* (minor updates) to AIX. Your users may have loaded a different set of patches from you.

In both cases, the way around the problem is to link statically. This provides greater control over the actual code that appears in your program and creates a greater certainty that you're testing what the user will receive, but it dramatically increases the size of the resulting executable files. The Motif and other X Window libraries tend to be quite large, increasing the size of your executable files by more than a megabyte each. If you link statically, your program burdens the user with extra RAM and disk consumption.

Linking with System Libraries

To link with a system library (or any library for that matter), use the -l option to the **cc** command. The following command links in the X11 (graphics) and m (math) libraries:

```
$ cc -o foo foo.c -lX11 -lm
```

With the -l option, **cc** expects to find a file named **libX11.a** (or something like **libX11.so** for a shared library) in the standard set of library directories, normally **/usr/lib** and **/lib**.

Due to the huge size of the X Window libraries for developing graphical user interfaces, these libraries are often stored in other areas of the file system, such as **/usr/X11R6/lib** (on Linux), **/usr/X11R5/lib** (on Hewlett-Packard HP-UX), or **/usr/openwin/lib** (on Sun Solaris). Sometimes **cc** will check these directories; sometimes it won't.

In addition, if your libraries appear anywhere else—a likely scenario— you need to use the -L option to tell **cc** other locations to find the libraries. To do this, include a directory after the -L parameter. For example:

```
$ cc -o foo foo.c -L/usr/X11R6/lib -lX11 -lm
```

 It's important to place the -L option before the libraries you reference, such as **-lX11**.

NOTE

For any major software project, you'll probably have your own library directories.

Creating Your Own Libraries with ar

The **ar** command (short for *archive*) provides the workhorse tool to create UNIX libraries.

While you can archive any sort of file with the **ar** command, most of the time, you'll use **ar** to create libraries of C and C++ routines.

A library in UNIX is merely a collection of object (**.o**) files in one file, normally sporting the **.a** (for *archive*) extension.

Use the **ar** command to add (or replace) **.o** files into one **.a** file. Then link this **.a** file into your programs, just like the libraries listed in Table 2.3.

The following command adds (or replaces) three object files into the library archive file **mylib.a**:

```
$ ar rv mylib.a module1.o module2.o module3.o
```

If the library file **mylib.a** doesn't exist, **ar** will create it. If any of the **.o** files are already in the library, **ar** will replace the version in the library with the **.o** file passed on the command line. That's what the r option is for.

The main options appear in Table 2.4.

Table 2.4 ar Options

Option	Usage
r	Replace files in archive with new files
s	Update symbol table
t	Print table of contents
v	Verbose mode; print out actions

Normally, you only need the r option to add or replace files in the archive. You can look in the online manual entry for **ar** for more information on this.

On systems derived from Berkeley UNIX, such as FreeBSD, you need to run a program named **ranlib** to update the symbol table in the beginning of the archive (**.a**) file. If your library is named **mylib.a**, use the following command:

```
$ ranlib mylib.a
```

Normally, you run **ranlib** after adding .o files to a library archive file with the **ar** command. Usually **ranlib** performs the same task as the s command-line parameter to **ar**, as shown in Table 2.4. See the online manual entry for **ar** for more information on whether you need to call **ranlib** on your system.

Quick Insertions

The q command-line parameter to **ar** tells **ar** to quickly append the .o file to the end of the library archive file. For large libraries, the q option can speed the **ar** command up quite a bit. The problem with just appending .o files is that there is no way to tell if the library already has the .o file, which may result in an error during linking. In addition, the q option doesn't rebuild the necessary symbol table, which means you'll need to run **ranlib** or **ar** with the s command-line parameter.

Shared Libraries

Shared libraries—unfortunately—work differently on different flavors of UNIX. Sun Solaris shared libraries differ from Hewlett-Packard shared libraries, and so on. This adds to the confusion when creating and using shared libraries.

Normally, to create a shared library, you need to perform two steps. First, you must compile to make position-independent code. The commands to do this depend on what system you're using. On Hewlett-Packard systems for example, use the +z option with **cc** to compile position independent code. Second, you need to use **ld** to create a shared library from the **.o** or **.a** files. On Hewlett-Packard systems, the –b option to **ld** creates a shared library.

I hate to be so general about shared libraries, but this information not only differs between systems, but major upgrades in UNIX versions also change how you build shared libraries. For example, Sun's migration from SunOS to Solaris 2, Hewlett-Packard's HP-UX 10, and the Linux upgrade from **a.out** to ELF (extended linking format) all changed the way these systems handle shared libraries. For best results, consult your system manuals.

Utilities for Working with Libraries

The **nm** command prints symbols and entry points (the beginnings of functions) in library and object files. This forms a useful, if cryptic, means to determine both the functions available in a library and the functions on which the library depends.

The output is exceedingly terse, however. For example:

```
$ nm libm.a


Symbols from /usr/lib/libm.a[acos.o]:
```

Name	Value	Scope	Type	Subspace
$global$		undef	data	
M$7	1073741824	static	data	$DATA$
S21acos	712	static	data	LIT
_acosd	592	extern	entry	$CODE$
_acosdf	648	extern	entry	$CODE$
_acosf	560	extern	entry	$CODE$
_dmatherr		undef	code	
_racos	680	extern	entry	$CODE$
acos	0	extern	entry	$CODE$
acosd	592	sdef	entry	$CODE$
acosdf	648	sdef	entry	$CODE$
acosf	560	sdef	entry	$CODE$
racos	680	sdef	entry	$CODE$
sqrt		undef	code	

With a library file, such as **libm.a**, **nm** goes through each **.o** file that was added to the library (with the **ar** command described earlier). Each function and global variable gets its own line of output.

nm becomes very useful when you're debugging strange libraries, but it isn't very good at creating a listing of which function comes from which library. For that, your UNIX system manuals are much more useful.

Unfortunately, I've learned through bitter experience that the system manuals don't always tell you which functions reside in which libraries. This can be very frustrating; sometimes you simply have to run **nm** as a means of last resort. If you find yourself in a similar situation, you can combine **nm** with **grep** (covered in Chapter 5) or look at the GNU automatic configuration package, autoconf (covered in Chapter 10).

Stripping Your Code

The -s option to **cc**, or the **strip** command, removes symbol table information from object files or executable programs. You need symbol table information to debug your programs, but when it's time to ship, most people strip the executables to shrink them—the symbol table information takes up a good bit of disk and memory space—and to prevent end users from being able to gain all the information that the symbol table has.

Graphical Applications with C and C++

Unlike Java, neither C nor C++ defines a graphical API as part of the language. Because of this, multiple APIs have flourished for creating graphical user interfaces. Just about every modern program sports such a beast, but there's no real standards—not in the language, or on the platform, at least not to the extent that QuickDraw dominates the Macintosh and Win32 dominates Windows.

So, as with a lot of UNIX, you're left with a choice of APIs, all of which are packaged into C and C++ libraries. For commercial versions of UNIX, the *de facto* toolkit of choice is the Motif toolkit mentioned in Chapter 1. But because Motif is a commercial product, very few freeware versions of UNIX, such as Linux and FreeBSD, provide Motif. (You need to determine whether or not this is an issue.)

CD-ROM

The CD-ROM comes with LessTif, a freeware clone of the Motif API. While you can compile and link many Motif programs with LessTif, LessTif is still far from ready for serious use, unfortunately.

In addition to Motif, there are several cross-platform toolkits that provide the ability to simply recompile to get your code running on Windows (and often Macintosh) systems. These toolkits include Galaxy from Visix and UNIX implementations of the Win32 and Microsoft Foundation Class (MFC) APIs from both Bristol and Mainsoft.

For freeware toolkits, there are several choices, including the Athena widget set (the Xaw library), which comes with X, as well as wxWindows and XView.

CD-ROM

The CD-ROM includes XView and wxWindows.

49

Because most graphical applications on UNIX use Motif, I'll concentrate on compiling Motif applications.

Compiling with Motif

All Motif programs require the Motif library, **libXm.a**; the X Toolkit Intrinsics library, **libXt.a**; and the low-level X library, **libX11.a**. Your UNIX system may require other libraries as well.

To test your system's libraries, you can use the following short Motif program:

```
/*
 *  motif.c
 *  A simple Motif program.
 */

#include <Xm/Xm.h>
#include <Xm/PushB.h>    /* XmPushButton */

/*
 * exitCB() is a callback for the
 * pushbutton widget we will create.
 */

void exitCB(Widget widget,
    XtPointer client_data,
    XtPointer call_data)

{   /* exitCB */

    exit(0);

}   /* exitCB */
```

```
int main(int argc, char** argv)

{   /* main */
    Widget          parent;
    XtAppContext    app_context;
    Widget          push;
    Arg             args[20];
    int             n;

    /*
     * Initialize the X Toolkit.
     */
    n = 0;
    parent = XtAppInitialize(&app_context,
            "UNIXtools",                /* app class */
            (XrmOptionDescList) NULL, /* options */
            0,                          /* num options */
            &argc,                      /* num cmd line */
            argv,                       /* cmd-line opts */
            (String*) NULL,             /* fallback rcs */
            args, 0);

    n = 0;
    push = XmCreatePushButton(parent,
            "quit", args, n);

    XtAddCallback(push,             /* widget */
        XmNactivateCallback,        /* which callback */
        (XtCallbackProc) exitCB, /* callback function */
        (XtPointer) NULL);          /* extra data to pass */

    XtManageChild(push);

    /*
     * Realize widget hierarchy, which
     * brings the top-level widget
     * (and all its children) to
     * reality. That is, create windows
```

```
    * for the widgets and then map
    * the windows.
    */
   XtRealizeWidget(parent);

   /* Process events forever. */
   XtAppMainLoop(app_context);

   return 0;

}   /* main */

/* end of file motif.c */
```

Save this program in a file named **motif.c**. Try to compile and link using the following command:

```
$ cc -o motif motif.c -lXm -lXt -lX11
```

On Hewlett-Packard workstations, you'll need to use the following command instead:

```
$ cc -o motif -I/usr/include/X11R5 \
   -I/usr/include/Motif1.2 \
   -Aa motif.c -L/usr/lib/Motif1.2 -lXm \
   -L/usr/lib/X11R5 -lXt -lX11
```

A backslash allows you to continue a long UNIX shell command on the next line.

N O T E

If you use X11 release 6 or higher, you're likely to require the Session manager, **libSM.a**, and Inter-Client Exchange, **libICE.a**, libraries. If so, you can use the following command:

```
$ cc -o motif motif.c -lXm -lXt -lX11 -lSM -lICE
```

Finally, many developers compile their Motif programs to use the Editres protocol, a means for allowing external programs to change Motif resources such as fonts and colors. If you do, or if you're using LessTif, which automatically sets this up, you need to link in the X extensions, **libXext.a**, library. Use the following command on X11 release 6 or higher:

```
$ cc -o motif motif.c -lXm -lXt -lXext \
   -lX11 -lSM -lICE
```

NOTE The Xext library also contains the code for the Shape extension, which allows for round windows. If you ever see a link error regarding a function that starts with *XShape*, then chances are that you need to link this library.

Table 2.5 lists the libraries required for the most common X APIs.

Table 2.5 Common X Library Orderings

Program Type	Libraries in Order
Athena	-lXaw -lXmu -lXt -lX11
Athena with X extensions, like Shape	-lXaw -lXmu -lXt -lXext -lX11
Motif	-lXm -lXt -lX11
Motif with X extensions, like Shape	-lXm -lXmu -lXt -lXext -lX11
OLIT	-lXol -lXt -lX11
Xlib	-lX11
Xlib with X extensions, like Shape	-lXext -lX11
XView	-lxview -lolgx -lX11

See Appendix A for a list of Motif and X Window System programming books.

Compiling and Running Java Programs

Java is a computer language based on C++ that uses the object model of Objective C. Unlike C++, however, the designers of Java removed many features they considered troublesome, including pointers, memory allocation and deallocation, and multiple inheritance.

Most programmers will agree that these features are often used incorrectly. Whether that justifies their exclusion remains to be seen.

The main benefit of Java is the promise of a future in which you no longer have to worry about system architectures, you don't care about the operating system, and you never worry about silly little details like RISC instruction sets.

The main ways Java achieves these benefits come from two features of how Java has been implemented. First, Java defines a standard API for many things that were left out of C++, the most important being a user interface API. This eliminates the differences among Macintosh QuickDraw, Windows Win32, and a whole host of X Window programming APIs on UNIX (such as Motif, OLIT, and Xview). By defining an API with the language, you know that any system that supports Java must support the same widget set (called *AWT*, short for Abstract Widget Toolkit).

Second, Java programs—in most implementations, anyway—get compiled to a form of byte codes, which are then interpreted at run time. The key factor that makes Java portable is that the byte codes are the same for all systems. This allows you to, for example, create a Java program on a Sun SPARC workstation and execute that same program on a PC running Windows 95. This does require that you have some form of Java run-time engine, an application that can read in and interpret the Java byte codes, executing the program on your system.

By compiling the Java program to a form of byte codes, you don't suffer from the performance hit incurred by strictly interpreted languages like Tcl. However, your Java applications will still run much slower than the equivalent compiled C or C++ programs.

To help solve this, many vendors sell just-in-time Java compilers. These compilers compile the already-compiled Java byte codes into native machine code at run time, giving your applications a great performance boost while maintaining the portability of the Java byte codes.

In the near future, I suspect that vendors will create native code Java compilers. This would require you to recompile on each system architecture you want to support, but you'd still gain the benefits of the Java API.

Another feature of Java, and perhaps the most written-about aspect of the language, is that you can write small applications, called *applets*, that execute from a Web browser. Thus, you can install applications on an Internet server and then execute those applications on any system that supports Java. In addition, because your applications reside on the server until they are used, this means you eliminate problems distributing your applications.

Right now, there's a host of products with coffee-related names, all of which provide Java environments. Because most of these products are relatively new, the easiest way to get started with Java is to download the Java Development Kit (JDK) from Sun (the company that created Java) or a related Internet site. You can also purchase books on Java, most of which come with a CD-ROM (my favorite is *Core Java*). See Appendix A for more on this.

 Most Java books come with versions of Java for Windows and Sun Solaris systems. For most UNIX systems, you'll need to download the Java Development Kit from the Internet. See Appendix A for more on this.

N O T E

Because the Java Development Kit is the most commonly available means to create Java programs, I'll stick to that here. Your Java manuals should describe any commands that diverge from this discussion.

The basic Java Development Kit comes with three programs and a host of support files. The programs appear in Table 2.6.

Table 2.6 Java Compilers and Run-Time Engines

Program	Usage
appletviewer	Executes applet HTML files
guavac	Freeware Java compiler
javac	Compiles Java source code into byte codes (**.class** files)
java	Executes Java byte codes
kaffe	Freeware program that executes Java byte codes

The Java Development Kit, in turn, assumes that you will name your files with certain extensions, as listed in Table 2.7.

Table 2.7 Java-Related File Extensions

Extension	Usage
.html	HyperText file that contains APPLET tags
.java	Java source code
.class	Compiled Java byte code

To make sense of this, we'll use the following short Java program to show how to compile and run Java applications on UNIX. Type in the following Java program:

```
//
// A simple first Java programming example.
//

public class UNIXProgTools
{
    public static void main(String[] args)
    {
        System.out.println( "Java application example." );
    }
}
```

Name the file **UNIXProgTools.java** (remember case counts in UNIX).

To compile a Java program to machine-independent byte codes, use the **javac** compiler:

```
$ javac UNIXProgTools.java
```

Because of Java's newness, many systems install it in **/usr/local/java/bin**. Chances are that this directory is not in your path. In the C shell, you can add this directory to your path with the following command:
N O T E   `% set path = ( $path /usr/local/java/bin )`

The **javac** command creates a byte code file named **UNIXProgTools.class**. You can execute this simple Java example using the **java** command:

```
$ java UNIXProgTools
```

You pass the full name of the **.java** file to **javac**, but just the class name (of the class that has the main function you want to execute) to **java**. The **java** command expects to find a file with the name of the class and ending N O T E   in **.class**.

When you run this program, you'll see the following output:

```
Java application example.
```

Creating Graphical Applications in Java

One of Java's best features is that the language defines a toolkit for creating graphical user interfaces. Many people complain about what's in the toolkit; I think it's nice to have a standard toolkit of any kind. This toolkit, called *AWT* (short for Abstract Window Toolkit), provides a small set of generic user interface components.

AWT is generic; your Java applications using AWT should work nearly the same on UNIX, Windows, or Macintosh systems. There will be some variance, as AWT conforms to the toolkit standards on each platform. On UNIX, most versions of AWT call Motif functions written in C, to implement the toolkit.

Creating Programs from Multiple Files

If your Java program requires multiple **.class** files (compiled from multiple **.java** files), then you need to set the CLASSPATH environment variable to tell **java** where to find the **.class** files.

The CLASSPATH environment variable contains a list of directories, separated by a colon, that tell **java** (and **javac**) where to look for **.java** and **.class** files. You can extend the CLASSPATH environment variable from the C shell with a command like the following:

```
% setenv CLASSPATH /home/erc/java
```

For both the **java** and **javac** commands, you can pass the class path as a command-line parameter as well:

```
$ java -classpath /home/erc/java UNIXProgTools
```

Java Applets

Java applets are different beasts from Java application programs. To run a Java applet, you can use a browser such as Netscape Navigator or run the appletviewer that comes with the Java Development Kit. The *appletviewer* is a primitive HTML file loader that executes Java applets.

With the appletviewer, you pass the name of the HTML file that calls up your applet, just like you would with a Web browser like Netscape Navigator. Use the following command as a guide:

```
$ appletviewer myapplet.html
```

Most Web browsers, such as Netscape Navigator, cache Web pages, including pages that contain applets. If you recompile your applet, you may not see the changes applied in your Web browser, because the caching may convince the Web browser it doesn't need to reload your applet. Because of this, you probably want to use the **appletviewer** command, instead of other Web browsers, during the initial stages of developing your applet.

Other Java Compilers

In addition to Sun's JDK for Linux and Solaris, the CD-ROM accompanying this book contains two other Java systems: guavac, a Java compiler and kaffe, a Java run-time engine. Both freeware tools are in their infancy. Kaffe, for example, does not yet execute Java's graphical interface toolkit functions.

When compiling guavac on your system, note that it requires a fairly recent C++ compiler and the Standard Template Library, or STL. Guavac compiles fine with **gcc** (also on the CD-ROM) but requires version 2.7.2 or higher and libg++ version 2.7.1 or higher.

Interpreters: Perl and Tcl

Most UNIX programs, especially those written in C and C++, are compiled into the native machine code instruction set. Shell scripts, however, are interpreted. The interpreter, in this case the shell, reads in the script file one line at a time, interprets what the command is telling it to do, and finally executes the command. Because of all the time needed to interpret the commands, interpreted scripts tend to run slower than compiled programs. But with interpreters, you can test your program right away, without having to wait for your C++ application to compile and link, which may require a significant amount of time for a large application.

So while interpreters are slower than compiled code, they give you quicker turnaround to run your programs. On UNIX, you use the shell interpreter for almost all of your commands. There are also two very popular scripting languages that I find useful: Perl and Tcl.

Perl

Perl, the practical extraction and report language, is an extremely powerful and complicated language, as reflected in Perl's official slogan: *There's more than one way to do it.* Even so, running Perl scripts from UNIX is relatively simple.

In this section, you'll learn how to run Perl scripts from the **perl** interpreter and how to make Perl scripts executable in their own right. The simplest Perl script is the ubiquitous Hello World script:

```
#
# hello.pl
#
# Hello World in perl.
print "Hello World.\n";
```

Enter this program using any text editor and save the file to the file name of **hello.pl**. All Perl programs are simply text files that get passed to the **perl** command. I use **.pl** as an extension for Perl scripts. While you can use any extension you like, **.pl** remains the most common extension in the Perl community.

Running Perl Programs

To run this program from a shell prompt, use the following command:

```
$ perl hello.pl
```

When you run this command, you should see the following highly original output:

```
Hello World.
```

N O T E If you get an error that the **perl** command is not found, then either you haven't installed Perl or the **perl** command is not in your command path. Your command path lists the directories where your system looks for commands. You need to extend the *PATH* environment variable.

In the C shell, use a command like the following, depending on where you installed Perl:

```
% set path = ( $path /usr/local/bin )
```

How Perl Runs Programs

When Perl first tries to run a script, it parses the entire script, compiling your commands into an internal format, and then it executes the script from this internal format. This means that most errors in the script, especially syntax errors, are reported before the script starts to run, even though Perl is considered an interpreted language.

This is very different from other scripting languages, like most UNIX shells and Tcl (covered soon), which parse each line separately and only report errors when executing a command.

This usually helps you detect errors in your script in advance, but sometimes errors remain undetected in this parsing stage.

Problems with Perl Scripts

To show how Perl detects problems, we can simply make an intentional error in a Perl script. We all probably have more than enough problems with unintentional errors to consider adding errors on purpose, but this example should help you track down the inevitable problems in Perl scripts.

One of the most common problems is forgetting a semicolon at the end of a Perl command. To show this, remove the semicolon after a Perl command, as shown in the **problem1.pl** script:

```
#
# problem1.pl
#
# Perl script that asks a question and
# gets user response.
#
# THIS SCRIPT HAS AN ERROR.
```

```
# YOUR MISSION IS TO FIND THIS ERROR.
#
# Note the extra space to print out.
print "What is your favorite scripting language? ";

$lang = <STDIN>;

# NOTE MISSING SEMICOLON BELOW.
chomp($lang)

if ( $lang eq "perl" ) {
    print "Congratulations, you chose perl!\n";
} else {
        print "Well, use $lang if you feel ";
        print "it's the right tool for the job\n";
}
```

When you run this script, you'll see the following error:

```
$ perl problem1.pl

syntax error at problem1.pl line 20, near "}"
Execution of problem1.pl aborted due to compilation errors.
```

WARNING

A common problem when starting Perl is forgetting the semicolon at the end of each command. If you do this, chances are Perl will report an error. The tough part is that Perl detects the error only *after* the line in which the problem occurred. So, when Perl reports a syntax error, the line number given is often only a guide. The error may have occurred on a line prior to the one listed.

In the **problem1.pl** script, the error is that the **chomp** command doesn't end with a semicolon. However, the error reported appears to be at the end of the `if-else` statement.

Making Your Scripts into Commands

On UNIX, you can convert your Perl scripts into commands that can be executed from the command line.

Making an Executable Script

Virtually all scripting languages (including Perl), use the # character to mark the start of a comment. (Some scripting languages require the # be in the first column.) In most UNIX shell scripts, you'll see a strange comment on the very first line:

```
#!/bin/sh
```

Comments are usually ignored. But this special comment names the program that should be used to run the script. This is useful because your shell, whether it be **csh**, **ksh**, or **bash**, can also run shell scripts. This special comment normally tells your shell to run a different program to execute the scripts. For example, I use the C shell (**csh**) for my daily work, but virtually all UNIX shell scripts are written in the Bourne shell (**sh**) language. This initial comment tells my **csh** to run **sh** for the script (rather than running another copy of **csh**).

This is just a convention, but it is followed on most UNIX command shells including **sh**, **csh**, and **ksh**. Because this convention is so widely followed, you can take advantage of this to ask the shell (usually **csh** or **ksh**) to run the **perl** interpreter. This allows you to type in the name of a Perl script alone, such as **hello.pl**, and have it execute, instead of typing **perl hello.pl**. You form a comment, like the one given earlier, with the location of your **perl** command, as in the following:

```
#!/usr/bin/perl
```

You need to add this line to your Perl scripts as the first line in the file.

If you installed Perl in a location other than **/usr/bin** (such as **/usr/local/bin**), you'll need to change this comment. Once you place the starting comment (and it *must* be the first line in the script), mark your Perl script as an executable file. In UNIX, an executable file has a file name that you can type in as a command. To do this, use the **chmod** (short for change mode) command:

```
$ chmod +x hello.pl
```

You should now be able to execute your script from the UNIX command line:

```
$ hello.pl
```

If you have any problems, chances are your command shell doesn't support this convention. If this is the case, you'll likely get a number of errors, as Perl commands are not compatible with most UNIX shell commands (but some are, which can lead to interesting results if you execute a Perl script as a Bourne shell script).

There's one main problem with this special first-line comment: some systems, especially Hewlett-Packard's HP-UX, only allow 32 characters in the path. Thus, long paths like **/usr5/local/perl/src/perl5.003/bin** won't work.

You can use the technique of the special comment on the first line to specify the program to run with any scripting language, including Tcl (covered soon). Of course, you'll need to change the comment to name the Tcl interpreter, instead of the Perl interpreter.

Finding out More about Perl's Commands

One of the best ways to track down problems in your Perl scripts is to look at the online documentation. Perl comes with extensive online documentation. In UNIX terms, this information is stored as online manual pages, which are accessible from the UNIX **man** or **xman** command and is shown in Figure 2.2.

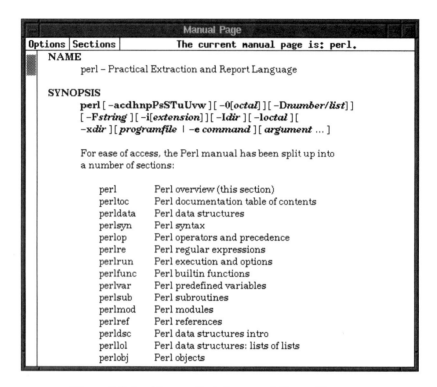

Figure 2.2 Looking up Perl documentation with **xman**.

CD-ROM

All of these Perl documents are also available on the CD-ROM as HTML
Web pages in the **doc** directory.

Table 2.8 lists the main topics of information.

Table 2.8 Online Reference Information on Perl

man Topic	Covers
perl	Main Perl overview
perlapi	Perl C application programming interface and glue routines
perlbook	List of some Perl books (see Appendix A)
perlbot	Object-oriented tricks and examples
perlcall	Calling conventions from C
perldata	Data structures
perldebug	Debugging
perldiag	Diagnostic messages
perlembed	How to embed Perl in your C or C++ application
perlform	Formats and reports
perlfunc	Built-in functions
perlguts	Internal functions for those doing extensions
perlipc	Interprocess communication
perlmod	Modules
perlobj	Objects
perlop	Operators and precedence
perlovl	Overloading semantics
perlpod	Plain old documentation
perlre	Regular expressions
perlref	References and nested data structures
perlrun	Execution and options
perlsub	Subroutines
perlsec	Security
perlstyle	Style guide
perlsyn	Syntax
perltrap	Traps for the unwary
perlvar	Predefined variables

In addition to the online documentation, there are a number of books available on Perl, including *Cross-Platform Perl*. See Appendix A for a list of Perl books.

Tcl

Tcl, the **Tool Command Language** (pronounced *tickle*), has captured the hearts and minds of tens of thousands of software developers worldwide. It's an easy-to-learn scripting language that runs under Windows (3.1 and 95), Windows NT, UNIX, and the Macintosh.

An associated add-on toolkit, **Tk** (short for toolkit), allows you to quickly create graphical applications without delving into arcane subjects like Win32, QuickDraw, Object Linking and Embedding or Motif, and the X Toolkit intrinsics. With a surprisingly small amount of code, you can quickly develop graphical applications.

There are a number of reasons for the great success of Tcl:

Tcl is a scripting language. While there are some Tcl compilers, most Tcl users run their programs as scripts. Scripts are easier to develop than full-fledged C or C++ programs, because scripting languages like Tcl tend to stand at a higher level than low-level languages like C, so you have to do less. Furthermore, because the language is interpreted, you get a really quick turnaround when testing your code. You don't have to compile or link; all you have to do is execute the Tcl interpreter, called **wish**, and run your script.

Tcl is easy to learn. The syntax is surprisingly simple. Each command has a command word and any number of arguments. Even **if** is a command in Tcl.

Tcl works on many different platforms. Ported to just about every version of UNIX (from Hewlett-Packard's HP-UX to Silicon Graphics' Irix and from SCO UNIX to Linux), Tcl works well in the UNIX environment, particularly because developing graphical applications on UNIX under Motif tends to be troublesome.

On the Windows side, versions of Tcl exist for Windows 3.1, Window 95, and Windows NT. The latest versions of Tcl also run on Apple's Macintosh platform. You can write complicated scripts in Tcl and execute those scripts on multiple platforms with the same results.

You can embed Tcl in your programs. The Tcl interpreter is merely a C function that you can link into your applications. This means that you can use Tcl as the application language in your C and C++ programs. For example, if you're developing a spreadsheet program, you can use Tcl as the built-in macro language.

Tcl is easy to extend. You can easily add commands to the base language of Tcl to extend the language. In fact, if you're embedding Tcl in your applications, chances are you'll need to add a number of commands that pertain to your application. This is one of the major uses of Tcl.

Tcl is free. Yep, you can get all this for free on the Internet or through a number of online services. This book comes with a CD-ROM that contains the Tcl source code, so you should be up and ready in just a few minutes.

Tcl works well with the Internet. Tcl includes a number of built-in features that make working with Internet World Wide Web pages easier. Tcl, like Perl, supports TCP/IP sockets for networking commands. In addition, the text widget supports tags that help if you want to create hypertext links in your text. Tcl is also good for CGI scripts, the code that Web pages execute for image maps and data retrieval.

All these reasons should convince you to join the Tcl bandwagon and program away.

Running Tcl Scripts

Tcl includes two interpreters (and you can build your own, as the Tcl interpreter is merely a C function): **wish** and **tclsh**. The **wish** interpreter comes with built-in graphics commands, called Tk, which allow you to create menus, scrolled lists, and so on. The **tclsh** interpreter only supports the base Tcl language. Because of this, most Tcl users run **wish** as the interpreter of choice.

To run a Tcl script, pass the name of the script file to **wish**:

```
$ wish filename
```

For example, the following short script creates a push button widget:

```
button .c -text "Hello World" -command { exit }
pack .c
```

If you save these two lines to a file named **hello.tk**, you can execute the script with the following command:

```
$ wish hello.tk
```

 Your UNIX system will probably not have Tcl installed. You can find Tcl on the CD-ROM that came with this book.

N O T E

 You mark Tcl scripts executable the same way as for Perl. Of course, you need to list the path to your **wish** command in the magic comment in the first line of the script, for example `#!/usr/local/bin/wish`.

N O T E

wish includes the Tk toolkit, which allows you to easily build widgets and create an X Window user interface. The whole concept of widgets is likely to be daunting unless you've programmed with one of the many X toolkits, such as Motif. Each widget acts as a part of your user interface, for example, a list of files or a push button to exit the program. If you have worked with Motif or the Athena widgets, you'll catch on to the concepts of Tk pretty fast. Even if you haven't worked with the Motif or Athena libraries, we found the basics of Tcl are easy to grasp. (There are some frustrating parts to Tcl, however.)

The Tk add-on to Tcl provides most of the standard widgets you'd expect. These widgets mirror most of the main widgets in the Motif toolkit, except for the handy Option menu, combo box, and notebook widgets. Tcl exceeds Motif in a number of areas, especially with the canvas widget, which allows you to place graphic "objects" such as lines, rectangles, Bezier curves, and even other widgets inside the canvas.

There are several books available on Tcl, including *Graphical Applications with Tcl and Tk*. See Appendix A for details.

When to Use Perl and Tcl

Many programmers devote considerable energy working with particular computer languages and *don't* like to be told which tool to use. In the end, use the tool that works best for you. The tips following should help you identify when one tool is better than another:

- Tcl is great as a glue language. That is, it is extremely easy to add your own commands, written as C functions, and to extend the Tcl language with your commands. You can do this in Perl, but it is more difficult. This means that Tcl would be a better choice for embedding an interpreter into your applications, especially if you need to call application-specific functions from the embedded interpreter. This is very useful for writing test programs for your C or C++ programs.

- Perl is a great tool to quickly automate tasks, especially tasks involving text files, due to Perl's very strong text-handling and text-searching functions.

- Tcl is better for creating graphical user interfaces. While there is a toolkit for Perl, called Perl/Tk, Tk seems better integrated with Tcl and works on more platforms under Tcl than Perl.

- Both languages provide syntax oddities. Perl tends to be more cryptic than Tcl (at least to me). This is probably because some people believe that Perl scripts should be as terse as possible and should use as many hidden side effects as possible. To me, this concept borders on insanity.

I mostly use Tcl to create programs that have a friendly user interface, look like Motif programs, and can run on a number of systems. Tcl and the Tk toolkit present something akin to the Motif look and feel—not close enough for purists, but close enough for most users. This is a great additional benefit because the Motif libraries don't ship with free versions of UNIX, like Linux, while Tcl does.

You should not discount the cross-platform abilities of Tcl either. You can create graphical applications that run on Windows, Macintosh, and UNIX systems.

I mostly use Perl to create scripts that parse text files. For example, convert a text file from one syntax to another, such as converting a C++ header file to formatted HTML output. Perl is also great for writing Common Gateway Interface, or CGI, scripts for Web pages.

Summary

Well, that's the whirlwind tour of creating C, C++, Java, Perl, and Tcl programs on UNIX.

The **cc** command compiles C programs into object, **.o**, files. **cc** can also call the UNIX linker, **ld**, to link the final executable. In fact, you'll almost never call **ld** directly.

For C++ programs, use **CC**, which acts in most respects like **cc**, but compiles C++ programs. For graphical programs, most UNIX developers use the Motif APIs with their C or C++ programs.

The **ar** command builds up libraries of **.o** files, so you can re-use routines. The **javac** command compiles Java programs into portable byte codes that can execute on any machine from the **java** command.

The **perl** command executes Perl scripts.

For Tcl, you have a choice of **tclsh** for nongraphical scripts and **wish** for graphics.

UNIX Commands Introduced in This Chapter

appletviewer

ar

CC

cc

chmod

java

javac

nm

perl

ranlib

tclsh

wish

CHAPTER 3

Using make to Automate Compiling and Linking

This chapter covers:

- **make**, a program that automates building programs
- **make** variables
- built-in variables
- **imake**, an extension to **make** used for X Window programs

Working with make

make manages a set of source code files and controls the compilation process to build your executable programs. As such, **make** is essential for building all but the most trivial UNIX programs. It has proven so useful that **make** has been ported to just about every computer in existence, and it forms the most important tool on UNIX after your text editor.

At its heart, **make** provides a simple rule-based inference engine that automatically determines which files that comprise your program need recompiling. Then it invokes the necessary commands. **make** can determine which files need recompiling from a set of rules you write in a file called a *Makefile*. For example, if you change an include, or **.h**, file, then all the C files that include the **.h** file must be recompiled. **make** provides a simple way to express this and other rules in the Makefile.

make originally became popular for managing C programs, but you can use **make** for any process in which some files depend on other files and the rules to follow for your task can be expressed in commands you can enter at the UNIX shell prompt.

make provides a number of advantages, which is why it is so popular:

- With **make**, you won't forget to recompile a file that needs it, avoiding a class of errors based on files getting out of sync.
- Because **make** only compiles what is needed, you save the time it would have taken to recompile all the files. For large programs, this can be a long time.
- You can automate much of your program's build processes with **make**, so you don't have to type in long commands.
- You can automate the installation and cleanup processes.
- You can use **make** for more than compiling and linking; you can launch any UNIX programs from **make**.

With all these good things, there are also some limitations to **make**:

- **make** uses file modification times to determine whether to rebuild a target. This doesn't really capture whether significant changes that require recompiling were made or if the file was just written. Thus, **make** will often recompile many files unnecessarily, especially when you make trivial changes to an include file, such as adding new comments.

- The Makefile syntax is far too rigid and prone to errors, especially in the use of **Tab** characters.

- **make** cannot handle platform differences by itself, although **imake**, covered at the end of this chapter, can help.

Dependencies and Targets

make is based on the concepts of dependencies, targets, and commands. A *target* is something you want to build, such as an executable program. In **make** parlance, the target *depends* on a number of other files, such as the source code **.c** and **.h** files that are compiled and linked together to create the executable program. When you modify any of these **.c** or **.h** files, **make** will rebuild the target by issuing the *commands* you specify in the Makefile.

In addition, some of the files the target depends on may in turn depend on other files. This is especially true for **.o** files, which depend on **.c** files, which depend on **.h** files. You can nest ever-deepening dependencies as far as necessary.

When **make** detects that a file has changed, and therefore a target needs to be rebuilt, **make** invokes the commands that rebuild the target. These commands are any number of UNIX commands necessary to create the target. In most cases, the command is simply a call to **cc** to recompile the **.c** file.

The commands, targets, and dependencies are all stored in a file named **Makefile**, using the following syntax:

target: *dependencies*
    command

You can have multiple commands; just place one command per line:

target: *dependencies*

    command

    command

    command

    ...

For example, we can take a simple hello world program and create a Makefile for it. Type in the following short program and save it under the name **hello.c**:

```
/* hello.c Simple hello world. */
#include <stdio.h>

int main(int argc, char** argv)
{
    printf("Hello world.\n");
}
```

Now, if we want to call the executable program **hello**, we know that **hello** depends on **hello.c**. In a **Makefile**, we can express this rule as follows:

```
#
# Simple Makefile for hello world.
#
hello: hello.c
    cc -o hello hello.c

# end of Makefile
```

Enter in this file and name it **Makefile**.

The preceding **Makefile** states that **hello** is a target. (You can have more than one target in a **Makefile**.) The **hello** target—really a file named **hello**, which is the executable program—depends on **hello.c**. If **hello.c** changes (is newer than **hello**), then **make** will invoke the rule on the following line, which calls **cc** to recompile **hello.c** into the **hello** executable.

To create a target in the **Makefile**, begin with a new line, you name the target—**hello**—then place a colon (**:**), some spaces, then list the files the target depends on. Starting on the next line, begin with a **Tab**, then place the UNIX command used to build the target. You can have multiple commands, each of which should go on its own line and every command line must start with a **Tab**.

The line that starts with **cc**, the command to rebuild the **hello** executable program, starts with a **Tab**, *not spaces*. You must use a **Tab**, or **make** will output a syntax error. This stupid limitation has always been in **make**.

WARNING

To try this, type **make**:

```
$ make
cc -o hello hello.c
```

make normally prints—or echoes—the commands it executes. This helps you stay aware of the progress through the commands.

You can also name the target you want built, as shown here:

```
$ make hello
cc -o hello hello.c
```

If you don't name the target, **make** looks at the first target it finds in the **Makefile**.

N O T E

When you try either of the two preceding commands, **make** should compile **hello.c** and create the new program **hello**. When you run **hello**, it just prints a dumb message:

```
$ hello
Hello world.
```

Now, to see how **make** works, type **make** again:

```
$ make
make: `hello' is up to date.
```

In this case, **make** does nothing, because the modification date of **hello** is later than that of **hello.c**. This is where **make** provides a measure of efficiency. But everything **make** does is based on the modification dates of files. Because of this, it is very easy to fool **make**.

Fooling make

Because **make** bases all its decisions on file modification dates, all you need to do to fool **make** is change the date of a file, for example:

```
$ make
make: `hello' is up to date.


$ touch hello.c


$ make
cc -o hello hello.c
```

The **touch** program merely updates the modification date of a file.

Now, chances are you have a number of files that depend on each other, which requires a more complicated **Makefile**.

A More Complicated Makefile

Chances are your **Makefile**s will need to compile multiple files and handle things like libraries of functions. The following example should show you how, without getting too bogged down in the details.

To start, consider the following **Makefile**:

```
#
# A more complicated Makefile.
#
```

```
myprog:      myprog.o libmylib.a
     cc -o myprog myprog.o -L. -lmylib

myprog.o: myprog.c myprog.h mylib.h
     cc -c myprog.c

# Dummy rule to prevent make errors.
myprog.h:

# note extra blank line above.

mylib.h:

# Rebuild a simple library.
libmylib.a: mylib.o
     ar rv libmylib.a mylib.o

mylib.o: mylib.c mylib.h
     cc -c mylib.c
# end of Makefile
```

Just going through this **Makefile**, we can determine a number of things about this program. The **myprog** program depends on **myprog.o** and a library, **libmylib.a**. (You usually start library names with **lib** to allow use of the –l syntax with **cc**.)

The file **myprog.o** depends on three files, **myprog.c**, **myprog.h**, and **mylib.h**. Note the dummy rules for **myprog.h** and **mylib.h**. Some versions of **make** try to invoke something on each target and we don't have to do anything to build an include file. Because of this, I usually put in dummy rules for all header files.

The library **libmylib.a** depends on just one object file, **mylib.o**. Normally, your libraries will depend on many source files. And **mylib.o** in turn depends on **mylib.c** and **mylib.h**.

Rather than bog down the text with dummy C programs, I'll leave it to your imagination to fill in all the files **myprog.c**, **myprog.h**, **mylib.c**, and **mylib.h**.

When you run **make** on the **myprog** target, you'll see the following results, presuming there are no errors in your files:

```
$ make myprog
cc -c myprog.c
cc -c mylib.c
ar rv libmylib.a mylib.o
a - mylib.o
cc -o myprog myprog.o -L. -lmylib
```

make Variables

In the preceding **Makefile**, the dependencies for the target **myprog** list all the object modules and libraries that **myprog** depends on. In the command in the next line, the object modules and libraries are listed again. Listing essentially the same data twice often leads to errors. If you add a new file, you may forget to add it to the dependency list and thereby not recompile the correct set of files on a change. To help with this problem, you can use **make**'s variables.

make's variables allow you to, for example, list all the object files and libraries that go into a program:

```
OBJS= myprog.o

myprog:     $(OBJS) libmylib.a
       cc -o myprog $(OBJS) -L. -lmylib
```

In most Makefiles, you'll see a variable like **OBJS**, **OBJ**, or **OBJECTS** used to hold the names of the object files needed for a program.

To define a variable in **make**, simply use the following syntax:

```
VARIABLE= value...
```

To use a variable, and this is where I always make typographical errors, you use the following strange error-prone syntax:

$(VARIABLE)

make also includes some handy built-in variables, which are very useful for creating generic rules. These variables appear in Table 3.1.

79

Table 3.1 Built-in make Variables

Variable	Holds
$@	The target of the rule
$<	The first dependency, usually the first file, in an implicit rule
$?	All dependencies that are newer than the target
$^	All the dependencies
$*	The stem used by an implicit rule
$(@D)	Directory part of the target file name, without a trailing /
$(@F)	The file part of the target file name
$(*D)	Directory part of the stem, without a trailing /
$(*F)	The file part of the stem

Many of these variables apply only to GNU **make**. Only $?, $@, $<, and $* seem to run on most versions of UNIX **make**.

Automatic make Rules

Because **make** was originally created to manage large C programs, it has a few built-in rules that you can take advantage of to shorten your Makefiles.

If you work on Windows, Microsoft's brain-dead **nmake** won't support any of these handy shortcuts.

Shortcuts Based on the File Suffix

The most common shortcut comes from a set of file suffixes that **make** understands, including **.c** and **.o**. You can use a simple suffix target and command, like the following:

```
.c.o:
    $(CC) $(CFLAGS) -c $<
```

The preceding rule states that each **.o** file depends on the corresponding **.c** file. If the **.c** file changes, **make** will issue the generic command, which uses the built-in **make** variables from Table 3.1 to compile the proper file.

This simple shortcut is supported on most versions of **make**.

To add to the built-in list of file suffixes that **make** understands, you can use a dummy target called **.SUFFIXES**:

```
.SUFFIXES: .java
```

WARNING

Different versions of **make** add useful enhancements, which, unfortunately, are not universally supported. The CD-ROM accompanying this book includes the source code for GNU **make**, an enhanced **make** from the GNU project (makers of GNU C and C++ compilers). GNU **make** adds a number of great shortcuts for **make**, but these short cuts are only supported by GNU **make**. Normal UNIX **make** won't accept these commands.

You may like these enhancements enough to install GNU **make** on all your systems. If you don't, you'll have to be careful to stick to what your system's **make** will accept.

Some of the handy shortcuts that GNU **make** supports include a set of % wildcards. In GNU **make**, for example, the following rule will manage all the recompiling for any files listed in the OBJECTS **make** variable:

```
OBJECTS = file1.o file2.o file3.o
```

```
$(OBJECTS): %.o: %.c
    $(CC) -c $(CFLAGS) $<
```

make Tricks

GNU **make** can also include other **Makefile**s in the current **Makefile**. This is very handy for defining **make** variables once for an entire project and then including these definitions into each **Makefile** used in the project. (For large projects, you'll likely have a lot of **Makefile**s.)

81

The `include` statement includes another file, right at that line. **make** suspends operation for a moment, finds the file or files, and reads them in at that spot. For example:

```
include gnu.mk project.mk common.mk
```

This GNU **make** command reads in the three files **gnu.mk**, **project.mk**, and **common.mk** into your **Makefile**.

You can also use shell wildcards, like the following:

```
include *.mk
```

 Don't use a **Tab** character in any of these include lines; **make** interprets **Tab**s as the beginning of commands.

WARNING

If the file names don't start with a slash, **make** will look first in the current directory. If the files can't be found there, **make** journeys abroad and starts looking in other directories. You can pass these directories to look in to **make** via the `-Idirectory` or `-include-dir directory` command-line parameters.

In addition, GNU **make** will search for your included files in the following directories, if the directories exist: **/usr/gnu/include**, **/usr/local/include**, and **/usr/include**.

If **make** can't find your files, it won't generate an error right away, but it will eventually exit with a fatal error. If you want **make** to ignore any include files it can't find, place a dash in front of `include`, for example:

```
-include *.mk
```

The dash tells **make** to silently ignore any errors in finding the files to be included.

More than One Makefile

make automatically looks for a file named **Makefile** or **makefile** (case counts) in the current directory.

GNU **make**, a popular **make** variant on the CD-ROM, also looks for a file named **GNUmakefile**.

N O T E

You can use a different name for the file that holds your rules, if you use the -f command-line parameter to **make**. For example:

```
$ make -f my_makefile
```

make supports a number of other useful command-line parameters, as shown in Table 3.2.

Table 3.2 make Command-Line Parameters

Parameter	Meaning
-f *newmakefile*	Uses the named file instead of **Makefile** for the rules
-n	Runs in no-execute mode. Only prints the commands, rather than compiling anything
-s	Runs in silent mode; doesn't print any commands **make** executes

Good Ideas with make

Over the years, UNIX developers followed some conventions with **make**, standardizing on **make** targets, something that you should also follow. Table 3.3 lists some of the common targets that experienced UNIX programmers expect to find in most Makefiles.

Table 3.3 Common make Targets

Target	Meaning
all:	Build everything, which may create multiple executable files
clean:	Remove all **.o**, **.a**, and **core** files, to clean up the disk space used in building the application
install:	Install the compiled program in its final resting place, perhaps **/usr/local/bin**
libs:	Build only the libraries that the programs depend on

Spanning Multiple Directories

Typically, you provide a **Makefile** for each directory in which you have code. You can also create a **Makefile** in a top-level directory and have the commands **make** executes change to each subdirectory and run **make** there.

Each command launched by **make** gets launched within its own shell—typically **sh**, the Bourne shell. Because of this, you have to be careful about placing multiple commands for a **make** target, as each command will get its own shell. To get around this, you can separate the commands with a semicolon (;) and place parenthesis around the whole combined command. For example:

```
all:
    (cd src; make)
    (cd math; make)
    (cd ui; make)
```

Using imake to Create Makefiles

When the creators of the X Window System started out, they used **make** to manage their very large project. However, they soon discovered a number of problems with **make**, and you will too if you work on multiple UNIX systems. This is because **make** has no real way to maintain system-specific customizations, and when you work with the X Window System, you'll need these customizations.

84

For example, Hewlett-Packard systems (not to pick on one vendor, but they broke many common conventions) place the X libraries in **/usr/lib/X11R5** and X include files in **/usr/include/X11R5**. The Motif libraries are located in **/usr/lib/Motif1.2** and the Motif include files in **/usr/include/Motif1.2**. Thus, every time you compile a Motif program on a Hewlett-Packard system, you need a command like the following:

```
$ cc -o foo -I/usr/include/X11R5 \
   -I/usr/include/Motif1.2 foo.c \
   -L/usr/lib/Motif1.2 -lXm \
   -L/usr/lib/X11R5 -lXt -lX11
```

NOTE To make this even more aggravating, to use ANSI C function prototypes on Hewlett-Packard systems, you must use the -Aa command-line parameter to **cc**.

It's hard to encapsulate all this information in a **Makefile** that you want to use on more than one system. Nor is Hewlett-Packard the only vendor that breaks established conventions. To help with this problem, the creators of the X Window System turned to a tool called **imake**.

imake, You make

The **imake** program generates a platform-specific **Makefile** for your system from a general set of rules stored in a file named **Imakefile** and from a set of system-specific configuration files that are normally installed when you install the X Window System.

NOTE Oddly enough, for many years Hewlett-Packard refused to ship **imake**, even though their HP-UX system was one of the worst offenders for odd X installations. If you're running an older version of HP-UX, chances are you won't have **imake**. You can find **imake** on the CD-ROM that accompanies this book.

The end result—if **imake** is configured properly—is a **Makefile** that should work on your system to build an X Window application. Then **make** takes over and compiles and links the X application.

imake starts by loading in a master template file called **Imake.tmpl** (the **.tmpl** stands for template). This file normally resides in **/usr/lib/X11/config**.

The master **Imake.tmpl** executes the following steps to build a **Makefile**. First, **Imake.tmpl** determines what sort of machine you have, such as a Sun SPARC, and includes, that is, executes the rules in, a file configured for your operating system. The Sun system file is named **sun.cf** (**.cf** stands for configuration). The Silicon Graphics (SGI) file is named **sgi.cf**, and so on. The **sun.cf** file, for example, contains variables to set the version of the operating system and other means to customize **imake** for Sun systems. (You'll only need to edit these operating system configuration files if your system has been misconfigured.)

These files, like all **imake** configuration files, are normally located in **/usr/lib/X11/config**. You may need to edit the *system.cf* file (e.g., **sun.cf**) when you install the X Window sources, but once you've done that, you probably won't need to edit the operating system file again. On systems where X comes pre-installed, you shouldn't need to edit this file.

Second, **Imake.tmpl** includes the file **site.def**, also in **/usr/lib/X11/config**. The **site.def** file should have local customizations. For example, if you want X programs to reside somewhere other than the standard **/usr/bin/X11**, you can configure this in the **site.def** file.

Third, **Imake.tmpl** includes a project-specific file named **Project.tmpl**. This is used mainly to build the X Window sources from the X Consortium.

Fourth, **Imake.tmpl** includes a set of rules to build X programs, stored in a file named **Imake.rules**. **Imake.rules** contains a set of generic rules used by **imake**. You shouldn't need to edit this file, but you may want to look at it to see what sort of rules are defined. The syntax won't make much sense, though, as it uses C preprocessor macros extensively.

Fifth, in the last step, **Imake.tmpl** includes the local directory's **Imakefile**. This file describes the high-level rules (using the low-level rules in the **Imake.rules** file) for building a particular X application.

In addition, there's a **Motif.tmpl** file, a template for Motif programs, and **Motif.rules**, the generic rules for building the Motif libraries and programs that use the Motif libraries.

When all this is done, **imake** uses a program called **makedepend** and all the configured rules to build the **Makefile**. The **makedepend** program creates **Makefile** rules for all files that your C code includes, such as **stdio.h**.

Unfortunately, **makedepend** can't really tell the difference between a system file that is unlikely to change and an include file created by you. Because of this, the **make** rules created by **makedepend** seem overly long and complicated.

Hopefully, you'll only have to configure **imake** once—if that. Many systems come with **imake** preconfigured.

imake Command-Line Parameters

imake supports the following command-line parameters, which we show in Table 3.4.

Table 3.4 imake Command-Line Parameters

Option	Meaning
-D*define*	Define the value following the –D
-I*directory*	Names the directory for the **Imake.tmpl** file
-T*template*	Names the master template file, which defaults to **Imake.tmpl**
-f *filename*	Names the local **Imakefile**, which defaults to **Imakefile**
-s *filename*	Names the output file, which defaults to **Makefile**
-e	**imake** should build and execute the **Makefile**, the default is to not execute the **Makefile**
-v	Turns on verbose mode, which prints **cpp** commands

While you can call **imake** directly, most users, though, use the **xmkmf** shell script to invoke **imake**.

xmkmf: A Wrapper Around imake

X includes a simple UNIX shell script called **xmkmf**, which serves as an easy front end to **imake**. If you have a directory with an **Imakefile**, you can use **xmkmf** to generate a **Makefile** by changing to the directory with the **Imakefile** and then using the simple command:

```
$ xmkmf
```

If **imake** is set up properly—a big if—you'll see the following output and you should now have a **Makefile** in the current directory:

```
imake -DUseInstalled -I/usr/lib/X11/config
```

The commands output to the screen are the commands you could use to invoke **imake** directly.

If you run **xmkmf** and there is already a **Makefile** in your local directory, **xmkmf** will save that **Makefile** to **Makefile.bak** before creating a new **Makefile**. Then the commands executed by **xmkmf** will look something like:

```
mv Makefile Makefile.bak
imake -DUseInstalled -I/usr/lib/X11/config
```

Creating Imakefiles

The easiest way to create an **Imakefile** is to use an existing working file as a template and then just fill in the differences. Most simple X programs can use the following file as a template:

```
#
#     As with Makefiles, lines starting
#     with a "#" are comments.
#
LOCAL_LIBRARIES1 = $(XAWLIB) $(XMULIB)\
         $(XTOOLLIB) $(EXTENSIONLIB) $(XLIB)

CDEBUGFLAGS = -g

SRCS1 = file1.c file2.c file3.c file4.c
OBJS1 = file1.o file2.o file3.o file4.o

INCLUDE_FILES = include1.h include2.h

PROGRAM = minicad
```

```
ComplexProgramTarget_1(minicad, $(LOCAL_LIBRARIES1), )
```

This **Imakefile** references a number of **imake** variables, including those shown in Table 3.5.

Table 3.5 imake Variables in the Sample imakefile

imake Variable	Used for
LOCAL_LIBRARIES1	Listing of the necessary libraries, using **imake** variables
SRCS1	C program files used to build the program
PROGRAM	Name of the program to build, **minicad** in this example
OBJS1	Object modules to link together to make the program
ComplexProgramTarget_1	**imake** command to build the whole thing

Unless you have special needs, you can use the **ComplexProgramTarget_1** macro to build your programs.

The library names are also **imake** variables, because these can have different names or locations on different platforms. Table 3.6 shows the most common X library variables.

Table 3.6 Examples of imake Library Names

imake Name	Description	Usual Library
XAWLIB	Athena widget library	**libXaw.a**
XMULIB	X miscellaneous utilities library	**libXmu.a**
XTOOLLIB	X Toolkit Intrinsics	**libXt.a**
EXTENSIONLIB	X extension library	**libXext.a**
XLIB	Low-level X library	**libX11.a**

Table 3.6 should help you decode the **imake** macros into the actual library names.

The preceding short 400-byte **Imakefile** generates a 10 Kilobyte **Makefile**.

Using the New Makefile

If all goes well, you shouldn't ever have to read the automatically generated **Makefile**. You should be able to just type **make** and the program should be built:

```
$ make
```

Summary

For software projects of any size, **make** can provide a great boon, both for organizing what files get built into what programs and for only recompiling the files that need it.

make bases its work on rules you provide in a file called **Makefile**. In a **Makefile**, each rule has a target, one or more dependencies, and the commands used to rebuild the target.

Different versions of **make**—especially GNU **make**—provide enhancements that make writing Makefiles easier, provided you only use GNU **make**.

For development of X Window applications, you can use **imake**, a program that generates a **Makefile** from a set of rules in a file named **Imakefile** and from a set of system-specific configurations.

UNIX Commands Introduced in This Chapter

imake

make

touch

xmkmf

## CHAPTER 4

Working with Text Files

This chapter covers:

- The most common text editor on UNIX, **vi**
- **emacs**, the all-singing, all-dancing editor
- Graphical text editors such as **nedit**
- Programming editors, like **xcoral**, that support C and C++ syntax
- Integrated development environments

Text Files

Whatever programming language you choose, you'll store your programs in text files. And UNIX, which is very text-oriented, provides a host of tools for working with text files.

This chapter covers a variety of text editors, special programming editors, and a number of UNIX utilities for manipulating text.

Your choice of editor depends on personal preference, I'm not inclined to recommend any of these editors. (I've been using **vi** for many years and find that my fingers have learned the **vi** commands to such an extent that it's very hard to migrate to another text editor, such as **emacs**.) Try the ones you think may fit your needs. Many are available on the CD-ROM that comes with this book. In addition, most UNIX systems provide text-based editors as well as windowed text editors, so you can pick from what's already available on your system.

One key criterion that you may want to consider is to stick to editors that run on all the platforms you use. For example, **vi** and **emacs** have been ported to just about every system in existence, including Windows. Other editors, like **nedit**, haven't. Another criterion may be that the editor works in text mode and in a graphic mode. I sometimes dial into UNIX systems or use **telnet**, and any work done in this manner requires text-only programs. Both **emacs** and **vi** work in text mode, which is one reason these editors are used by most UNIX programmers.

Almost all UNIX systems provide **vi**. Many also provide **emacs**. (**emacs** and a number of **vi** clones are on the CD-ROM that comes with this book.)

In addition to the ubiquitous **vi** and **emacs**, most UNIX systems provide some form of windowed text editor with a graphical interface. Table 4.1 lists some of the text editors that come with major UNIX systems.

Table 4.1 Graphical Editors Provided by Major UNIX Platforms

Editor	System	Interface
dtpad	HP, Sun, IBM, DEC	Common Desktop Environment
vuepad	HP	Motif
jot	Silicon Graphics	SGI/Motif
textedit	Sun, Linux	Open Look

There are also a number of freeware text editors, such as **emacs**, that may better fit your needs. Table 4.2 lists a number of freeware graphical text editors.

Table 4.2 Freeware Graphical Text Editors

Editor	Interface
emacs	Athena or Motif
nedit	Motif
tkedit	Tcl/Tk
xcoral	Xlib
xwb	XView

The next sections briefly introduce these editors, starting with **vi** and **emacs**, the most common text editors in the UNIX community. I hope to give you enough of a taste of an editor for you to decide whether you want to try it. Only by trying an editor will you know whether or not you like it.

One important aspect to **vi** and **emacs** is that both work in text mode and graphics mode. Thus, if you log on to a UNIX system through a text-based terminal interface, both **emacs** and **vi** will work fine, while the X-based graphical editors, such as **nedit**, require you to run the X Window System to work. This may be an issue. If so, stick to **vi** or **emacs**. (Even with all these other choices, most programmers on UNIX stick to either **emacs** or **vi**.)

vi

vi was one of the first screen mode, as opposed to line mode, editors. This means that **vi** uses your entire terminal to edit text. This advance was really something in the 1970s, but it seems rather primitive today. For some reason, though, **vi** has become the UNIX editor that's available on all systems.

NOTE Actually, I once found a system from Prime Computer that didn't come with **vi**. There are many other reasons you'd never want to use this system, though.

If you don't have **vi**, don't fret, there are a number of versions on the CD-ROM in the **editors/vi** directory.

vi bases its work on modes. At any time, you're in either command mode or input mode. In input mode, you enter text. In command mode, you can enter commands (a number of the commands start input mode, such as **i**).

To exit input mode, hit the **Escape** key.

Remembering which mode you're in can be tricky, but it really isn't all that hard (my fingers seem to have the memory for **vi** commands).

If you forget which mode you're in, simply hit the **Escape** key. If you were in input mode, **Escape** will take you to command mode. If you were already in command mode, **vi** will simply beep. Either way, after hitting the **Escape** key, you will know for sure that you're in command mode.

The most-used **vi** commands appear in Table 4.3.

Table 4.3 Common vi Commands

Command	Action
u	Undo last command
r	Replace text, enter input mode
i	Enter input mode, inserting new text
a	Enter input mode, appending new text
:e *filename*	Stop editing current file; load *filename* and start editing it
:r *filename*	Read *filename* and include it in the current file
:n	Jump to next file on command line
:n *filename*	Jump to named file
:w	Save current file
:w *filename*	Save under new name
:rew	Rewind to beginning of file list
yy	Yank a line to copy buffer
5yy	Yank five lines to copy buffer

*N*yy	Yank *N* lines to copy buffer, where *N* is a number
p	Paste copy buffer
ZZ	Save current file and quit
:wq	Save current file and quit
:q	Quit without saving
Escape	Exit input mode
/*text*	Search ahead for *text*
?*text*	Search backward for *text*

NOTE The **vi** clone called **vim** implements undo differently. Instead of one level of undo, **vim** provides multiple levels of undo. Thus, **u u** does not redo the last undone command with **vim** like it does with normal **vi**.

Editing Many Files with vi

You can edit a number of files with **vi**, but only one at a time. To start **vi** with a number of files, pass all the files on the command line. For example, the following command edits all the files in the current directory ending in **.c**:

```
$ vi *.c
```

vi calls up the first file. To jump to the next file, use the **:n** command. To go back a file, use **:e#**. To start again in the file list, use **:rew**. To save any file, use **:w** to save to its current name.

Copy and Paste with vi

If you run under the X Window System, you'll run **vi** in a shell window, such as that provided by **xterm**, **dtterm**, and so on. You can then take advantage of the graphical environment, even while using a text-mode editor such as **vi**.

In **xterm**, **dtterm**, **hpterm**, **winterm**, and most other windowed shell programs, you can select text with the leftmost mouse button. Clicking the middle mouse button pastes the selected data. If you have **vi** in insert mode—this is very important to avoid potentially destructive **vi** commands—click the middle mouse button to paste the selected data into the **vi** editor. This is a very handy way to combine the best of the windowed environment with old text-mode tools like **vi**. Figure 4.1 shows an example of pasting text into **vi**.

When comparing **vi** to **emacs**, there always seems to be a battle over which editor is better, but it all boils down to what editor makes *you* the most productive. That's always the best choice.

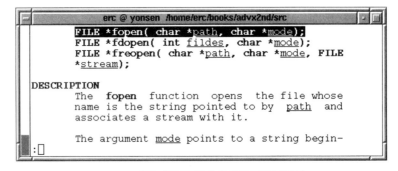

Figure 4.1 Pasting data into **vi**.

emacs

emacs is one of the most advanced, complicated, and frustrating editors in existence. With a built-in LISP compiler, there's not a lot you *can't* do in **emacs**. The only problem is figuring it out. **emacs** is famous for lots of **Ctrl**, **Escape**, and **Alt** key commands, more cryptic than anything you ever imagined. Even so, **emacs** provides its devotees a very productive full-blown software development environment.

Unfortunately, my fingers retain the **vi** commands so well that it makes it hard to quit **vi**. You'll probably find that as well, and stick to the first editor you became really productive with.

emacs works well in a text-based terminal or on an X Window screen. It provides a number of useful features in a text editor, including:

- Multiwindowed: Emacs allows you to edit files in multiple windows at the same time.

- Customizable: You can redefine keys and create other customizations in **emacs**.

- Extensible: Users have written **emacs** packages to read and send email, add C- and C++-specific commands for editing code files, view **tar** files as directories, and grab files over a network.

- UNIX-oriented: You can launch shell commands from **emacs** and even edit directories in an **emacs** window.

- Self-documenting: **emacs** comes with extensive online help material (and frankly, **emacs** needs it). Just type **Ctrl-h**.

Figure 4.2 shows **emacs** in a windowed environment in all its glory.

98

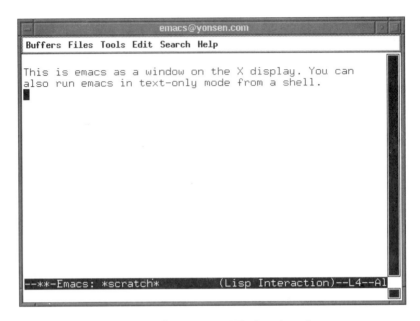

Figure 4.2 The **emacs** X Window interface.

emacs works off the concepts of buffers. Each separate window is a *buffer*. You can save buffers to disk, load up files into buffers, and generally edit text in buffers.

emacs allows you to split the screen to display more than one buffer at a time. You can also cycle between buffers, allowing you to edit many files at the same time, if you want.

emacs implements undo functions by reserving one buffer as the *kill* buffer. This allows you to see old deleted text and restore it, if you want.

At any given time, only one buffer—or window—is active.

Control and Meta Keys

Just about every **emacs** command starts with a **Ctrl** or **Meta** key combination. As you look up **emacs** commands in the extensive online help, *C* stands for *Control* and *M* for *Meta*. The **Meta** key won't exist on your keyboard as *Meta*; it's usually the **Alt** key or sometimes the **Escape** key.

Thus the **C-x C-c** command, to save your files and exit **emacs**, is really **Ctrl-x Ctrl-c**. The **emacs** documentation uses the shorthand notation **C-x** for **Ctrl-x** and **M-x** for **Meta-x**.

The reason for these odd commands is that when you're editing text in **emacs**, you just start typing. All the characters you enter go into the buffer. This is unlike **vi**, which requires you to be in input mode. You can just type in **emacs**. This makes entering commands harder in **emacs** than in **vi**, though.

Table 4.4 covers some of the most common editing commands in **emacs**.

Table 4.4 Common emacs Commands

Keyboard Shortcut	Action	Long Command
C-x C-c	Save buffers and kill emacs	save-buffers-kill-emacs
C-x u	Undo	undo
C-l	Clear screen, redraw	recenter
C-t	Transpose two characters	transpose-chars
Del	Delete character to left	delete-backward-char
C-d	Delete character to right	delete-char
C-k	Delete to end of line	kill-line
M-d	Delete word	kill-word
M-Del	Delete word to left	backward-kill-word

emacs also includes a set of navigation commands, shown in Table 4.5.

Table 4.5 Navigating in emacs

Keyboard Shortcut	Action	Long Command
C-a	Jump to beginning of line	beginning-of-line
C-e	Jump to end of line	end-of-line
C-f	Jump forward one character	forward-char
C b	Jump backward one character	backward char
M-f	Jump forward one word	forward-word
M-b	Jump backward one word	backward-word
C-n	Jump down one line	next-line
C-p	Jump up one line	previous-line

Entering Commands the Long Way

For any **emacs** command, there is a long command name and, often, a keyboard shortcut. If you prefer, you can enter commands the long way, using the syntax **M-x** *commandname*, such as:

```
M-x forward-char
```

Some commands don't have keyboard shortcuts, making the **M-x** command essential.

Getting Help in emacs

Ctrl-h calls up help mode in **emacs**. This is very useful. **emacs** provides a huge amount of online documentation to help you figure out this very large, complex program. Table 4.6 lists some handy help commands.

Table 4.6 Getting Help in emacs

Keyboard Shortcut	Action	Long Command
C-h k *key*	Provides help on given key	describe-key
C-h C-h C-h	Help on help	
C-h a *text*	Lists commands containing text	command-apropos
C-h b	List key bindings	describe-bindings
C-h c *key*	Name command bound to key	describe-key-briefly
C-h t	Show tutorial	help-with-tutorial
C-h w *command*	Lists keys that run *command*	where-is

Searching

Searching in **emacs** is easy. Type **Ctrl-s** and then start typing the text you want to search for. As you type each character, **emacs** jumps to the next occurrence where the text starts.

Table 4.7 lists the main search commands.

Table 4.7 Searching in emacs

Keyboard Shortcut	Action	Long Command
C-s	Search forward	isearch-forward
C-r	Search backward	isearch-backward

Buffers and Windows

emacs does most of its work in buffers, what most of us would call a window. Each file you edit goes into its own buffer. You can display one or more buffers in a single **emacs** window or create new windows (when running graphically).

Table 4.8 lists the most common window and buffer commands.

Table 4.8 Window and Buffer Commands

Keyboard Shortcut	Action	Long Command
C-x b	Jump to next buffer	switch-to-buffer
C-x b *buffer_name*	Jump to named buffer	switch-to-buffer
C-x 4 b	Jump to next buffer, create new window	switch-to-buffer-other-window
C-x 4 b *buffer_name*	Jump to named buffer, create new window	switch-to-buffer-other-window
C-x C-f *filename*	Load file into buffer	find-file
C-x 4 f *filename*	Load file into new window	find-file-other-window
C-x C-s	Save current buffer	save-buffer

To load a file into a buffer, type **C-x C-f** and then the file name. If **emacs** already loaded the file, **emacs** makes that buffer active. Otherwise, **emacs** creates a new buffer for that file.

To save the current file, type **C-x C-s**.

In an X Window environment, **emacs** works well with the mouse. You can place the cursor with the mouse, select text, and activate buffers.

Launching UNIX Commands from emacs

You can launch UNIX shell commands or simply launch a shell from **emacs**. The **M-!** command reads in your UNIX command and launches it.

The **M-x shell** command launches a subshell in an **emacs** buffer. You can then launch any UNIX command and edit your commands before execution—a very handy trait. You can copy text and paste it to make up a command, turning **emacs** into an enhanced UNIX shell.

Editing Directories

A special mode in **emacs** starts up the directory editor, called *dired*. With this, you view the files in a directory, delete files, and so on.

The **C-x d** command enters directory mode, or the **C-x 4 d** command enters directory mode in a new window.

Once in directory mode, you can load up a file with the **f** key. Simply select the file and type an **f**. Using **o** (*oh*) instead of **f** brings up the file in another window.

You can delete files in directory mode. First, you mark each file for deletion with the **d** key. (The **u** key unmarks a file.) Then, delete all the marked files with the **x** key.

Compiling Code from emacs

emacs is a highly integrated environment. You can literally do anything from **emacs**. Because a lot of people do a lot of program development, there are **emacs** commands to make life easier.

To compile code, use the **M-x compile** command. Error messages appear in an emacs buffer named *compilation* (note the asterisks).

You can run the **grep** command from within **emacs** with the command **M-x grep**. **grep**'s output also goes into the buffer named *compilation*.

The handy **C-x** ` (that's a back-tick character) jumps to where an error occurred or where **grep** found a match. Each time you type **C-x** `, **emacs** jumps to the next entry.

It's hard to provide even the barest flavor of **emacs**. I urge you to at least try this program; you may find it essential.

Graphical Editors

Aside from the great old text-mode editors, many UNIX systems also provide graphical text editors, so that, if you like, you can use the version that comes with your system. Any system that provides the Common Desktop Environment (CDE) provides an editor called **dtpad**, available from the CDE front panel and shown in Figure 4.3.

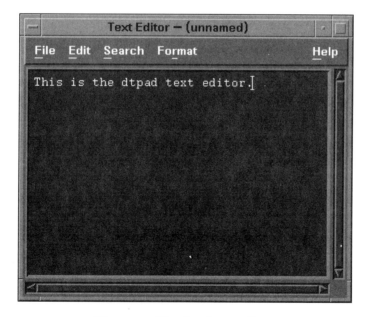

Figure 4.3 The **dtpad** text editor.

dtpad is very similar to **vuepad**, which is common on Hewlett-Packard systems. The interface follows standard Motif conventions.

Some users still run a number of Open Look applications. You'll find **textedit**, an Open Look text editor shown in Figure 4.4, available on Sun and Linux systems. On Linux, you need to install the OpenWindows applications.

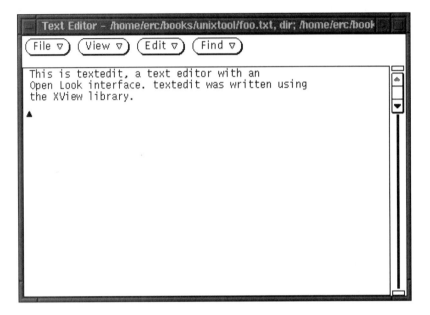

Figure 4.4 The **textedit** text editor.

By far the best graphical editor I've seen, though, is **nedit**, which unfortunately requires the Motif libraries to compile. Most commercial UNIX systems provide Motif, most free UNIX systems do not. If you have the Motif programming APIs and you like graphical editors, **nedit**, shown in Figure 4.5, is for you.

Even on many systems that don't include the Motif APIs, such as Linux, you can get binary versions of **nedit** over the Internet (at *ftp.fnal.gov* in the **/pub/nedit** directory) or from Linux CD-ROMs. See Appendix A for more on Linux.

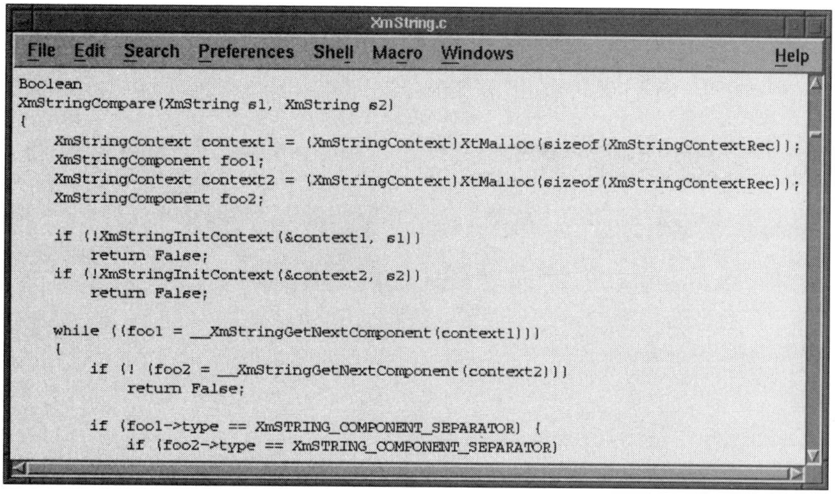

Figure 4.5 The **nedit** text editor.

Along with **nedit** comes a client-server mode program called **nc. nc**, short for **nedit** client, calls up **nedit** (acting in server mode in this usage) with a given file. You can also request that **nedit** place the cursor at a certain line within the file. This is very useful for calling up a file and placing the cursor at the line number of the first error detected by the compiler.

If you use an integrated development environment, often called an IDE, you may want to replace the editor in the environment with one of your own choosing, such as **nedit**. To integrate **nedit** into the environment, you can use the **nc** command, like the following example:

```
$ nc -line 11 -noask hi_unix.c
```

This command calls up **nedit** to display line 11 of the file **hi_unix.c**. The **-noask** command-line parameter tells **nc** not to ask whether or not to launch **nedit** (if it isn't already running). If **nedit** is already running, **nc** will cause **nedit** to call up the file in the current window.

In addition to **nedit**, I've had some luck with **tkedit**, an editor written entirely in Tcl/Tk (which you need to run the program). **tkedit**, shown in Figure 4.6, provides some limited programming add-ons. **tkedit** supports C, Tcl, and FORTRAN coding with a few extra functions, such as highlighting curly brace (open and close) and an option to add C-style comments.

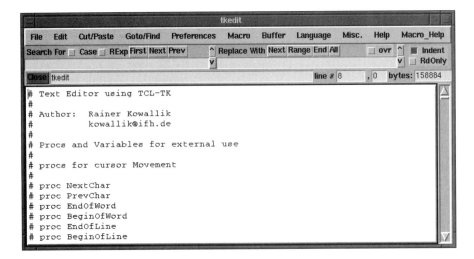

Figure 4.6 The main **tkedit** window.

While not a true source code editor, **tkedit** provides a number of nice features for C and C++ programmers.

Source Code Editors

Some text editors directly support editing source code. Most such editors add special commands to jump between the beginning and ending braces or parenthesis (depending on the language involved), automatically indent levels of code, and perhaps browse C++ classes.

One such editor is **xcoral** (**emacs** is another). **xcoral**, shown in Figure 4.7, provides a C and C++ browser that allows you to jump from function to function.

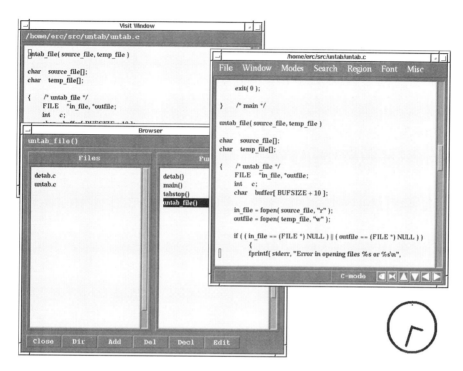

Figure 4.7 xcoral browsing a C program.

Choose the **Add** button in the browser window to add more files to the list of files **xcoral** browses. You can then select a class or function in the browser window and instantly see that class or function in an **xcoral** window. This is very handy, especially if you are modifying code written by someone else.

Programming Environments

In addition to source-code editors, you can find a few integrated development environments. Very common in the Macintosh and Windows worlds, these are not as common on UNIX. The main reason is that each UNIX vendor sells its own IDE, such as Hewlett-Packard's SoftBench. This IDE only runs on the one vendor's systems, detracting from portability.

By far, most UNIX programmers don't use one of these environments. Instead, most UNIX programmers tend to use shell commands like **make** and **cc**.

On the free software front, there's **xwpe**, a clone of the old Borland IDE for MS-DOS. It's a somewhat primitive program, but it provides a link to source code control systems such as RCS (see Chapter 8) and **make**, covered in Chapter 3.

xwpe appears in Figure 4.8.

Figure 4.8 xwpe, a Borland-like IDE.

xwb is another such programming environment, based on the XView API. You can launch **make** or other UNIX commands from **xwb**. You can see an **xwb** window in Figure 4.9.

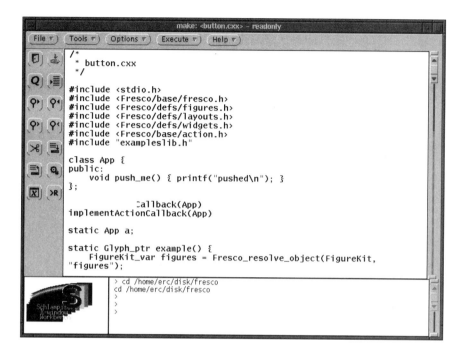

Figure 4.9 xwb in action.

 With **xwb**, you need to copy the file **xwb.config** to **.xwbrc** in your home directory, or **xwb** will not start up properly.

N O T E

If you are using an integrated development environment, you should be able to customize the environment to call up your favorite editor in place of the IDE's choice of editor. The way you do this differs for each environment, but some of the concepts are the same. You'll need to enter the command line for your editor, with suitable placeholders for the file name and line number to call up.

Other Editing Tools

UNIX comes with a number of other tools that can aid your editing tasks. The stream editor, **sed**, is a form of offline version of **vi** (or the **ex** engine that sits underneath **vi**). By this, **sed** allows you to specify some edits to make in batch mode rather than interactively. For example, **sed** is very good at going through a file (or set of files) and converting one reference to another, a company name perhaps, should your company get bought out.

awk is another text file tool, although it's most used for creating files, or reports on data kept in files. Finally, Perl is the mother of all scripting languages. You can do almost anything in Perl, including writing scripts to automate file edits.

Summary

This chapter just touched on the editing options available on UNIX. The CD-ROM, in the **editors** directory, contains a number of other editors that I've had mixed luck with. The ones covered in this chapter have worked best, compiled with the least hassles, and generally run better than the others. As always, though, editors are a matter of taste. Use the one that works best for you.

While this chapter covered how to edit text files on UNIX, the next chapter delves into a very common need: finding data from your program text files.

CHAPTER 5

Finding That Code

This chapter covers:

- Finding files
- Using **grep** to search for data
- **grep** and pipes
- **egrep**, an enhanced **grep**
- Searching the file system with **find**
- Viewing files
- Finding data in binary files
- Sorting files
- Counting lines of code

Text Tools on UNIX

In addition to the plethora of text editors introduced in the last chapter, UNIX provides many tools that work with text files, performing tasks such as searching and sorting.

This chapter introduces the most useful UNIX text file tools and shows how they help the programming task.

UNIX Tools—A Philosophy

The UNIX philosophy favors small tools that you pipe together using the shell pipe command, |. Because of this philosophy, you won't find many do-everything tools. Instead, you'll find little tools that you're supposed to put together the way you'd like. For example, one tool searches files for particular data (**grep**) while another tool sorts its input (**sort**). You can combine the two for a sorted list of found data using a pipe.

So, often you won't find the tool you're looking for—you'll need to build it. Luckily, UNIX provides a lot of technology to help in this regard.

Finding Files

One of the most common tasks I do is to find a particular piece of code. For any large software project, this task tends to quickly become burdensome.

UNIX provides three main tools for searching: **ls**, covered in Chapter 1; **grep**; and **find**. Despite its odd-looking name, **grep** is far more useful than **find** for programming-related tasks.

Using grep to Search for Data

grep is a handy tool with a bizarre name—shorthand for a general regular expression parser. The basic function of **grep** is to print lines that match a pattern. For example, to find all occurrences of the function call XOpenDisplay (which connects to the X server) in all files ending in *.c* in the current directory, you can use the following command:

```
$ grep XOpenDisplay *.c
chap2.c:     display = XOpenDisplay( displayname );
chap3.c:     display = XOpenDisplay( displayname );
chap4.c:     display = XOpenDisplay( displayname );
chap5.c:     display = XOpenDisplay( displayname );
colort.c:    display = XOpenDisplay( displayname );
dinfo.c:     display = XOpenDisplay( displayname );
display.c:   display = XOpenDisplay(display_name);
gumby.c:     display = XOpenDisplay( (char*) NULL);
mchat.c:     display = XOpenDisplay(widget->text);
notesend.c:   display = XOpenDisplay( displayname );
restest.c:   display = XOpenDisplay( displayname );
shape.c:     display = XOpenDisplay( displayname );
toolkit.c:   display = XOpenDisplay( displayname );
visinfo.c:   display = XOpenDisplay( displayname );
```

Each line represents one occurrence of the string XOpenDisplay. With multiple files of input, **grep**—by default—prints the file name and the line of text where **grep** detected the string.

If you use **grep** on one file, it returns only the matching text:

```
$ grep XOpenDisplay notesend.c
  display = XOpenDisplay( displayname );
```

The basic syntax for **grep** is:

grep *options pattern files*

As such, **grep** is very useful for tracking down where a particular function gets called or in simply finding the files you need to modify, based on some text string contained within the file.

There's a problem with **grep**, that isn't readily apparent in the preceeding examples. **grep** just looks for text strings; it doesn't pay any attention to the context. Thus, if you search for a particular string, **grep** will report all occurrences, not only those that are actual C function calls. For example, to find all occurrences of the function call XCreateWindow (which creates a window under the X Window System), you can use the following command:

```
$ grep grep XCreateWindow *.c
crtwind.c: * CreateWindow calls XCreateWindow to create an X window.
crtwind.c:    window = XCreateWindow( display,
```

The response shows which file the text string XCreateWindow was found in, but note that it found an occurrence that is obviously within a C comment. **grep** doesn't know anything about C (or any other programming language) syntax. All **grep** knows about is text.

grep searches text files for patterns, but it offers more than the simple ability to search for literal text strings like XCreateWindow.

Special Patterns with grep

grep also supports a complicated regular expression language that makes extreme use of most of the punctuation characters on your keyboard. You'll find **grep** soon becomes so complicated that it becomes unwieldy.

Table 5.1 lists some regular expressions and how to use them with **grep**.

Table 5.1. Regular Expressions with grep.

Expression	Matches
[0123456789]	Any single digit
[0-9]	Shorter form for above: matches any single digit
[A-Z]	Any uppercase letter, *A* to *Z*
[0-9A-Za-z]	Any alphanumeric character, 0 to 9, *A* to *Z* or *a* to *z*
[^0-9]	Any character *not* a digit

A caret, ^, converts a bracket expression to match anything not in the expression. For example, [^A-Z] matches any character that is not an uppercase letter.

grep prints out whole lines for what it matches. Thus, when you look for the pattern [^A-Z], **grep** prints any line that has a non uppercase character. These lines may also have uppercase characters—they just have to have at least one character that isn't uppercase.

The preceeding expressions cover more than most **grep** usage. Even so, there are more complicated expressions you can build with **grep**. See the online manual entry for **grep** for more on this subject.

Special Characters

The UNIX shell intercepts some the characters *,.,?,[, and], so you need to place these characters in quote marks, ", to pass them to **grep**. In addition, **grep** looks for command-line parameters that start with -. If your pattern contains a -, precede it with a backslash, for example \-, to tell **grep** to look for a dash. Otherwise **grep** will assume you're passing another command-line parameter.

The following example command looks for the pattern -m-:

```
$ grep "\-m\-"
```

Command-Line Parameters for grep

grep supports a number of command-line parameters. The parameters most useful that are available in most versions of **grep** appear in Table 5.2.

Table 5.2 Command-Line Parameters for grep

Command -Line Parameter	Meaning
-i	Ignore the case, so that *me* matches *Me*, *ME*, and *mE*
-l	Don't list the lines of text that match, just file names
-v	Select lines that don't match
-w	Only select lines that contain whole words

With the -i command-line parameter, **grep** ignores case in both the text string it looks for and the data in the files.

Searching for What Isn't There: A Zen Koan

With the -v command-line parameter, **grep** prints those lines in the files it searches that *don't* have the pattern you're looking for.

This option is useful for filtering data when you can determine a good filtering criteria.

grep with grep

For a realistic example of using the -v command-line parameter, many graphical programs require fixed-width fonts, usually for numeric input. **grep** helps find what fonts are available and filter the list to a manageable size. You can find out the name of all available X Window fonts with the **xlsfonts** program. Typing **xlsfonts** will result in a great deal of output, with very long font names:

```
-adobe-courier-bold-o-normal—10-100-75-75-m-60-iso8859-1
-adobe-courier-bold-o-normal—11-80-100-100-m-60-iso8859-1
-adobe-helvetica-bold-r-normal—17-120-100-100-p-92-iso8859-1
-adobe-new century schoolbook-bold-r-normal—0-0-100-100-p-0-iso8859-1
-adobe-symbol-medium-r-normal—10-100-75-75-p-61-adobe-fontspecific
-adobe-times-bold-r-normal—34-240-100-100-p-177-iso8859-1
-adobe-times-medium-i-normal—0-0-75-75-p-0-iso8859-1
-adobe-times-medium-r-normal—24-240-75-75-p-124-iso8859-1
-b&h-lucida-bold-i-normal-sans-34-240-100-100-p-215-iso8859-1
-b&h-lucidabright-medium-i-normal—17-120-100-100-p-96-iso8859-1
-b&h-lucidatypewriter-medium-r-normal-sans-34-240-100-100-m-200-iso8859-1
-bitstream-charter-medium-i-normal—12-120-75-75-p-65-iso8859-1
-daewoo-gothic-medium-r-normal—0-0-100-100-c-0-ksc5601.1987-0
-jis-fixed-medium-r-normal—16-150-75-75-c-160-jisx0208.1983-0
-schumacher-clean-medium-r-normal—6-60-75-75-c-60-iso8859-1
```

Among the output of **xlsfonts** shown earlier, fixed-width fonts usually have a -m- in the very long font name, for example:

```
-adobe-courier-bold-r-normal—14-100-100-100-m-90-iso8859-1
```

(The -m- stands for mono-spaced fonts.) To find all fixed-width fonts, you can use the following command:

```
$ xlsfonts | grep "\-m\-"
```

You'll see a lot of output. Note that most of these fonts are some variation of a style called Courier. Perhaps you don't want Courier fonts but are looking for something different. In this case, you'd use the -v command-line parameter with **grep** to find all fonts that don't have the text string *courier*. Try the following command:

```
$ xlsfonts | grep "\-m\-" | grep -v courier
-b&h-lucidatypewriter-bold-r-normal-sans-11-80-100-100-m-70-iso8859-1
-b&h-lucidatypewriter-bold-r-normal-sans-12-120-75-75-m-70-iso8859-1
-b&h-lucidatypewriter-bold-r-normal-sans-14-100-100-100-m-80-iso8859-1
-b&h-lucidatypewriter-bold-r-normal-sans-14-140-75-75-m-90-iso8859-1
-b&h-lucidatypewriter-bold-r-normal-sans-17-120-100-100-m-100-iso8859-1
-b&h-lucidatypewriter-bold-r-normal-sans-18-180-75-75-m-110-iso8859-1
-b&h-lucidatypewriter-bold-r-normal-sans-19-190-75-75-m-110-iso8859-1
-b&h-lucidatypewriter-bold-r-normal-sans-20-140-100-100-m-120-iso8859-1
-b&h-lucidatypewriter-bold-r-normal-sans-24-240-75-75-m-140-iso8859-1
-b&h-lucidatypewriter-bold-r-normal-sans-25-180-100-100-m-150-iso8859-1
-b&h-lucidatypewriter-bold-r-normal-sans-26-190-100-100-m-159-iso8859-1
-b&h-lucidatypewriter-bold-r-normal-sans-34-240-100-100-m-200-iso8859-1
-b&h-lucidatypewriter-bold-r-normal-sans-8-80-75-75-m-50-iso8859-1
-b&h-lucidatypewriter-medium-r-normal-sans-10-100-75-75-m-60-iso8859-1
-b&h-lucidatypewriter-medium-r-normal-sans-11-80-100-100-m-70-iso8859-1
-b&h-lucidatypewriter-medium-r-normal-sans-12-120-75-75-m-70-iso8859-1
-b&h-lucidatypewriter-medium-r-normal-sans-14-100-100-100-m-80-iso8859-1
-b&h-lucidatypewriter-medium-r-normal-sans-14-140-75-75-m-90-iso8859-1
-b&h-lucidatypewriter-medium-r-normal-sans-17-120-100-100-m-100-iso8859-1
```

The preceeding command searches for all fixed-width fonts (with a -m- in the long font name) that don't have the text string *courier* in the name. This is one way you can use **grep** with **grep** and UNIX pipes to filter your data.

 In addition to -m-, X supports another type of fixed-width font, called a *character* cell font. These fonts are identified by a -c-. See the section on **egrep** to see how to combine two searches together. For more on X Window fonts, see Appendix A for a listing of X Window books.

N O T E

Finding Whole Words

One of the tricks with **grep** is that you often get a lot more output than you bargained for. For example, if you search for Window, **grep** will gladly match any occurrence of *Window*, including XCreateWindow and XDestroyWindow. If you want to find only the data type *Window*, you can use the -w command-line parameter. This forces **grep** to select only those lines with the pattern as a whole word. For example:

```
$ grep -w Window *.c
apndprop.c: * X Window Applications Programming, 2nd ed.
apndprop.c:    Window window,
sendevnt.c: * X Window Applications Programming, 2nd ed.
sendevnt.c:Window   send_to_window; /* Window to send events to. */
sendevnt.c:    Window window, char* string);
```

egrep, an Enhanced grep

egrep is an enhanced **grep** that allows you to specify multiple search strings. For example, to find all occurrences of XOpenDisplay or XCreateWindow in files ending with .c, you can use the following command:

```
$ egrep "XOpenDisplay|XCreateWindow" *.c
chap2.c:    display = XOpenDisplay( displayname );
chap3.c:    display = XOpenDisplay( displayname );
chap4.c:    display = XOpenDisplay( displayname );
chap5.c:    display = XOpenDisplay( displayname );
colort.c:    display = XOpenDisplay( displayname );
crtwind.c: * CreateWindow calls XCreateWindow to create an X window.
crtwind.c:    window = XCreateWindow( display,
dinfo.c:    display = XOpenDisplay( displayname );
display.c:    display = XOpenDisplay(display_name);
gumby.c:    display = XOpenDisplay( (char*) NULL);
mchat.c:    display = XOpenDisplay(widget->text);
notesend.c:    display = XOpenDisplay( displayname );
restest.c:    display = XOpenDisplay( displayname );
shape.c:    display = XOpenDisplay( displayname );
toolkit.c:    display = XOpenDisplay( displayname );
visinfo.c:    display = XOpenDisplay( displayname );
```

The pipe character, |, tells **egrep** to report all lines that match either XOpenDisplay or XCreateWindow. You can also use **egrep** to search for fonts. Remember that -m- signifies one kind of fixed-width X Window font. The pattern -c- signifies another kind of fixed-width font. You can combine a search as follows:

```
$ xlsfonts | egrep "\-m-|\-c-" | more
```

There's also a program called **fgrep**, short for fast **grep**. The problem is, **fgrep** is slower than **grep**. For that reason, I normally stick to **grep** or **egrep**.

NOTE

While **grep** is a tool that searches within files, **find** looks for file names, file dates, and other criteria, not the actual content of files.

Searching the File System with find

The **find** program searches through the file system looking for files that match a certain criteria. **find** then performs some action on the files found. Sometimes you just want to get a list of the files that match the criteria; other times you may want to delete old files or back up changed files to tape. You can do all this with **find**, but **find** isn't very intuitive.

The basic syntax for **find** is as follows:

find *path expression actions*

find searches all files from the path on down, using the expression to decide whether the files match and then performing the actions on the files that match the expression.

For example, to find all files on disk that have a name **shape.c** and print the file names (with their paths), you can use the following command:

```
$ find / -name shape.c -print
find: /var/spool/cron: Permission denied
find: /var/spool/atjobs: Permission denied
find: /var/spool/atspool: Permission denied
find: /var/lib/uucp/taylor_config: Permission denied
find: /var/lib/uucp/hdb_config: Permission denied
find: /var/games/sasteroids: Permission denied
find: /usr/doc/emacs-19.31: Permission denied
find: /root: Permission denied
/home/erc/books/advx2nd/src/shape.c
```

The preceeding **find** command starts in the root directory, /, to search for everything on disk. It looks for only those files with a name of

shape.c (the expression) prints the name of all files found (only **/home/erc/books/advx2nd/src/shape.c** in this case).

Note the large number of directories in the example that **find** couldn't search. This is because I, a lowly user, don't have permission to mess in a number of system directories, although there seems to be no reason why the emacs-19.31 and games directories are among those I have no permission to mingle.

Most UNIX systems have a *lot* of files and directories. If you search from the root directory, /, expect **find** to take a long time to find things. On a network, **find** may have thousands of directories to look through. If you can narrow the search, for example, to your user account, you'll help **find** do a lot less work. To do this, start searching from your home directory, such as **/home/erc**, instead of /.

It may seem idiotic, but by default, **find** does nothing with what it finds. **find** won't even print the file names unless you ask it to. At first glance, this seems completely devoid of reason. But **find** was intended as a tool to be run in the background, often from **cron** (see Chapter 1 on **cron**).

Because background tasks run by **cron** aren't supposed to print data to the screen (you may not even be logged in when **cron** runs the task), **find** by default won't print any data. Thus, you always need to remember the -**print** action.

Table 5.3 lists the most commonly used expressions.

Table 5.3 Common Expressions for find

Expression	Meaning
-name *pattern*	Search for files with given name; can use wildcards like * and ?
-newer *filename*	Find files that were modified more recently than *filename*
-user *username*	File is owned by given user

The most common actions appear in Table 5.4.

Table 5.4 find Actions

Actions	Meaning
-exec *command*	Executes *command* for each file; replaces {} in the *command* with current file name
-fprint *filename*	Prints name of each file found into *filename*; GNU **find** only
-print	Prints file name

There are a number of different versions of **find** available. Not all versions support all the options.

NOTE

There's a lot more to **find**, mostly of importance to system administrators. See the online manuals for **find** for more on this.

Scrolling the Output of grep and find

As you work with **grep** and **find**, you'll often see more output than you can handle. To make the output scroll one screenful at a time, pipe the output to **more**. For example:

```
$ grep foo *.c | more
```

The output of the **grep** command will get paged by the **more** program, the standard UNIX tool for presenting a text file a page at a time.

You can then hit the **Spacebar** to go forward a page, the **Enter** key to go forward one line, and the letter **q** to quit.

For example, try the following command:

```
$ xlsfonts | grep adobe | more
```

On most UNIX workstations, **xlsfonts** will display copious amounts of information.

 xlsfonts only works in the X Window environment.

NOTE

You can also use **more** to view a file a page at a time, for example:

```
$ more shape.c
```

more and less

The main problem with **more** has always been that it only scrolls forward. Once you go past an area, you can't get back to it. This problem led to a program called **less** (a pun on **more**). With **less**, you can go forward and backward.

For example, try a command like the following:

```
$ less shape.c
```

less supports all the commands of **more**, such as the **Spacebar** to move forward. It also supports some simple navigation commands which are listed in Table 5.5.

Table 5.5. Navigation Commands in less

Command	Meaning
f	Go forward a full page
b	Go backward a full page
d	Go forward (down) a half page
u	Go back (up) a half page

You can also use **Cntrl-f**, **Cntrl-b**, **Cntrl-d**, and **Cntrl-u**, just like the navigation commands in the **vi** text editor.

N O T E

124

Sometimes you don't want to view an entire file. In those cases, the **head** and **tail** programs come in handy.

head and tail: Viewing the Top of Files

head prints the top few lines of a file—10 lines by default. For example:

```
$ head shape.c
```

You can change the number of lines printed with the -n command-line parameter. To display the first 20 lines, for example, use the following command as a guide:

```
$ head -n 20 shape.c
```

tail works the same way, but it displays the last few lines of a file. **tail** also supports the -n command-line parameter:

```
$ tail -n 20 shape.c
```

Some older versions of **tail** use a -1 command-line parameter instead of -n.

N O T E

Sometimes you want to view the end of a data file that's growing. For example, if you ever build a large software package, such as the X Window System, it's common to redirect the output of all the **make** commands into a large log file. Such a log file grows and grows. You can use **tail -f** (short for forever) to view the log file:

```
$ tail -f logfile
```

With the `-f` command-line parameter, **tail** loops forever awaiting new data at the end of the file. You can kill **tail** with **Cntrl-c**.

Finding Data in Binary Files

In addition to the programs that work with text files, UNIX offers the **strings** command to look for ASCII text strings within binary files.

The **strings** command prints all printable strings in a file. Normally, you call **strings** on a binary file, such as an executable program. (If the file is a text file, it is more convenient to use a text editor.)

When running **strings** on an executable file, you'll find interesting information buried within the file. For example:

```
$ strings shape | more
libXext.so.6
printf
_DYNAMIC
__environ
_init
XFree
XShapeQueryVersion
XShapeCombineMask
_fini
atexit
XFlush
_GLOBAL_OFFSET_TABLE_
exit
libX11.so.6
XSetWMProtocols
memmove
XCloseDisplay
memcpy
_IO_stderr_
XSetWMProperties
XFilterEvent
sprintf
XInternAtom
Shape extension not supported.
ERROR: Usage is:
```

126

This highly edited output shows a number of printable strings from an X Window application. Because the program was compiled with the -g option that includes debugging information, every function called in the program has a text entry in the executable file.

In addition, all literal strings used in the file, such as the error messages, also appear when you run **strings** on a program.

I've used **strings** mostly as a method of last resort. If I have an errant binary-only program with no source code or a strange data file that does not seem to be correct, I use **strings** to verify as much of the data as I can. In binary programs, you can often figure out what files and directories the program is trying to find by looking at the path names embedded in the binary executable.

NOTE I once came across a really weird side effect of using **strings**. Any message with **Cntrl-d** (ASCII character 4) will not print properly. In my case, I was searching through a binary file, verifying that a number of strings with the text *END* existed in the file. The file had the odd format of placing the string length first—as a number—then the text string. In this case, the length was 4 (*E-N-D* plus a trailing NULL character), making the UNIX end-of-file character **Cntrl-d** (ASCII 4). Because of this **Cntrl-d** character, **strings** ignored the whole string (^DEND in this case), and I never saw the END statement I was looking for. I spent a lot of time tracking down a bug that didn't exist, due to this strange quirk of **strings**. The moral of all this is not to place too much trust on the output of **strings**.

The tools described so far offer some generic abilities when dealing with files, but UNIX offers even more for dealing with code files in particular.

Ways to Look Up Code

I make very effective use of **grep** when tracking down where functions are defined, structures are used, and so on. If you have some time to prepare, though, UNIX offers better tools when working directly with source code files.

The **ctags**—for **vi**—and **etags**—for **emacs**—programs work almost the same. Both programs search through source code files for language constructs. For C and C++ programs, this is usually where each function is defined.

The **ctags** program was created to work with the **vi** text editor. **ctags** goes through a list of files and creates a file named **tags** in the current directory. Inside this **tags** file, **ctags** places an alphabetized list of tag names—usually function names. With each function, **ctags** places the file name and a search string needed to find where the function was defined. For example, try the following command in a directory of C code:

```
$ ctags *.c *.h
```

The **ctags** command builds up a list of functions and places the data in a file named **tags**. Next, use the **vi** editor to call up a function name. The syntax follows:

vi -t *functionname*

For example, using a function I wrote called `ReadProperty`, I can call up the proper file and place the text cursor at the start of the function with the following command:

```
$ vi -t ReadProperty
```

The `-t` command-line parameter tells **vi** to look for the given tag. The nice part about this is that you don't have to know which file contains the function definition; **ctags** finds it for you. This is *very* useful when you need to edit code written by someone else and you're not familiar with the file organization.

Inside the tags file created by **ctags**, you'll see one function name per line, followed by the file name and a search string to find the function inside the file. For example, here's a few lines from a **ctags** file:

```
AllocNamedColor color.c /^AllocNamedColor(Display* display,$/
AppendProperty apndprop.c    /^Bool AppendProperty(Display* display,$/
ReadProperty    mchat.c /^void ReadProperty(MchatInfo* info)$/
```

etags works similarly for **emacs** users, creating a file named **TAGS** in the current directory that contains much the same information.

Until now, the tools have queried files and directories. UNIX also offers a several tools that directly manipulate files.

Manipulating Files

UNIX provides a several commands for manipulating files. The most common task is to concatenate files.

Concatenating Files

The **cat** command concatenates files. For example:

```
$ cat *.c
```

This command concatenates all files ending in **.c** and prints them to the screen, one after another.

On its own, **cat** isn't very useful. In most cases, though, you'll use **cat** with some other tool, piping together the output of **cat** as the input of the other tool, such as **sort** for sorting files.

Sorting Files

The **sort** command sorts all the lines of text in a file or files, sending the sorted data to the screen. Usually you redirect the output of **sort** into a pipe or file. For example:

```
$ sort foo.txt > sorted.data
```

Sorting source code files is not very helpful. I mostly sort text files.

N O T E

Often, you'll combine **sort** with **cat**. Use **cat** to concatenate a lot of files and then **sort** to manipulate the results into an easier-to-read format. For example:

```
$ cat *.txt | sort > sorted.data
```

In the **sorted.data** file, you'll most likely see a lot of repeated lines. To get rid of those, you can use the program called **uniq**.

Looking for Unique Strings

The **uniq** command, short for *unique*, removes duplicate lines from a sorted file. In virtually all cases, you need to use **uniq** with **sort**. As you probably guessed, this hews closely to the UNIX philosophy of combining many small tools.

For example, to sort all the data in a number of text files and then remove all the duplicate lines, you can use the following command:

```
$ cat *.txt | sort | uniq > uniq_str.data
```

The resulting file **uniq_str.data** then contains the sorted results, with all duplicated lines removed. Sorting some of the text for this book gets me results like the following:

```
$ sort foo.txt > sorted.data
$ strings shape | more
$ touch hello.c
$ vi *.c
$ vi -t ReadProperty
$ wc -l foo.c
$ wc foo.c
$ xlsfonts | grep "\-m\-"
$ xlsfonts | grep "\-m\-" | grep -v courier
$ xlsfonts | grep adobe | more
```

Counting Lines of Code

The **wc** command reports the number of lines, words, and bytes in a text file. With source code files, the word count (based on white space separating words) is obviously suspect. But the number of lines is useful in determining lines of code, giving you a rough idea of how large a software project is. (Of course, some lines of code are more equal than others.)

If you pass no command-line parameters, **wc** provides all three values: lines, words, and bytes. For example:

```
$ wc foo.c
    265     988    6952 foo.c
```

The first value—the smallest—is the number of lines of text. The second is words, and the third is bytes.

If you just want lines, use the `-l` command-line parameter:

```
$ wc -l foo.c
    265 foo.c
```

Summary

This chapter covered the most useful UNIX commands for delving into and manipulating text files. Because all programs start out as source code in text files, UNIX offers a lot for programmers.

grep searches for data in files. **find** searches for files that match a pattern, usually a file name or a date. **egrep** is an enhanced **grep**, while **fgrep**, the so-called fast **grep**, isn't.

less offers more than **more**—the ability to go forward and backward in a file. UNIX is full of puns.

strings prints any text string it finds in files—even binary files. And, depending on your editor, **ctags** (**vi**) or **etags** (**emacs**) searches source code files and creates a form of database of C functions and place them in the files where the functions are defined.

In the next chapter, you'll discover what UNIX offers for installing software and find out how to improve your installation scripts.

UNIX Commands Introduced in This Chapter

cat

ctags

egrep

etags

fgrep

find

grep

head

less

more

uniq

sort

strings

tail

xlsfonts

CHAPTER 6

Installing Programs

This chapter covers:

- Archiving directory hierarchies with **tar**
- Using **tar** with pipes
- Shell archives, or **shar** files
- Splitting text files with **split**
- The **uuencode** and base 64 encoding methods
- **compress** and **gzip** for compressing files
- The **install** program
- **make** install targets
- Where to install your programs on UNIX systems

What You Need to Do

134

Whenever you provide software to someone, that person needs to install the program and any necessary support files. To do this, you need to:

- Bundle the files together.
- Compress the bundle.
- Decide where the files should be installed.
- On delivery, uncompress the bundle and copy the files to the proper locations.

This chapter covers a plethora of UNIX options for bundling, compressing, and delivery.

Bundling Your Software Together

The easiest and most-used method for bundling a large number of files is called **tar**, short for *tape archive*, although **tar** has nothing to do with tapes. (The reason for this is that **tar** deals with files. Under UNIX, most devices, including tape drives, are represented as files. Because **tar** works with files, **tar** works with tape devices; it also works with any other files on your hard disk.)

You may use **tar** to make backups to tape; **tar** manages archive files. A **tar** archive file contains any number of files you care to include.

tar allows you to place files in the archive, extract files, and list the contents. Each **tar** archive is itself a plain old UNIX file, so you can copy that file, delete it, and so on.

One of the best things about **tar** is that you can place entire directory hierarchies into **tar** archives. **tar** can then faithfully extract the entire hierarchy. This makes **tar** the best UNIX tool for bundling a large directory hierarchy and delivering that hierarchy to end users.

Working with tar

There are only three basic operations you perform with **tar**:

- Copying files into a **tar** archive file.
- Extracting files from a **tar** archive file.
- Listing the files inside a **tar** archive file.

To create a new **tar** archive file, you need to place some files into the archive, as shown in the following command:

```
$ tar cvf mytar.tar *.c
a apndprop.c 3 blocks
a chap2.c 6 blocks
a chap3.c 7 blocks
a chap4.c 7 blocks
a chap5.c 9 blocks
a checkarg.c 2 blocks
a checkgeo.c 3 blocks
a color.c 2 blocks
a colort.c 10 blocks
a crtwind.c 4 blocks
a cursor.c 2 blocks
a delwind.c 4 blocks
a dinfo.c 10 blocks
a display.c 4 blocks
a error.c 7 blocks
a filtevnt.c 3 blocks
```

This command places all files that end in **.c** into a new **tar** archive file named **mytar.tar**. The v command-line parameter puts tar into verbose mode, a handy way to check what's going on.

WARNING

Don't try any command that places the **tar** archive file inside itself, or **tar** will run recursively and eventually fill your disk. For example, *don't* try the following command:

```
$ tar cvf mytar.tar *.tar
```

This command is problematic because the ***.tar** pattern matches the **tar** file itself.

To see what's in our new **tar** archive file, you can use the **t** command-line parameter to list a table of contents—the names of all the files in the archive. For example:

```
$ tar tvf mytar.tar
rw-r—r— 367/10    1252 Aug 16 20:21 1994 apndprop.c
rw-r—r— 367/10    2717 Jun  3 22:02 1994 chap2.c
rw-r—r— 367/10    3165 Jun  8 20:03 1994 chap3.c
rw-r—r— 367/10    3312 Jun  8 20:03 1994 chap4.c
rw-r—r— 367/10    4602 Jun  8 20:15 1994 chap5.c
rw-r—r— 367/10     925 Apr 14 18:41 1994 checkarg.c
rw-r—r— 367/10    1478 Jun  3 20:24 1994 checkgeo.c
rw-r—r— 367/10     906 Jul  7 17:01 1994 color.c
rw-r—r— 367/10    4945 Jun 12 19:08 1994 colort.c
rw-r—r— 367/10    1545 Jun  3 20:24 1994 crtwind.c
rw-r—r— 367/10     655 Jun  8 20:21 1994 cursor.c
rw-r—r— 367/10    1825 Aug 16 19:58 1994 delwind.c
rw-r—r— 367/10    5035 Apr 14 18:44 1994 dinfo.c
rw-r—r— 367/10    1815 Mar 21 20:37 1994 display.c
rw-r—r— 367/10    3233 Jul 14 19:52 1994 error.c
rw-r—r— 367/10    1447 Jun  5 12:42 1994 filtevnt.c
```

To extract the files from the archive, you can use the x command-line parameter:

```
$ tar xvf mytar.tar
x apndprop.c, 1252 bytes, 3 tape blocks
x chap2.c, 2717 bytes, 6 tape blocks
x chap3.c, 3165 bytes, 7 tape blocks
x chap4.c, 3312 bytes, 7 tape blocks
```

```
x chap5.c, 4602 bytes, 9 tape blocks

x checkarg.c, 925 bytes, 2 tape blocks

x checkgeo.c, 1478 bytes, 3 tape blocks

x color.c, 906 bytes, 2 tape blocks

x colort.c, 4945 bytes, 10 tape blocks

x crtwind.c, 1545 bytes, 4 tape blocks

x cursor.c, 655 bytes, 2 tape blocks

x delwind.c, 1825 bytes, 4 tape blocks

x dinfo.c, 5035 bytes, 10 tape blocks

x display.c, 1815 bytes, 4 tape blocks

x error.c, 3233 bytes, 7 tape blocks

x filtevnt.c, 1447 bytes, 3 tape blocks
```

NOTE

In each of the preceding commands, the f command-line parameter names the file we're using as a **tar** archive. If you omit the f command-line parameter, **tar** defaults to using a tape drive, such as **/dev/rmt0**. This default is very handy for making backups, but not for installing software—unless the software resides on a tape.

Table 6.1 lists the most important command-line parameters for **tar**.

Table 6.1 tar Command-Line Parameters

Parameter	Usage
c	Create a new **tar** archive file.
r	Add files to the end of an existing **tar** archive.
t	List the files in a **tar** archive file.
x	Extract files from a **tar** archive file.
f *filename*	Use *filename* for the **tar** archive file, instead of the default file, which is normally a tape drive.
f -	Write to standard output or read from standard input.
o	Change file ownership to that of the user issuing **tar** command.
v	Verbose mode; print information on what **tar** does.

tar will archive and extract full directory hierarchies. You just need to pass a directory name to **tar** on the command line. For example, to archive an entire directory named **src**, you can use the following command:

```
$ tar cvf mytar.tar ./src
a ./src/apndprop.c 3 blocks
a ./src/chap2.c 6 blocks
a ./src/chap3.c 7 blocks
a ./src/chap4.c 7 blocks
a ./src/chap5.c 9 blocks
a ./src/checkarg.c 2 blocks
a ./src/checkgeo.c 3 blocks
a ./src/color.c 2 blocks
a ./src/colort.c 10 blocks
a ./src/crtwind.c 4 blocks
a ./src/cursor.c 2 blocks
a ./src/delwind.c 4 blocks
a ./src/toolkit.h 7 blocks
a ./src/dinfo.c 10 blocks
a ./src/display.c 4 blocks
a ./src/error.c 7 blocks
a ./src/filtevnt.c 3 blocks
```

This **tar** command archives everything in the **src** subdirectory into the **tar** file.

WARNING

Never use a full path from the root directory with **tar**. For example, don't place the contents of the **/usr/local** directory into a **tar** archive. Why? Because when you extract the data, it will go directly into **/usr/local**. If you only work on one machine, this is OK. But, if you extract the **tar** archive file on another machine, it could overwrite important system data.

Some versions of **tar** automatically remove the leading / from a directory name, ensuring that this problem won't occur. Don't depend on this.

If you avoid the full path and instead use a relative path, **tar** will extract into the current directory. For example, if you need to archive **/usr/local**, first change to the root directory and then archive the data in **usr/local** (when you're in the root directory, **/usr** is really a subdirectory of the current directory). If you do this, then you can extract the data without over-writing key files on your hard disk. Later you may want to copy those files into the real **/usr/local**, but you have time to check things out first.

Using tar with Pipes

tar recognizes the file name **-** as a special file; it tells **tar** to use either standard input—if reading—or standard output—if writing. This allows you to use **tar** with UNIX pipes.

The most common usage of this special file name is to create a special command to copy a whole directory hierarchy to another directory. To copy all data from a directory named **from_dir** to a directory named **target_dir**, you can use the following command:

```
cd from_dir; tar cf - . | (cd target_dir; tar xf -)
```

This command is somewhat complicated. Each semicolon ends a complete shell command. The semicolon causes all the commands to be executed from the same shell. (If you didn't do this, the **cd** command would change the directory for a different shell and you'd run **tar** in the wrong directory.

The first part of the command changes to the **from_dir** directory and then runs **tar** on all the files in the current directory (.):

```
cd from_dir; tar cf - .
```

The `cf` - command-line parameters tell **tar** to create a new archive and use standard output as the file to write to. The period tells **tar** to archive the current directory.

The output of the first part is then sent as input to the second part:

```
(cd target_dir; tar xf -)
```

The second part is a bit trickier. The commands must be placed inside parenthesis to ensure that the shell gets the **tar** data as standard input. Otherwise, the **cd** command would get the entire **tar** archive as standard input and would ignore the data, because **cd** doesn't deal with standard input. By using the parenthesis, the input data gets passed on to **tar**.

The xf - command-line parameters tell **tar** to extract all the files in the **tar** archive and that the archive file is in standard input.

Putting the entire command together, you can copy all the contents of **/usr/local/include** to a backup directory, such as **include.backup**, with the following command:

```
cd /usr/local/include; tar cf - . | \
    (cd /home/erc/include.backup; tar xf -)
```

This is a very handy way to copy file hierarchies from a network-mounted disk. **tar** creates binary archive files. Sometimes, though, you need a text-only archive.

Shell Archives

The **shar** program creates a shell archive, which you can use to bundle your files. A *shell* archive is merely a shell script that, when run, extracts a number of files. All the data for all these files resides within the shell archive. Virtually every shell archive I've seen holds source code files.

The main purpose of these shell archives, or **shar** files, is to create a text-only bundle that can be mailed as one unit and then extracted by the recipient. If you use **tar**, you'll need to convert the binary **tar** file into an ASCII-printable file using **uuencode** or **uuenview**—described which are in the section on dealing with binary files). **shar** works with text files and creates a text-only archive.

shar expects all the input files to be text files. It expects files to have lines of text; you're asking for trouble if you feed **shar** a binary file.

N O T E

The basic syntax is as follows:

shar *input_files* > *output_file.sh*

For example, the following command bundles all the files ending in **.c** and **.h** in the current directory into an archive called **myshar.sh**:

```
$ shar *.c *.h > myshar.sh
```

A shell archive is really a large shell script with the files as data embedded within the script. Because **shar** files are shell scripts, the usual extension is **.sh**, (sometimes **.shar**). That's right, **shar** files are really Bourne (**sh**) shell scripts. This makes **shar** archives easy to extract for the recipients of your archives.

WARNING

Be sure that the output file is not included in the input. If this happens, **shar** will run over and over, filling the output file and then trying to insert the contents of the output file into the output file. Eventually, this will fill your disk. For example, the following command is dangerous:

```
$ shar *.sh > myshar.sh
```

Here, **myshar.sh** is the output file. But, because the file name ends in **.sh,** **myshar.sh** is also an input file. Don't run a command like this!

As **shar** runs, it will print the names of the files it archives, as in the following:

```
shar: Saving apndprop.c (text)
shar: Saving chap2.c (text)
shar: Saving chap3.c (text)
shar: Saving chap4.c (text)
shar: Saving chap5.c (text)
shar: Saving checkarg.c (text)
shar: Saving checkgeo.c (text)
```

Inside the **shar** file, **myshar.sh** in this example, you'll see a bona-fide shell script. The shell script starts with comments identifying the files inside, as in the following:

```
#!/bin/sh
# This is a shell archive (produced by GNU sharutils 4.1).
# To extract the files from this archive, save it to some FILE, remove
# everything before the '!/bin/sh' line above, then type 'sh FILE'.
#
# Made on 1996-09-19 19:30 GMT by <erc@yonsen>.
# Source directory was '/home/erc/books/unixtool/shar'.
#
# Existing files will *not* be overwritten unless '-c' is specified.
#
# This shar contains:
```

```
# length mode        name
# ──  ────  ─────────────────
#   1251 -rw-r-r- apndprop.c
#   2717 -rw-r-r- chap2.c
#   3165 -rw-r-r- chap3.c
#   3312 -rw-r-r- chap4.c
#   4602 -rw-r-r- chap5.c
#    925 -rw-r-r- checkarg.c
```

After the initial comments, you'll see some shell commands and then the start of the first file. Each line normally gets an *X* added to the beginning of the line, as in the following:

```
X    SetWMHints(display, window, x, y, width, height,
X        argc, argv,
X        "My Window Name",
X        "my icon",
X        "chap2",
X        "AdvX2nd");
```

The *X*es are removed when you unpack the shell archive. At the end of the file, you'll see the **shar** end-of-file marker: SHAR_EOF. Then you'll see a few more shell commands and the start of the next file.

Unpacking a Shell Archive File

To unpack a shell archive file, you can run the file from the Bourne shell. For example:

```
$ sh myshar.sh
```

As **sh** executes the **shar** file, you'll see the name of each file extracted, as follows:

```
sh myshar.sh
x - extracting apndprop.c (text)
x - extracting chap2.c (text)
x - extracting chap3.c (text)
x - extracting chap4.c (text)
```

```
x - extracting chap5.c (text)
x - extracting checkarg.c (text)
x - extracting checkgeo.c (text)
```

Sending Shell Archives via Email

One of the main purposes of the shell archive format is that you can send such a file via email. The key is that a **shar** file is made entirely of text.

NOTE I know that the wonderful world of MIME is supposed to make email attachments the easiest thing in the universe. MIME should ensure that you can attach binary files to email messages and take care of all the sundry issues about sending binary files. But the fact of the matter is that many email systems still treat attachments differently. Many popular packages don't use MIME, don't understand MIME attachments and don't send proper attachments. Because of this, I find it better to be safe than sorry.

If you get a **shar** file via email, there's likely to be an email header that interferes with the syntax expected by **sh**. The topmost lines of the file contain a number of email fields, such as From: and Subject: fields:

```
From erc@yonsen.com  Thu Sep 19 19:40:00 1996
Return-Path: erc
Received: (from erc@yonsen.com) by yonsen.com
Thu, 19 Sep 1996 19:39:59 GMT
From: "Eric F. Johnson" <erc@yonsen.com>
Message-Id: <199609191939.TAA00703@yonsen.com>
Subject: Source code
To: erc@yonsen.com (Eric F. Johnson)
Date: Thu, 19 Sep 1996 19:39:59 +0000 (GMT)
X-Mailer: ELM [version 2.4 PL25]
MIME-Version: 1.0
Content-Type: text/plain; charset=US-ASCII
Content-Transfer-Encoding: 7bit
Status: RO

#!/bin/sh
# This is a shell archive (produced by GNU sharutils 4.1).
```

```
# To extract the files from this archive, save it to some FILE, remove
# everything before the `!/bin/sh' line above, then type `sh FILE'.
#
# Made on 1996-09-19 19:30 GMT by <erc@yonsen>.
# Source directory was `/home/erc/books/unixtool/shar'.
```

Note how the **shar** file starts about 16 lines down in the email file. In this case, you have two options: you can edit the email file in a text editor, stripping off the email header, or you can pass the file—email header and all—to **unshar**.

The **unshar** program scans a file for the start of a shell script—usually a line starting with #!/bin/sh—and then spawns a shell that executes the script. For example, assuming you saved your email message to a file named **myshar.email**:

```
$ unshar myshar.email
```

The only problem is that many UNIX systems don't come with **unshar**.

Don't worry. The source code for **shar** and **unshar** are in the **install** directory on the CD-ROM.

CD-ROM

Every UNIX system should have **sh**. This is another advantage to using shell archives: all UNIX users can unpack the archive. No special software is required.

Dealing with Large Archives

Many email systems limit the size of a message, often counting by the number of lines. You'll often discover this after you send a message and the recipients only get part of the data.

The issue normally isn't your or the recipient's email system. Chances are the problem lies in an email system between the two machines. Somewhere along the chain of systems that make up the Internet, some system cut off your message.

NOTE

I find this problem most acute when sending email to users far away, such as when I send messages from the United States to Japan. Again, modern email systems are supposed to take care of this problem; in my experience, though, they don't.

The simple solution to this problem is to create a number of smaller **shar** files and send each smaller file as a separate email message. Of course, this method results in a lot of work to send an email message.

UNIX provides a handy tool called **split** to get around this. **split** splits apart text files into a set of smaller text files.

The basic syntax for **split** follows:

split -l *lines input_file output_prefix*

WARNING

split only works with text files. Do not attempt to **split** a binary file.

By default, **split** divides a file into smaller files, each with 1000 lines. The last chunk will likely be smaller than 1000 lines.

The output prefix is used to identify the files. For each file **split** creates, **split** appends a code, such as *aa*, *ab*, or *ac*, onto your prefix.

For example, to split the **shar** file created earlier, you could use the following command:

```
$ split -l 300 myshar.sh split
```

This command creates the following smaller files:

```
splitaa
splitab
splitac
```

When you list the split files, they appear in alphabetical order. **split** ensures that this is the file order, so the typical suffixes start at *aa*, then *ab*, up to *az*, and then starting with *ba*, *bb*, to *bz*, and so on.

146

Restoring split Files

To restore the original file, you need to concatenate all the **split** files. For the earlier example, the following command restores the original file:

```
$ cat split* > original.sh
```

After executing this command, the **original.sh** file and the **myshar.sh** file should match exactly.

Restoring split Files Sent via Email

If you receive a set of **split** files via email, you can expect to have an email header at the top of each file. You first need to save each file—likely in a separate message—to disk. If you save all the **split** files separately, then you can concatenate the files together with **cat**.

But there's a problem: all the files have email headers. To get around this, you can manually edit the files. Search for the text From:, which starts every email message. Delete all the email header lines.

For a large number of **split** files, the manual editing approach can be a real hassle. To get around this, a number of programs, including **uudeview** (covered later) will automatically remove the email headers for you. Many email programs also do this.

Dealing with Binary Files

The traditional UNIX email system requires all messages to be in text format. Even with new standards such as MIME, which allows for binary files attached to email messages, the actual data transmitted must still be text. If you send a binary file, your email system should transform the data into printable text. This is done through an encoding mechanism that ensures all nonprintable data is transformed into printable characters.

 You'll see a lot of messages on the Internet Usenet news encoded in this fashion.

N O T E

The two standard methods for this task are called *base 64*, used for MIME messages, and **uuencode**, an older encoding system. Both methods result in files that are entirely ASCII-printable.

To use the **uuencode** method, you use a program named **uuencode**. The basic **uuencode** syntax follows:

uuencode *input_filename name > output_file*

The *input_filename* is the name of the input file. The name is placed within the uuencoded file and is usually the same name as the input file. All the data gets written to the output file.

If you skip the *input_filename*, then **uuencode** takes input from the shell, usually from input redirection (<) or a pipe (|).

For example, you can use the following command on a **tar** file named **mytar.tar**:

```
$ uuencode mytar.tar mytar.tar > mytar.uu
```

Yes, you repeat the input file name. The first **mytar.tar** names the input file. The second **mytar.tar** names the file inside the output, **mytar.uu**. This second name is the *decoding name*, the name the user will see after decoding the encoded file.

When done, the **mytar.uu** file will contain data like the following:

```
begin 644 mytar.tar
M(R$J($&FEN+W-H"B,5&$I<R%I<R%A('-H96QL(&%%R8VVI=F4=F4@*'$!R;V1U8V5D
M(&&Y($$$($&Y=YUU96Y90R4!R``5=V5`%S:&`L%9%U96%%!2U$E!2%F;'-`]
...
```

(encoded data continues)

The first line of the data contains the decoding name. At the end of the data, you'll see an end statement to signify the end of the data:

```
M.38@)WAS=')I;F<N8R<@)B8*("!C:&UO9"`P-C0T("="=X<W1R:6YG+F,,G('Q\
M"B`@96-H;R`G<F5S=&]R92!O9B!X<W1R:6YG+F,,@9F%I;&55D)PH@('-H87=7)?
M8VQU;G;G01(F!W8R`M8R`\("="=X<W1R:6YG+F,,G8("`("!T97;T-T(#(#((Y.3D@+65Q
M("#(<VAA<E]C;W5N=";("@@?'P**("``@(5C:&\@(G((GQAGAG(GQIGG(G(('H:F<N8R<@;;VW9)GX8E9
M86P@G:#<VER92`R(#(:R;++G!C=7)I^]R96U92!YT;W!R(F,,G(#(Y8];L;U?;<l>F]Y4@)?8V]B"F89)"F89)X
%:70@,`IZ
```
```
`
```

end

> The word *end* is very important. **uudecode** won't recognize the file as complete without *end*.

NOTE

To decode a uuencoded file, use the **uudecode** program. Its syntax follows:

uudecode *filename*

The *filename* is the name of the encoded file. The first line in this file, as shown earlier, names the output data file. For example:

```
$ uudecode mytar.uu
```

The base 64 format is similar to the **uuencode** format, but it is different enough to require its own encoding and decoding programs. You won't usually need to deal with base 64-encoded data; most of this data comes in the form of email messages. I hope your email system can automatically decode such data for you. If not, there are options.

A handy program called **uudeview** can encode and decode both the uuencoded and base 64 formats.

uudeview is located in the **install** directory on the CD-ROM.

CD-ROM

To convert an encoded file with **uudeview**, simply pass the file name on the command line. For example:

```
$ uudeview news.uu
Loaded from news.uu:  requirements.doc part 1   Base64

Found 'requirements.doc' State 16 Base64 Parts 1 OK

 -rw-r—r— requirements.doc    is OK   [d] (?=help)
    File successfully written to /home/erc/requirements.doc
```

uudeview will tell you what it thinks is in the encoded file and ask you to confirm the name for writing the file. **uudeview** comes with **uuenview**, which encodes files to either base 64 or **uuencode** formats.

Putting this all together, I've often used **tar** to archive a number of directories, **compress** or **gzip** to compress the binary file as small as possible (see the section on packing everything in), **uuencode** to create an ASCII-printable file, and **split** to split the large text file into smaller chunks that are acceptable for the Internet email system.

The recipient of such a file then needs to apply the same process in reverse: concatenate the split pieces together into one large text file, **uudecode** the text to create a binary file, use **uncompress** or **gunzip** to uncompress the file, and then use **tar** to extract a copy of the original files. This may seem like a long drawn-out process, but it allows you to transfer data via a simpler email link with UNIX systems at each end. Many countries provide less convenient access to the Internet than the United States, so I often use this method to communicate with customers overseas.

Packing Everything in

After figuring out all the issues with bundling your files, you'll probably note how large the package becomes. Especially on RISC architecture systems, executables tend to take up a lot of disk space. To help get around this, you can compress your bundle of files.

The main UNIX compression program is called **compress**. To compress a file, simply pass the file name to **compress**:

```
$ compress filename.c
```

The **compress** program compresses the file and then replaces the file with the compressed file. This compressed file has the same name as the original file, but with a **.Z** (that's an uppercase *Z*) extension.

compress removes the original file when it's finished. You're left with only the compressed file ending in **.Z**.

WARNING

For text files, **compress** often cuts the file size by 50 percent. For source code files, you can usually get even better compression.

To uncompress a compressed file, pass the compressed file name to **uncompress**:

```
$ uncompress filename.c.Z
```

uncompress restores the original file, **filename.c** in this case, and deletes the compressed file.

GNU Zip

In addition to **compress** and **uncompress**, which use a patented compression algorithm, you can use the freeware GNU Zip programs **gzip** and **gunzip**.

The GNU Zip programs generally compress files even smaller than compress, and they use a free algorithm.

Both **gzip** and **gunzip** reside on the CD-ROM in the **archive** directory.

CD-ROM

With the GNU Zip programs, you compress a file with **gzip**:

```
$ gzip filename.c
```

Unlike compress, **gzip** creates a file with a **.gz** extension, **filename.c.gz** in this case.

To uncompress a file made by **gzip**, you can use **gunzip**:

```
$ gunzip filename.c.gz
```

You can also use **gzip -d** to decompress files.

The GNU Zip programs have no relation to a separate package called Zip or PKZip for Windows systems. Ironically, both **gzip** and Zip use the same "deflate" algorithm, but they use different file formats.

If you have a file made by a Zip program on Windows, you can use the **unzip** UNIX program to extract the files from the **.zip** archive:

```
$ unzip filename.zip
```

unzip resides on the CD-ROM in the **archive** directory.

This version of **unzip** won't properly handle the long file names often used in newer Zip files on Windows 95 and NT.

Now that you've seen numerous ways to bundle your files and compress them to the smallest possible size, the next step is to deliver this data to the user and actually install your software. The first part of this task is to decide where to install the software.

Deciding Where to Install Your Software

The best software packages allow the user to choose in which directory to install the software. Of course, that doesn't let you off the hook completely.

Some tips for deciding where to install your software include:

- Pick a reasonable default, such as **/usr/local**.
- It's generally not a good idea to install your software into system directories like **/usr/bin**, **/usr/lib** or **/etc**. When the user upgrades to a new version of UNIX, your software may get trashed.
- Try to keep your files from spreading all over the file system. For example, if most of the files go into **/usr/local**, you shouldn't place other files in **/etc**.
- Try to avoid dependencies on file locations. If you can't, the common default location for these files is in a new subdirectory—named for your application—in **/usr/local/lib**.
- Try to keep all dependent files in one directory hierarchy, such as in **/usr/local/lib**.

Installing Your Software

If you distribute programs to users, you need to create a way for them to install your programs. Of course, for best results, you should follow the conventions on your particular platform. For example, Hewlett-Packard provides an installation program called **update**. which will load software from tape or CD so long as the software supports the update format.

Sun systems, many other UNIX systems based on UNIX System V R4, and Slackware Linux offer a program called **pkgadd**, which is part of the system's package management. A related **pkgrm** program removes such packages.

It seems that each UNIX platform supports different means and conventions for installation programs. While this is handy for users who are familiar with just one system, this can make it difficult for those who have to support multiple systems. Because of this, and because of the simple hassle of supporting many installation methods, you may want to diverge from what the vendor recommends and create some form of generic installation script.

Writing Installation Scripts

Unlike the Windows system with its fancy **setup** programs, most UNIX installation programs are simple shell scripts. There are two main reasons for this. First, UNIX systems support multiple processor architectures. This means you must provide a compiled installation program on each architecture you support, including Sun SPARC, HP PA-RISC, and Intel Pentium.

The second main reason is that UNIX systems don't provide graphics by default. While many systems provide an X Window login screen, you're never sure if the system administrator is logging in over a text-only line (such as via the **rlogin** or **telnet** program or a direct serial link). UNIX installation programs are expected to have a text-only installation if you provide a graphical installation.

Because of all this, and because the Bourne shell is standard equipment on all UNIX systems, virtually every installation script uses the Bourne shell. Installation scripts need to perform the following tasks:

- Create any necessary directories on the user's hard disk.

- Copy the files from the source media, such as CD-ROM or tape, to the final destination on the user's hard disk.

- Configure the software if necessary, for example, to look in the directory in which the user chose to install the program.

- Run any other setup utilities, such as licensing.

Inside your installation scripts, you need to copy the files from the source media, such as CD-ROM or tape, to the final destination on the user's hard disk, creating any necessary directories. For this task, you can use **tar**, described earlier, to unarchive a tar file, or the install program.

The install Program

The **install** program copies files to their final destination. Acting very much like an enhanced **cp** copy program, **install** creates directories as needed and sets the file attributes of the target software. As a safety feature, **install** refuses to overwrite files.

The basic syntax of **install** follows:

install *options source destination*

install *options* -d *directory*

The -d command-line parameter creates the given directory. Table 6.2. lists the most useful command-line parameters to **install**.

Table 6.2 Command-Line Parameters for install

Parameter	Usage
-c	Installs a file only if it does not already exist in the target directory.
-d *directory*	Creates named *directory*, if needed.
-g *group*	Set the file's owning group to *group*.
-m *mode*	Set file *mode*, usually an octal value such as 0644.

There are many versions of the **install** program. Not all these versions support all the command-line parameters. Because of this, it is important that you test your install scripts on each platform.

If you find a platform that doesn't support **install**, you can always use **cp**, **mkdir**, **chmod**, and other UNIX commands to simulate the effects of **install**.

When to Use install and When to Use tar

If you're starting from a large archive of files, **tar** is the better approach. **tar** creates directories and places files in them without a lot of individual install commands.

The **install** program works better if you're starting with a number of separate files. For example, if you distribute source code to your applications, after building the program with **make**, the Makefile *install* target would likely call **install** instead of **tar**. In this case, **install** copies the newly-built executable programs and support files to the proper directories.

Makefile Targets for Installation

If you distribute source code, all your Makefiles should all have an *install* target. This target should copy the executable programs and support files to the proper directories.

You should always allow the user to change the directory into which the software is installed. The software, after all, is going on the user's hard disk and the user should have some control over this.

 If the program hasn't been built yet, the *install* target should build the software first. You can handle this through a **make** dependency. The *install* target should depend on the target that builds the software, typically the

N O T E name of the main executable program.

For example, the following snippet of a Makefile handles the installation chores for a mythical software package called *WunderWord*:

```
#
# Makefile for WunderWord
#

# Base installation directory.
INSTALL_BASE=   /usr/local

all: wword

install: wword
    install -c wword $(INSTALL_BASE)/bin
    install -c ww.support $(INSTALL_BASE)/lib
```

Note how the install target in this **Makefile** ensures that the software gets built before **make** installs it. Note also that the **make** variable INSTALL_BASE identifies the base directory in which to install the software. This makes it easy for someone to modify the installation directory.

See Chapter 3 for more on **make**.

Configuration And Licensing

After all the files are in the right place, your software may require some special configuration or licensing program before becoming workable software. If so, your installation scripts should launch whatever is required to let the user finish the task of installing and configuring the software.

If some form of licensing is involved, this may require the user to call the vendor for a license string or other magic value that unlocks the program. If so, you should allow the user to install without finishing the licensing. By separating the two steps—at the user's option—the user will be able to make the call when convenient. If the vendor and user are in two different time zones, for example, this may be mandatory.

Summary

This chapter covered all sorts of options for bundling, packaging, compressing, and installing your software. One of the great strengths of an open system like UNIX is in the many choices you have available.

One of the great weaknesses of UNIX lies in the plethora of options you have to choose from. There's no standard way to install software.

The **tar** command allows you to archive entire directory hierarchies into **tar** archive files for later retrieval. This forms the handiest method for distributing large numbers of files and directories to other systems.

The **gzip** and **compress** programs can both shrink you data, allowing you to fit more on a CD-ROM or tape. Compressing files also frees up more space on your hard disk.

All installation scripts should be written in the Bourne shell (**/bin/sh**) syntax. This is the only scripting language available on all versions of UNIX.

UNIX Commands Introduced in This Chapter

compress

gunzip

gzip

install

shar

split

tar

uncompress

unshar

unzip

uudecode

uudeview

uuencode

uuenview

SECTION 2

Maintaining Your Programs

Maintaining software is often a daunting task. There's a lot of work to do to keep things up to date and track down bugs. This section covers UNIX tools that help debug, manage, analyze, and otherwise maintain your programs.

Chapter 7 covers the painful task of debugging and testing your software. UNIX offers a number of debuggers, both textual and graphical. Chapter 7 also discuses a number of tools to help test your code for code coverage and to detect hard-to-track down memory errors.

Chapter 8 shows how to compare files, for example, to see what changes were necessary to fix a particular bug.

Chapter 9 helps you manage your releases by delving into UNIX configuration management and version control tools, including the Revision Control System, or RCS.

All UNIX systems differ. Chapter 10 shows how to get the most mileage out of programs by writing cross-platform code. It's much easier to design in cross-platform capability than to add it later. In addition, Chapter 10 covers a number of topics that are necessary for porting code to other systems such as Windows NT.

Chapter 11 helps speed your software by analyzing performance, tracking down bottlenecks, and then improving the slowest parts of your code.

## CHAPTER 7

Debugging and Testing

This chapter covers:

- Common debuggers, including **dbx**, **gdb**, and **xdb**
- Compiling for debugging
- Using debuggers to find errors in your programs
- Graphical front ends to debuggers
- Memory leak libraries that help find memory problems
- Measuring test coverage
- Debugging Java applications

Debugging

Debugging is the long, painful, arduous task of removing bugs from software. Debugging is never fun, but using the right tools can go a long way toward making it less tedious.

This chapter covers debugging and testing C, C++, and Java applications. Most UNIX tools aim at C and C++ developers, but Java developers aren't left in the cold; you can make effective use of the Java debugger **jdb**.

The chapter starts with C and C++ coverage, and ends with Java.

Debuggers

The main debugging tool is a program called a *debugger*. A debugger lets you examine the internal workings of your code while a program runs. You can examine variables and data structures. In some debuggers, you can even execute functions.

Debuggers allow you to set breakpoints, which stop the program's execution at a particular point of interest. Once the program is stopped, you can examine variables and verify whether your program is working correctly or—hopefully—find out why the program misbehaves.

To work with a debugger, you first need to recompile your programs with the proper debugging options.

Compiling with Debugging Options

Most C and C++ compilers aim at creating compact, fast executables. This means any extraneous data, such as symbol table information, is removed. For a debugger to work, however, your program must contain this extra information.

The main purpose of this debugging information is to provide a connection between the code that is executed and the actual location—usually a line number—in a source code file. Remember, programs are compiled to machine code, so all relations to the original lines of code are lost in the compilation process. If you compile with the debugging option, the compiler inserts this information into your program.

The debugging option also tells the compiler to insert information that maps between variable and function names, such as `write_database`, and the actual address in the code. This allows you to query the value of a variable or to stop at a function by using the name rather than trying the impossible task of figuring out the memory address assigned by the compiler.

To place debugging information in your code, you need to use the -g command-line parameter to **cc** or **CC**. For example:

```
$ cc -g -c foo.c
$ cc -g -o foo foo.o
```

These commands compile the file **foo.c** and place debugging information into the resulting executable, **foo**.

You need to compile each source code file with the -g command-line parameter, and you need to link together the whole program, also using the -g command-line parameter. The -g command-line parameter is required for both steps.

NOTE

Except for the GNU C compiler, almost no compiler allows you to mix the -o optimize option with the -g debugging information option. In most cases, this isn't a problem, but I've seen a few cases where the bug was not in the program but in the compiler's optimizer. Thus, the debugger never saw the error. Only when the program was compiled with optimization did the program generate an error. This is something to watch for. With most C and C++ compilers, you can turn off optimization entirely or use a lower level of optimization for problematic files.

Typically, the -o command-line parameter turns on full optimization. Using a lower level of optimization, such as -o1 or -o2, can often cut out the part of the optimizer that generates the bug.

NOTE

Don't use the -s command-line parameter when compiling for debugging. This option strips out all the symbol table information you just added with the -g option.

Once you've compiled your program with debugging information, you can then use a debugger.

Using a Debugger

You can use UNIX debuggers in two ways. You can run the debugger on your program, executing the program from within the debugger and see what happens. Or you can use a debugger in post-mortem mode. In this mode, after your program has crashed and core dumped—leaving a file named **core**—the debugger can examine both your program's executable file and the core file to try to figure out what went wrong.

In post-mortem debugging, you often won't be able to find out exactly what happened, but you can usually get a stack trace. A *stack trace* shows the chain of function calls where the program exited ungracefully. Such information can usually pinpoint where the program went down.

But a stack trace does not always pinpoint what caused the problem. Memory problems or stack corruption can both exhibit the behavior where the program continues for a while after an error. In this case, the place the program went down may have nothing to do with the cause of the error.

In most cases, the stack trace shows you the offending routine. It's up to you to examine the parameters to the routine that crashed the program and to see if you can determine what went wrong.

The Major Debuggers

There are many different debuggers in the UNIX community. Generally, each platform provides a primary debugger. In most cases, the debugger is closely tied to the compiler and linker. So, for example, Sun and Silicon Graphics systems provide a debugger named **dbx**, although the **dbx** on each platform is unique. Hewlett-Packard systems provide a very different debugger called **xdb**. Linux systems provide the freeware GNU debugger, **gdb**, which also runs on most UNIX platforms. These three form the main debuggers on most UNIX platforms.

While most debuggers offer similar features, such as breakpoints, and stack traces, each debugger uses a different set of cryptic commands—making your life difficult if you use multiple UNIX platforms.

To help cut through the differences, I'll show the main debugger commands for these three debuggers: **dbx**, **gdb**, and **xdb**, which should help you go from one to the other. To start, Table 7.1 compares the commands in these three debuggers.

Table 7.1 dbx, gdb, and xdb Commands Compared

dbx	gdb	xdb	Meaning
where	bt	t	Display stack trace.
where	backtrace	t	Display stack trace.
where	where	t	Display stack trace.
where	info stack	t	Display stack trace.
quit	quit	quit	Quits debugger.
run	run	run	Runs program.
run *args*	run *args*	run *args*	Runs program with *args* as command-line parameters.
stop in *func*	break *func*	bp *func*	Sets breakpoint at start of function *func*.
stop at *line_num*	break *line_num*	b *line_num*	Sets breakpoint at line number.
file *filename.c*	list *filename.c:func*	v *filename.c*	Views *filename.c*
c	c	c	Continues from breakpoint.
step	step	s	Executes next program line.
print *var*	print *var*	p *var*	Prints value of variable *var*.
help	help	help	Gets help.

In most debuggers, you can just type in the first letter of a command, or a short abbreviation, instead of the full text. For example, **q** for *quit* or **bt** for *backtrace*. Be careful, though, some commands start with the same letter.

gdb supports most **dbx** commands. **gdb** supports quite a few commands for the same operations. This makes the migration from **dbx** to **gdb** much easier.

N O T E

All these debuggers provide online help. This is very useful because few programmers are more than casual users of any debugger program. If you're having trouble with the syntax, try the **help** command within the debugger.

To help get a better feel for how debuggers work, I'll start with a small C++ program sporting a clear bug and show how you can help track down the source of the problem with each of **dbx**, **gdb** and **xdb**. All of these debuggers act similar to each other, so it isn't very hard to go from one to the other.

The following C++ program, **buggy.cc**, contains a nasty bug: it writes to memory that was never initialized. (Do not write your C++ classes like this.) The code for the **buggy.cc** program follows:

```
//
// Sample buggy C++ program.
//
#include <string.h>

class Buggy {
public:
    Buggy() { }
    ~Buggy(){ }

    char*   Bug() { return &_ptr[100]; }

private:
    char*   _ptr;
};

void function_6(Buggy& object)
{   // BUG
    char* ptr;
```

```
    ptr = object.Bug();

    ptr[1000] = '\0';  // BUG

}
```

```
void function_5(Buggy& object)
{
    function_6(object);
}

void function_4(Buggy& object)
{
    function_5(object);
}

void function_3(Buggy& object)
{
    function_4(object);
}

void function_2(Buggy& object)
{
    function_3(object);
}

void function_1(Buggy& object)
{
    function_2(object);
}

int main(int argc, char** argv)

{
    Buggy   object;

    function_1(object);
}
```

This program should compile fine, but it will crash when it's run. You can compile the **buggy.cc** program with a command like the following:

```
$ CC -g -o buggy buggy.cc
```

Remember to compile your code with the –g command-line parameter. If you don't, none of the debuggers will be able to provide much information.

After compiling and linking, try running the **buggy** program. You should see an error like the following:

```
$ buggy
Segmentation fault (core dumped)
```

The bug in the **buggy.cc** file, which wrongfully writes data into memory that was not allocated, runs OK on a Silicon Graphics Irix 5.3 system. Thus, you may need to create your own buggy code for SGI systems.

This is why I'm a strong proponent of cross-platform development. If your primary development machine is forgiving for certain types of errors, you may end up creating a lot of problems in other places in your code.

Now that we have a program in error, the next step is to run it from a debugger. The basic command for **dbx**, **gdb**, and **xdb** is the following:

```
debugger program
```

You need to replace *debugger* with the name of your debugger, such as **dbx**, **gdb**, or **xdb**, and *program* with the name of your program, such as **buggy**. With the **dbx** debugger, you enter a command like the following:

```
$ dbx buggy
```

At the **dbx** prompt—(dbx)—type in the **run** command:

```
(dbx) run
```

The program should crash. However, because you're running in a debugger, you can find out more about what went wrong. At the next **dbx** prompt, you can find out where the program crashed with the **dbx where** command:

```
(dbx) where
>  0  function_6(Buggy&)(object = 0x7fffaf0c) ["buggy.cc":23, 0x400d60]
   1  function_5(Buggy&)(object = 0x7fffaf0c) ["buggy.cc":29, 0x400da0]
   2  function_4(Buggy&)(object = 0x7fffaf0c) ["buggy.cc":34, 0x400dec]
   3  function_3(Buggy&)(object = 0x7fffaf0c) ["buggy.cc":39, 0x400e38]
   4  function_2(Buggy&)(object = 0x7fffaf0c) ["buggy.cc":44, 0x400e84]
   5  function_1(Buggy&)(object = 0x7fffaf0c) ["buggy.cc":50, 0x400ed0]
   6  main(argc = 1, argv = 0x7fffaf2c) ["buggy.cc":59, 0x400f50]
   7  __start() ["crt1text.s":133, 0x400b9c]
```

The **where** command in **dbx** provides a stack trace, a list of all the function calls on the stack at the time of program termination (or any time the program is stopped in the debugger). This is very useful for figuring out which function has the error.

 You must be careful; the function where the error manifests itself is not always the function where the error occurred.

WARNING

The top function is the deepest in the stack trace, and the likely cause of the error. At the very least, you should check the top function for bad data.

Sometimes the top function comes from a library for which you don't have the source code. In that case, you need to go down the stack trace until you find a function for which you do have the source code. Start looking for errors at this point. Note that the debugger provides the file name and line number.

In the **gdb** debugger, you'll see a stack trace like the following:

```
$ gdb buggy

(gdb) run
Program received signal SIGSEGV, Segmentation fault.
0x80484b3 in function_6 (object=@0xbffff650) at buggy.cc:23
23              ptr[1000] = '\0';  // BUG
```

```
(gdb) where
#0  0x80484b3 in function_6 (object=@0xbffff650) at buggy.cc:23
#1  0x80484c8 in function_5 (object=@0xbffff650) at buggy.cc:29
#2  0x80484dc in function_4 (object=@0xbffff650) at buggy.cc:34
#3  0x80484f0 in function_3 (object=@0xbffff650) at buggy.cc:39
#4  0x8048504 in function_2 (object=@0xbffff650) at buggy.cc:44
#5  0x8048518 in function_1 (object=@0xbffff650) at buggy.cc:50
#6  0x804853b in main (argc=1, argv=0xbffff674) at buggy.cc:59
#7  0x804844b in ___crt_dummy__ ()
```

And, in **xdb** you'll see a stack trace like the following:

```
$ xdb buggy

>run
bus error (no ignore) at 0x00002188
buggy.cc: function_6: 23 +0x00000008: ptr[10] = '\0';  // BUG
>t
  0 ::function_6 (object =    00000000)     [buggy.cc: 23]
  1 ::function_5 (object =    00000000)     [buggy.cc: 30]
  2 ::function_4 (object =    00000000)     [buggy.cc: 35]
  3 ::function_3 (object =    00000000)     [buggy.cc: 40]
  4 ::function_2 (object =    00000000)     [buggy.cc: 45]
  5 ::function_1 (object =    00000000)     [buggy.cc: 51]
  6 ::main (argc = 1, argv = 0x7b03aa44)    [buggy.cc: 60]
```

In all these debuggers, you can call up the file in which the error occurred (if you have the source code) and then set breakpoints in the code.

A breakpoint is a place you want the debugger to *break*—or stop. Usually you set a breakpoint at a line number in a file or at the beginning or end of a particular function.

In the preceding example, we probably want to break at line 23 in the file **buggy.cc**, where the error occurs:

```
(dbx) stop at 23
Process     0: [3] stop at "/devfiles/johnsone/buggy.cc":23
```

Next, run the program. The debugger stops the program at the given place in the source file:

```
(dbx) run
Process 24819 (buggy) started
[3] Process 24819 (buggy) stopped at [function_6(Buggy&):23 ,0x400d60]
  23  ptr[1000] = '\0';  // BUG
```

The **list** command displays parts of the current file:

```
(dbx) list
>    24
     25  }
     26
     27  void function_5(Buggy& object)
     28  {
     29          function_6(object);
     30  }
     31
     32  void function_4(Buggy& object)
     33  {
```

You can print variable values with the **print** or **p** command:

```
(dbx) p object._ptr
0x7fffaf2c = "\177\377\257\340"
(dbx) p ptr
0x7fffaf90 =
"\177\377\263\313\177\377\263\371\177\377\264\017\177\377\264\030\177\377\264%
"
```

To continue executing from the breakpoint, use the **c** command:

```
(dbx) c
Process 24819 (buqqy) terminated
```

And, of course, this buggy program stops at the bug.

In **gdb**, you can try the following commands. First, set the breakpoint at line 23 with the **break** command:

```
$ gdb buggy
(gdb) break 23
Breakpoint 1 at 0x80484ab: file buggy.cc, line 23.
```

Run the program. The program automatically stops at the breakpoint:

```
(gdb) run
Starting program: /home/erc/books/unixtool/buggy

Breakpoint 1, function_6 (object=@0xbffff650) at buggy.cc:23
Source file is more recent than executable.
23
(gdb) list
18      void function_6(Buggy& object)
19      {   // BUG
20          char* ptr;
21
22          ptr = object.Bug();
23
24          ptr[1000] = '\0';   // BUG
25
26      }
27
```

The *list* command shows the source code around the breakpoint. At this point, you can print the value of variables:

```
(gdb) p object._ptr
$2 = 0x0
```

The **c** command continues execution:

```
(gdb) c
Continuing.
```

```
Program received signal SIGSEGV, Segmentation fault.
0x80484b3 in function_6 (object=@0xbffff650) at buggy.cc:23
```

The program crashes after the breakpoint.

The **xdb** debugger uses different commands. To set a breakpoint at a given line number, use the **b** command:

```
>b 23
Overall breakpoints state:   ACTIVE
Added:
 1: count:   1  Active    ::function_6(Buggy &): 23: ptr[1000] = '\0';  // BUG
```

The **run** command runs the program until it hits the breakpoint, the same as **dbx** and **gdb**:

```
>run
Starting process 12363:   "buggy"

breakpoint at 0x00002180
>
```

xdb presents a form of multiwindowed display inside a text-only window. To see parts of the source code, use the **v** command, as shown in the prompt at the bottom of the following output:

```
16:
      17: void function_6(Buggy& object)
      18: {       // BUG
      19:         char* ptr;
      20:
      21:         ptr = object.Bug();
      22:
*>    23:         ptr[1000] = '\0';  // BUG
      24:
      25: }
      26:
      27: void function_5(Buggy& object)
```

```
28: {
29:             function_6(object);
30: }
File: buggy.cc    Procedure: function_6    Line: 23
2 ::function_4 (object =    00000000)    [buggy.cc: 35]
3 ::function_3 (object =    00000000)    [buggy.cc: 40]
4 ::function_2 (object =    00000000)    [buggy.cc: 45]
5 ::function_1 (object =    00000000)    [buggy.cc: 51]
6 ::main (argc = 1, argv = 0x7b03aa48)     [buggy.cc: 60]
>v
>v 23
```

Also like **dbx** and **gdb**, the **p** or **print** command prints variable values:

```
>p object._ptr
_ptr = <null pointer>
```

And the **c** command continues execution. Like before, the program stops at the bug:

```
>c
bus error (no ignore) at 0x00002188
buggy.cc: function_6: 23 +0x00000008: ptr[1000] = '\0';  // BUG
```

As you can tell, all these debuggers provide similar interfaces.

emacs and gdb

The **M-x gdb** command in **emacs** starts the **gdb** debugger from within an **emacs** window. Using the **buggy.cc** program, **emacs** automatically places the cursor where the program crashes:

```
void function_6(Buggy& object)
{   // BUG
    char* ptr;

    ptr = object.Bug();
=>
    ptr[1000] = '\0';   // BUG

}

void function_5(Buggy& object)
{
    function_6(object);
}
```

This tight integration provides a nice front end to **gdb**. There are also other programs that provide even better interfaces to various UNIX debuggers.

Graphical Front Ends to Debuggers

By now, you probably find the standard UNIX debuggers difficult, frustrating, and examples of ancient technology. There are of graphical front ends for the debuggers we've discussed.

First, if you've purchased a development environment, from Sun, Hewlett-Packard, Silicon Graphics, and so on, that environment should come with some form of graphical debugger. In addition, a number of freeware debuggers include graphical interfaces.

On the commercial product front, Sun offers a graphical front end to the **dbx** debugger called (appropriately enough) **debugger**. This debugger forms one of the best graphical interfaces for debugging, as shown in Figure 7.1.

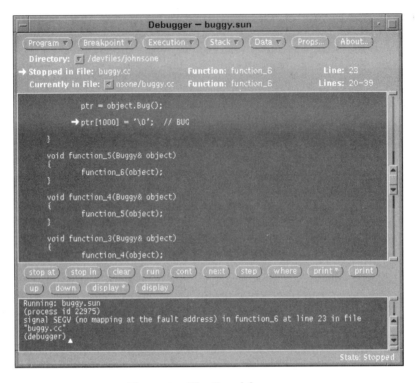

Figure 7.1 The Sun debugger.

Because the **debugger** works with **dbx**, you can use all the familiar **dbx** commands or select elements in the graphical interface.

Hewlett-Packard offers a similar debugger with its SoftBench product, called **softdebug**. Silicon Graphics and other UNIX vendors also sell graphical debuggers as part of development environments.

Tk and gdb

The **gdbtk** debugger includes the full version of **gdb** and adds a graphical interface written in Tcl/Tk (see Chapter 2 for more on Tcl/Tk).

If you build this debugger (available on the CD-ROM in the **debug/gdb-4.16** directory), you run the program with the command name **gdb**, just like the normal **gdb**. However, this new **gdb** presents a graphical interface by default. To use this **gdb** in text-only mode, you need to add the -nw command-line parameter, short for *no window*. For example, to run this new **gdb** in text-only mode, you can use the following command:

```
$ gdb -nw
```

The whole point of this new debugger is to present a graphical interface, as shown in Figure 7.2.

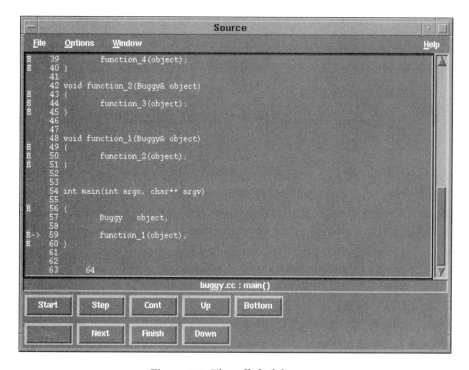

Figure 7.2 The **gdbtk** debugger.

Inside the graphical interface, you can still run all the standard **gdb** commands, as shown in Figure 7.3.

178

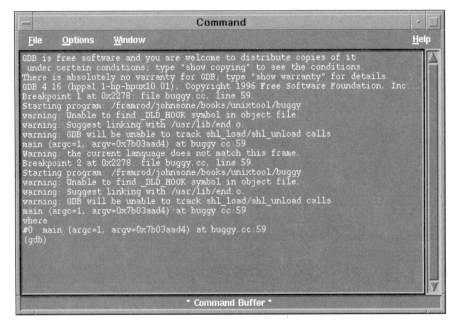

```
                              Command
  File    Options    Window                                    Help
 GDB is free software and you are welcome to distribute copies of it
  under certain conditions; type "show copying" to see the conditions.
 There is absolutely no warranty for GDB; type "show warranty" for details.
 GDB 4.16 (hppa1.1-hp-hpux10.01), Copyright 1996 Free Software Foundation, Inc...
 Breakpoint 1 at 0x2278: file buggy.cc, line 59.
 Starting program: /framrod/johnsone/books/unixtool/buggy
 warning: Unable to find _DLD_HOOK symbol in object file.
 warning: Suggest linking with /usr/lib/end.o.
 warning: GDB will be unable to track shl_load/shl_unload calls
 main (argc=1, argv=0x7b03aad4) at buggy.cc:59
 Warning: the current language does not match this frame.
 Breakpoint 2 at 0x2278: file buggy.cc, line 59.
 Starting program: /framrod/johnsone/books/unixtool/buggy
 warning: Unable to find _DLD_HOOK symbol in object file.
 warning: Suggest linking with /usr/lib/end.o.
 warning: GDB will be unable to track shl_load/shl_unload calls
 main (argc=1, argv=0x7b03aad4) at buggy.cc:59
 where
 #0  main (argc=1, argv=0x7b03aad4) at buggy.cc:59
 (gdb)


                          * Command Buffer *
```

Figure 7.3 Entering **gdb** commands in **gdbtk**.

N O T E

The **gdbtk** package uses an older version of Tcl/Tk, specifically Tcl 7.4 and Tk 4.0. If you have installed a newer version of Tcl/Tk, you will need to set the TCL_LIBRARY and TK_LIBRARY environment variables to point to the directories with the support files for the older versions of Tcl and Tk, respectively.

Virtually all these debuggers are a graphical interface program acting as a front end to the old text-mode debugger. For example, **xxgdb** launches **gdb** from a UNIX pipe and then presents the **gdb** output to you in a friendlier format, as shown in Figure 7.4.

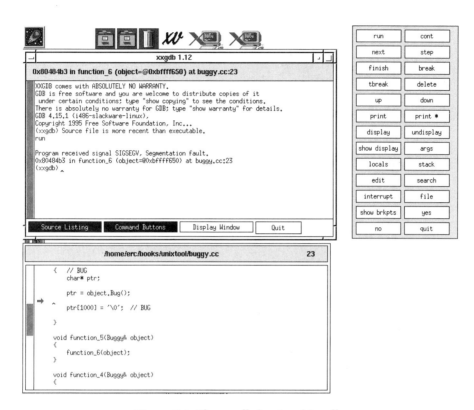

Figure 7.4 The **xxgdb** front end to **gdb**.

Other freeware debuggers include DDD, which requires the GNU C++ compiler and the Motif libraries.

All the freeware debuggers mentioned so far reside on the CD-ROM in the **debug** directory.

CD-ROM

Cleaning Up Your Code

lint is a C program checker that aims to remove the yucky stuff—called *lint*—from your C programs. Most of what **lint** does is complain about C program constructs that seem dangerous, not portable, or violate type safety rules.

As a program, **lint** takes much the same arguments as the C compiler, **cc**. For example, to specify an include directory, you can use the `-I` command-line parameter, as for **cc** (as described in Chapter 2).

The basic syntax of **lint** follows:

lint *options files*

The options come from **cc** and the files should be any of your C source code files. For example, you can use the following command on a Hewlett-Packard system to run **lint** on a C file named **motif.c**:

```
$ lint -Aa -I/usr/include/Motif1.2 -I/usr/include/X11R5 motif.c
```

You'll find **lint** complains copiously, as shown here (with about 400 lines removed):

```
lint: "motif.c", line 16: warning 828: argument "widget" unused in function
"exitCB"
lint: "motif.c", line 17: warning 828: argument "client_data" unused in func-
tion "exitCB"
lint: "motif.c", line 18: warning 828: argument "call_data" unused in function
"exitCB"


==============
name used but not defined
     XtAppInitialize     motif.c(42)
     XmCreatePushButton          motif.c(54)
     XtAddCallback       motif.c(58)
     _XmStrings          motif.c(59)
     XtManageChild       motif.c(64)
     XtRealizeWidget     motif.c(74)
     XtAppMainLoop       motif.c(78)
name declared but never used or defined
     XtSetTypeConverter          Intrinsic.h(725)
```

```
XtRemoveActionHook          Intrinsic.h(845)

XtRemoveEventHandler        Intrinsic.h(971)

XtRemoveRawEventHandler     Intrinsic.h(991)

XtRemoveGrab          Intrinsic.h(1037)

XtRemoveTimeOut       Intrinsic.h(1111)

XtRemoveInput         Intrinsic.h(1136)

XtRemoveCallback      Intrinsic.h(1363)
```

Most of **lint**'s complaints can be ignored. The most useful complaints are those where a variable was used before being set—a serious bug. Whenever you use **lint**, you have to be willing to sort through all the copious complaints to find the ones that are important.

Checking for Memory Leaks

One of the most common errors for C and C++ has to do with pointers and memory allocation problems. You can often use a tool that tracks memory usage and reports *leaks*—memory blocks that are allocated but not freed—to help track down memory errors in your code.

Purify, from Pure Atria, forms the most popular tool on UNIX for tracking down memory leaks and other pointer-related bugs in C and C++ programs. This commercial package is well worth looking into if you develop on mainstream UNIX systems such as Sun, Hewlett-Packard, IBM, and Silicon Graphics.

In addition to Purify, there are many of libraries that help track down memory leaks in C and C++ programs, such as Insure++ from Parasoft. Most of these libraries replace the system versions of the `malloc` and `free` functions with special instrumented versions. These instrumented versions of `malloc` and `free` track memory allocations and deallocations. If your program doesn't free an allocated block of memory, these libraries can point out the offending code.

Plumber, a memory leak library on the CD-ROM (in the **mem_leak** directory), acts similarly to Purify. Plumber tracks all calls to `malloc` and `free` using its own versions of these functions and then writes out a log file when your program quits. The log file contains information about memory blocks allocated but not freed, and so on.

However, with Plumber, you need to modify your source code. In your main function, you need to add a call to `plumber_init` at the beginning and `plumber_shutdown` at the end.

I had some problems with Plumber on Linux systems. You should have better luck on Sun systems.

N O T E

Other memory leak detectors include Electric Fence and Checker. Electric Fence uses the virtual memory hardware of your system to try to detect overruns of memory boundary. If your program overruns a memory boundaries, Electric Fence stops the program, which makes it easier to track down such errors with a debugger, because you know where the error occurred.

Electric Fence runs on Sun, Hewlett-Packard, IBM, Digital Equipment, Silicon Graphics, Linux, and other UNIX systems. See the **mem_leak** directory on the CD-ROM for the Electric Fence source code.

Checker acts as a more traditional `malloc` and `free` library that searches for memory errors. Unfortunately, Checker only runs on Sun Solaris and Linux systems. Checker looks for the following specific cases:

- You try to free a pointer that has not been allocated with `malloc`, `realloc` or `calloc`.
- You try to free a pointer that has already been freed.

If you run on Linux, you also need the Checker libraries, found in the **mem_leak/checker** directory on the CD-ROM.

N O T E

Test Coverage

The Sun **tcov** program and compiling option allow you to check for test coverage. This checks for what lines of code in your program are actually executed when you run a test. The idea is that the more of your code you cover, the better the test—with all else being equal.

So, the **tcov** option outputs a large set of data files. Then the **tcov** program combines the data files with the original source code to output an annotated source code listing. For each block or line of code executed, **tcov** prints the number of times the block of code was executed. This is the *number of times* executed, *not* the *amount of time* it took. Thus, if an `if` statement was checked 5002 times, **tcov** prints out 5002. This has no relation to performance.

Instead, **tcov** looks to whether the code was executed at all. If a line of code was never executed—a bad thing for test programs—**tcov** prints a warning, normally in the form of a number of # characters, such as #####, to alert you that the code was not tested.

To use **tcov**, you must first recompile your code, using the -xa command-line parameter (on Sun systems—I have not found **tcov** on other systems) to **cc**. Then, relink—also using -xa—and then run your program. As the program runs, it will output lots of data into **.d** files, for example, **motif.d**, or **buggy.d**. The first part of the name comes from the corresponding source code file.

When you're finished running the program, use the **tcov** program to format the results. **tcov** outputs a **.tcov** file that contains this annotated listing.

For example:

```
$ cc -xa -o foo foo.c
$ foo
$tcov foo.c
```

Even though **tcov** is only available on Sun systems, there's a freeware tool called ATAC on the CD-ROM in the **debug** directory. ATAC acts very much like **tcov** in that it displays test coverage information. Again the goal is the same: to see how much of your code the test program actually tested.

To work with ATAC, though, you must compile your C programs with **atacCC**. **atacCC** builds the information tables it needs, instruments your code to collect data at run time and then calls the C compiler, **cc**, to actually compile the code.

Debugging Java Applications

In addition to C and C++, Java provides a debugger, built on many of the same assumptions as **dbx**. **jdb**, the Java debugger that comes with the Java development kit, is a text-mode application much like **dbx**. (There are a number of commercial Java development packages that offer more friendly Java debuggers.)

184

Also like **dbx**, you must first recompile your Java code with the –g command-line parameter in order to work with a debugger.

To test **jdb**, I'll revisit the small Java application shown in Chapter 2, **UNIXProgTools.java**:

```
//
// A simple first Java programming example.
//

public class UNIXProgTools
{
    public static void main(String[] args)
    {
        System.out.println( "Java application example." );
    }
}
```

To compile this file with debugging information, you can use the following command:

```
$ javac -g UNIXProgTools.java
```

Remember, you must compile your Java code with the –g command-line parameter to work with a debugger.

N O T E

Then you can run this application in the debugger:

```
$ jdb UNIXProgTools
Initializing jdb...
0x404c4628:class(UNIXProgTools)
```

At the **jdb** prompt, >, you can enter any of **jdb**'s commands, listed in Table 7.2.

Table 7.2 jdb's Commands

Command	Usage
print *object*	Print data.
print *object.field*	Print data.
dump *object*	Print all object information.
locals	Print all local variables.
classes	List all classes—a large list.
methods *class*	List a class's methods.
stop in *class.method*	Set breakpoint at method.
stop at *class:line_num*	Set breakpoint at line number in class.
clear *class:line_num*	Clear breakpoint.
step	Execute current line.
cont	Continue execution from breakpoint.
up *num_frames*	Move up a thread's stack.
down *num_frames*	Move down a thread's stack.
catch *class*	Break on exception for class.
ignore *class*	Ignore exception for class.
list *line_num*	Print source code—did not work.
load *class*	Load class into debugger.
run *class args*	Run program.
!!	Repeat last command.
help	Get information on available commands.
exit	Quit **jdb**.
quit	Quit **jdb**.
use *source file path*	Change source file path.

Table 7.2 jdb's Commands (continued)

use	List source file path.
memory	List memory usage.
gc	(Garbage collect) free unused objects.
threads	List threads.
thread *id*	Set default thread.
suspend *id*	Suspend thread.
resume *id*	Resume thread.
threadgroups	List thread groups.
threadgroup *name*	Name current thread group.
where *id*	List a thread's stack.
where *all*	List all thread stacks.

Because Java is a multithreaded language, this makes the debugger quite complex. Most of the commands in **jdb** relate to threads. Most of the problems you have with Java will probably also deal with threads, because concurrent programming is a tough task.

The use of threads also makes the stack trace tougher, because each thread has its own stack. To try **jdb**, you can enter some of the available commands listed in Table 7.2.

The **methods** command lists all the methods for a class. For example:

```
$ jdb UNIXProgTools
Initializing jdb...
0x404c4628:class(UNIXProgTools)
> methods UNIXProgTools
void main(String[])
void <init>()
```

You can also run this on the built-in Java classes:

```
> methods java.io.DataOutput
void write(int)
void write(byte[])
void write(byte[], int, int)
void writeBoolean(boolean)
void writeByte(int)
void writeShort(int)
void writeChar(int)
void writeInt(int)
void writeLong(long)
void writeFloat(float)
void writeDouble(double)
void writeBytes(String)
void writeChars(String)
void writeUTF(String)
```

You can use the **method** command to find out a lot about various Java classes, although for the built-in classes, the Java documentation is probably a better bet.

The **dump** command prints information on a class:

```
> dump UNIXProgTools
UNIXProgTools = 0x404c4628:class(UNIXProgTools) {
    superclass = 0x404b8018:class(java.lang.Object)
    loader = null
}
```

For objects, the **print** command is less useful than dump:

```
> print UNIXProgTools
UNIXProgTools = 0x404c4628:class(UNIXProgTools)
```

print works much better at printing data members of an object.

You can view the current source code file path with the **use** command:

```
> use
.:/usr/local/java/bin/../classes:/usr/local/java/bin/../lib/classes.zip:/usr/l
ocal/java/bin/../bin/../classes:/usr/local/java/bin/../bin/../lib/classes.zip
```

You can also change the source file path with **use**.

The **memory** command lists the amount of memory used:

```
> memory
Free: 608384, total: 1048568
```

And, most importantly, the **run** command runs the application:

```
> run
run UNIXProgTools
running ...
main[1] Java application example.


The application has exited
$
```

Note that when the application quits, the debugger also quits, which is not always the behavior you want.

Breakpoints work much like those in **dbx** or **gdb**, except that because all functions are members of a class, all breakpoints must be in a class. For example:

```
> stop in UNIXProgTools.main
Breakpoint set in UNIXProgTools.main
> run
run UNIXProgTools
running ...
main[1]
Breakpoint hit: UNIXProgTools.main (UNIXProgTools:11)
main[1]
```

In a breakpoint, the **cont** command continues execution:

```
main[1] cont
Java application example.
```

And the **exit** or **quit** command exits the debugger:

```
> exit
pid 650 status 0
Received sigchild for 650 exit=0
```

This should give you a head start for when you need to debug your Java applications.

Summary

This chapter covered debugging, never a fun task. Each UNIX system seems to offer its own incompatible debugger, although the main contenders are **dbx**, **gdb**, and **xdb**. Debuggers help you find out why your program crashed, and hopefully tell you where the crash occurred.

In addition to text-mode debuggers, UNIX offers a number of different graphical debuggers. Many of these graphical debuggers are merely front ends to the existing text-mode applications. The graphical front-end program then communicates with the debugger via a UNIX pipe.

You can use a memory leak library to check your programs for memory leaks and bad pointer accesses. A test coverage tool can tell you how well your test programs actually test your code.

The Java debugger, **jdb**, allows you to debug Java programs.

The next chapter will delve into comparing files to help you keep track of versions of files and to find differences in code.

UNIX Commands Introduced in This Chapter

dbx

debugger

gdb

tcov

xdb

CHAPTER 8

Comparing Files

This chapter covers:

- Using **diff** to compare files
- Other diff-related programs: **sdiff**, **bdiff**, **diff3**, **cmp**, **comm**, and **dircmp**
- Graphical **diff** programs
- Merging files
- Using **diff** from **emacs**
- Updating files with **patch**
- Creating patches

The UNIX diff Program

The main UNIX program for comparing files is called **diff**, short for *differential file comparator*—a hefty moniker. For such a seemingly simple program, **diff** provides one of the most-used UNIX tools. **diff** compares two text files and shows which lines are different.

The basic syntax follows:

diff *file1 file2*

For example, to compare files named **buggy.cc** and **buggy1.cc**, you can use the following command:

```
$ diff buggy.cc buggy1.cc
11c11
<         char*    Bug() { return &_ptr[100]; }
___
>         char*    Bug() { return _ptr; }
18c18
< {       // BUG
___
> {
22,23d21
<
<         ptr[1000] = '\0';   // BUG
```

Interpreting diff Output

To interpret the output of **diff**, you need to look at the < and > characters that begin the output lines. Any line starting with < refers to the first file, and any line starting with > refers to the second file. The lines that are different get printed, along with some positional information.

Thus, you can tell that in the preceding example, the file **buggy.cc** has the following line:

```
char*    Bug() { return &_ptr[100]; }
```

But, the file **buggy1.cc** has the following line:

```
char*   Bug() { return _ptr; }
```

Using diff on Directories

If one of the files you pass to **diff** is a directory but the other is not, **diff** is smart enough to look for a file of the same name in the directory. For example, the following command compares two versions of the header file **stdio.h**:

```
$ diff /usr/include stdio.h
28c28
< #define _STDIO_USES_IOSTREAM 1
—
> #define _STDIO_USES_IOSTREAM 0
```

If both files passed to **diff** are directories, **diff** compares the files of the same name in the directories, one at a time, in alphabetical order.

Other diff Programs

The **bdiff** program, short for *big diff*, calls **diff**, but first it divides the two files into smaller, more manageable chunks. I'd suggest using this program only if for some reason **diff** fails due to the size of the files you are comparing. This is because dividing files can confuse **diff**, obscuring the output.

The **sdiff** program acts like **diff** but presents both files side by side. You can then use this information to try to merge the data between the two files. By default, **sdiff** prints every line of both files, side by side. For text files, this means you should have a very wide terminal setting, such as 163 characters, to fully see the output of both files. (That's 80 columns for each file, with three characters in between.)

To see how **sdiff** works, it's best to start with two simple files. One file, **a**, has the following lines:

```
a
a
b
c
d
e
```

The other file, **b**, differs slightly:

```
a
b
c
dd
  e
f
```

When you run **sdiff** on the files, you'll see the following output:

```
$ sdiff a b
a                       a
a                   <
b                       b
c                       c
d                   |   dd
e                   |     e
                    >   f
```

A | in the gutter between the two files indicates that the lines differ. A <
indicates that only the first file, **a** in this case, has that line. A > indicates
that only the second file, **b** in this case, has that line.

The -b command-line parameter tells **sdiff** to ignore changes in white
space—spaces, tabs, carriage returns, and new lines.

Extending the **diff** paradigm further, the **diff3** program compares three
files. It uses spacers to tell you which file differs, as shown in Table 8.1.

Table 8.1 Spacers Used by **diff3**

Spacer	Meaning
====1	File 1 differs.
====2	File 2 differs.
====3	File 3 differs.
====	All three files differ.

For example, to compare three files, you can use the following command:

```
$ diff3 a b c
====1
1:2c
  a
2:1a
3:1a
====2
1:5,6c
3:4,5c
  d
  e
2:4,6c
  dd
  e
  f
```

In addition to the **diff** family of programs, UNIX offers even more. The **cmp** program compares two files and prints the first place the files differ. For example:

```
$ cmp a b
a b differ: char 3, line 2
```

UNIX users often use **cmp** in silent mode, with the –s command-line parameter. This causes **cmp** to print nothing. The way you tell whether the files differ is to check the program's exit code, which is one of those listed in Table 8.2.

Table 8.2 cmp Exit Codes

Code	Meaning
0	The files are identical.
1	The files differ.
>1	An error occurred.

You can use **cmp** with **make**, because **make** treats all exit codes other than 0 as an error and a reason to stop processing. This way, you can verify whether a task succeeded if you can compare an output file with a known master file. If the files differ, you may have an error.

Unlike **diff** and most diff-like programs, **cmp** works on both text and binary files.

N O T E

comm compares two sorted files. It prints three columns that contain lines unique to the first file, lines unique to the second file, and lines both files have in common, respectively. For example:

```
$ comm a b
                a
a
                        b
                        c
d
        dd
            e
e
        f
```

Only the first, third, and fourth lines are the same.

Comparing Directories

Unlike the rest of the comparison programs, the **dircmp** command compares two directories. **dircmp** lists files found only in the first directory, files found only in the second directory, and files common to both directories.

Graphical diff

The **diff** program and its compatriots all cry out for some form of windowed user interface so that you can scroll through the results and better see the output. The best all-around graphical **diff** I've seen is called **gdiff**; unfortunately, is available only on Silicon Graphics systems.

One of the best features of **gdiff** is the colored display along the side margin, showing you at a glance where the major changes in the file reside, as shown in Figure 8.1.

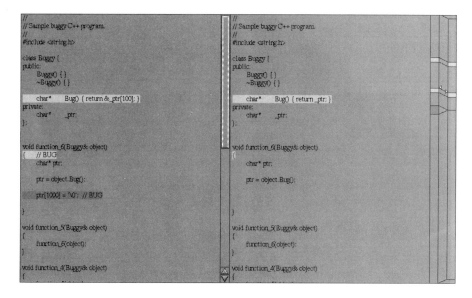

Figure 8.1 The **gdiff** graphical **diff** program.

gdiff helps you merge files (see the section on file mergers). In fact, **gdiff** is one of the best tools for merging files.

A similar Motif-based program called **mgdiff** operates on most versions of UNIX.

mgdiff resides in the compare directory on the CD-ROM. **mgdiff** requires the Motif libraries to compile.

CD-ROM

To launch **mgdiff**, you can use the following command:

```
$ mgdiff buggy.cc buggy1.cc &
```

You'll then see a window like the one shown in Figure 8.2.

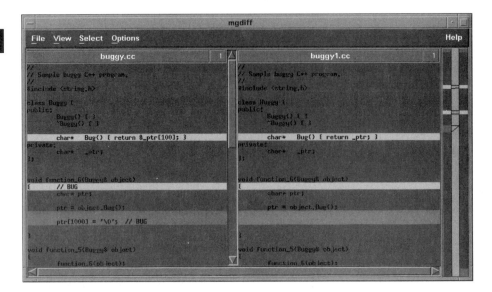

Figure 8.2 The **mgdiff** graphical **diff** program.

Like **gdiff**, **mgdiff** presents a colored bar in the far right margin showing what's different between the files.

File Mergers

One of the main reasons to use a graphical **diff** program—other than the differences are easier to see—is to aid the merging of files. When you merge files, you try to combine the differences between two versions of the same file.

For example, if a colleague and I are editing the same file for two different projects, we will eventually need to merge the different versions of the file. We both presumably added new features or fixed bugs. We need to capture both sets of changes and place them into the master copy of the file.

Most graphical **diff** programs allow you to merge the two files. Basically, the two source files are combined to create a third. The merger can be manual or automatic; it is usually a little of both.

Some graphical **diff** programs try to automatically perform as many operations as possible. For example, if I changed the top of a file and my colleague changed the bottom of the file, chances are our changes won't collide. An automated program can merge the results with—you hope—few problems.

Call me a Luddite, but I'm scared of automatic mergers; some scary decisions have been made by merger programs. So I usually insist on examining each difference and approving each change into the merged file. This process is far more tedious, but I've found it to be more correct in the end.

Figure 8.3 shows a file merger in progress in the **gdiff** application.

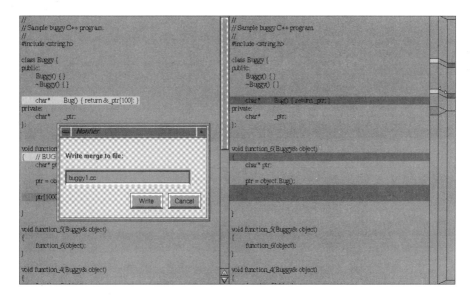

Figure 8.3 A file merger with **gdiff**.

Using diff from emacs

The **ediff** extension to **emacs** allows you to use **diff** from within the **emacs** environment. This is very handy for **emacs** users. If you're running the graphical version of **emacs**, you can select **Compare** or **Merge** from the Tools menu. Otherwise, you can enter one of the commands listed in Table 8.3.

Table 8.3 The Most Common **ediff** Commands for **emacs**

Command	Usage
M-x ediff-files	Compare two files.
M-x ediff-buffers	Compare two buffers.
M-x ediff-directories	Compare two directories.
M-x ediff-merge-files	Merge two files.

For example, you can merge files within **emacs**, as shown in Figure 8.4.

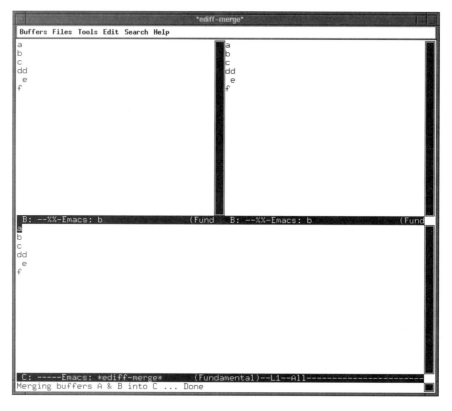

Figure 8.4 emacs merging two files.

When you compare two files, you'll see a window like the one in Figure 8.5.

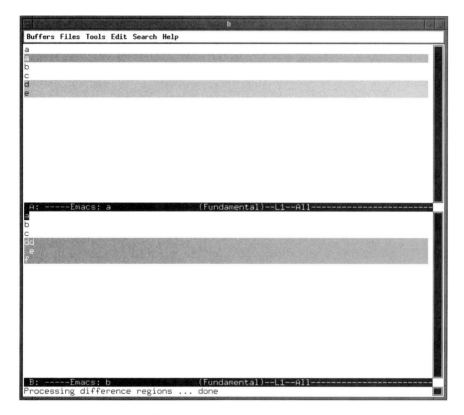

Figure 8.5 emacs in **ediff** mode.

There's a lot more information available on **ediff** from within the **emacs** help system.

Patching Your Code with patch

Many X Window programs tend to come in huge distributions, even in source code form. Because of this, program modifications often come in *patch files* instead of rereleasing the whole shebang. This is very useful for any kind of source code distributions. The main reason to use **patch** is that you can distribute only the changes rather than the entire file.

A *patch file* is a file that was produced by the UNIX **diff** utility. Armed with the differences between the new version and the old version, the **patch** program can apply the proper changes to update your old program to the latest version.

Thus, **patch** is a very handy utility, even for non-X programs. And if you work much with free X programs, you'll need to learn how to use **patch**, because there are many program updates (this is a good thing; you get bug fixes and new features for free).

Basically, you change the program's directory and then run **patch**:

```
$ patch < patchfile
```

This command feeds the patch file named *patchfile* as standard input to the **patch** program. When run, **patch** will pump out a lot of status information and may ask a few questions. Generally, the process completes fairly quickly.

All the periodic fixes to the X Window System source code and updates to most free X applications come in the form of patch files.

Using diff with patch

The **patch** program is smart enough to take any form of **diff** output that describes the differences in the files and to apply that to an older version of the same file.

To create a patch file, keep a copy of the original files you sent out. Then, when you release a new version, run **diff** on the files that have changed. The differences are what you will then send to your users, who will apply **patch** to update their files, which are the old versions. **patch** updates the old versions, creating up-to-date files.

When **patch** changes a file, it first copies the original to the same file name, but with a **.orig** extension.

Creating Patches

For best results, use context **diffs**, produced by the –c command-line parameter to **diff**. This causes **diff** to output a few lines around each difference to provide some context to help **patch** figure out where the lines are really located.

 Remember to apply **diff** to the old file first and the new file second. It's easy to get this backward.

N O T E

For example, we can build a patch file to update the file **a** to the file **b** using the following command:

```
$ diff -c a b > patchfile
```

Here, **diff** outputs the differences, along with extra context, into the file **patchfile**, which looks like the following:

```
$ more patchfile
*** a    Thu Sep 26 19:04:57 1996
--- b    Thu Sep 26 19:06:24 1996
***************
*** 1,6 ****
  a
- a
  b
  c
! d
! e
--- 1,6 ---
  a
  b
  c
! dd
!  e
! f
```

You can then apply **patch** to update the file **a** using the following command:

```
$ patch < patchfile
```

```
Hmm...  Looks like a new-style context diff to me...
The text leading up to this was:
--------------------------
|*** a  Thu Sep 26 19:04:57 1996
|--- b  Thu Sep 26 19:06:24 1996
--------------------------
Patching file a using Plan A...
Hunk #1 succeeded at 1.
done
```

When **patch** finishes, the file **a** will be updated to that of **b**, and the original **a** file is renamed **a.orig**.

When testing, you normally don't want to run **patch** in a directory that already has the old and new files. This will confuse **patch** into patching the wrong file.

WARNING

If you plan on using **patch**, you should follow the convention of creating a **patchlevel.h** file. Basically, this file contains the patch level number—a form of version number. Each patch file you send out should update the **patchlevel.h** file and increment the number. This way, users can tell whether or not they loaded a given patch.

If your UNIX system doesn't provide **patch**, look in the **compare** directory on the CD-ROM.

CD-ROM

Summary

This chapter showed how to compare files, using many different UNIX tools. Because software development results in many small changes to many files, tools that compare files are essential.

The main UNIX tool for comparing files is **diff. diff** compares two files and prints the lines that are different.

Graphical **diff** programs, such as **gdiff** and **mgdiff**, make your life much easier by presenting the **diff** output in a far more readable form. You can even use these programs to help you merge the differing files together.

The **patch** program allows you to send out source code updates without sending out entire new files. **patch** automatically updates files from the differences produced by **diff**.

205

UNIX Commands Introduced in This Chapter

bdiff

cmp

comm

diff

diff3

dircmp

gdiff

mgdiff

patch

CHAPTER 9

Controlling Versions

This chapter covers:

- Revision control
- RCS, the Revision Control System
- Getting started with RCS
- Comparing versions
- Merging branches
- CVS, the Concurrent Version System
- PRCS, the Project Revision Control System
- Aegis, a transaction-based configuration management tool

What Is Version Control?

Whenever you create software, you edit source files. As time passes, you'll often return to the same source files, making changes to add new features or fix bugs or just to keep up with ever-changing APIs. Each time you revise your software, there's a chance that things will go wrong. In that case, you may need to back out the new changes and restore a previous version of the software.

If others edit the same files you do, you also need to merge the multiple versions of the same file, creating a new harmonious whole.

Version control is the task of managing revisions to software. You can make this task as hard or as easy as you'd like, but sooner or later every software project needs some way to manage revisions to files.

Once you've released software, you need the ability to fix bugs reported on one release while working on the next release. In fact, you may release interim maintenance versions of your software based on minor changes to the most recent release, all the while adding bells and whistles for the next release. With any significant software project, you need to do all this and more.

This chapter covers RCS, the Revision Control System. RCS provides the main method for managing versions on UNIX. You'll find out how to use the various RCS commands and you'll delve into three other packages built on top of RCS that extend it to allow for more developers to work on the same source code base.

Even if you use other version control systems, such as SCCS, the Source Code Control System that comes with some versions of UNIX, or ClearCase from Pure Atria, most of the concepts remain the same. With any version control system, you need to be able to:

- Store and retrieve different versions of the same file.
- Maintain a history of all versions of each file in the RCS system.
- Re-create an earlier version of your software, say release 1.0, restoring all files to their state in that version.
- Use a check-in and check-out system to prevent two users from editing a file at the same time.
- Help merge separate revisions of the same file.
- Help identify revisions.

How Version Control Systems Work

All version control systems maintain a form of database for each file you want to control. Virtually all of these files are source code files, that is, text. If you use third-party libraries, you may sometimes need to archive binary files, but most usage of version control tools sticks to text files. Because most of the files you'll manage are text, you can make extensive use of the UNIX utilities for managing text files. For example, the primary tool used with version control packages is a **diff** program, like those discussed in Chapter 8.

At certain times, for example, when you're at a good stopping place and things work, you may want to make a snapshot or checkpoint for your files, placing them into the version control system's database. Whenever you make a checkpoint, you're saving a version of your files that you can recover later.

If you're using a manual form of version control, checkpointing your code requires making a copy of the current directory hierarchy and archiving that copy somewhere. While this may work for small projects, it soon becomes unworkable for large projects; you usually need something more.

RCS: The Revision Control System

RCS provides the main version control suite for UNIX. It includes a number of utilities for working with files under version control and an established convention for numbering versions and creating branches.

CD-ROM

The CD-ROM contains RCS in the **src_cntrl/rcs** directory. RCS does not ship with commercial UNIX systems, but many sites install it anyway. To see if you have RCS installed already, check for the **ci** (check in), **co** (check out), and **rcs** commands. If you have these, you probably have RCS installed.

RCS scales quite well, going from simple check-in and check-out control to allowing you to add version labels and manipulate the versions of your code in complicated ways. That's a great feature of RCS. You can get started with very little effort and a few simple commands.

209

The Only RCS Commands You Really Need

For most usage, you really only need to create the **RCS** directory and use two RCS commands. To get started with RCS, you need to create a directory named **RCS** in each directory where you have files of which you want to manage versions. Usually, this is every source code directory. Create a directory named **RCS**:

```
$ mkdir RCS
```

The **RCS** directory will hold all the version control information on your files. Once you start checking files in, as described in the next section, you'll start filling the **RCS** directory with specially formatted copies of your files using the **ci** command. To save space, RCS stores the latest version of each file, along with the difference information needed to re-create any previous version.

The key point to remember is that RCS requires a subdirectory named **RCS** in every source code directory you work on. For example, if you have three libraries, named **a**, **b**, and **c**, and each library has its own source code directory, you'll need a directory structure like the following:

```
a/
a/RCS/
b/
b/RCS/
c/
c/RCS/
```

That is, each of the library directories—**a**, **b**, and **c**—needs an **RCS** subdirectory.

The next step is to check in all your source code files for the first time, placing each file under version control by RCS. To do this, you can use the following command:

```
$ ci -u filename.c
RCS/filename.c,v  <--  filename.c
enter description, terminated with single '.' or end of file:
NOTE: This is NOT the log message!
>> Initial version
>> .
```

When you first check in a file, **ci** prompts you for a descriptive message. Your message may span a number of lines and continues until you enter a period all alone on a line to end the message.

When you check in the same file again, **ci** prompts you for a log message, which you enter the same way and end with a period all alone on a line.

The **ci** command copies the file into the **RCS** directory, with a **,v** extension. (Yes, that's a *comma v*.) When you first check in a file, the **,v** file contains the full text of the original file plus any RCS log messages. When you check in later versions, the **,v** file changes. RCS stores all the revision history for the file in the **,v** file and keeps the full text of the latest version and the differences necessary to re-create any earlier version.

By keeping the full text of the latest version, RCS assumes you'll most likely want to check out the latest version. Checking out earlier versions involves more work, because RCS must re-create the earlier versions from the difference information stored in the **,v** file.

By keeping only the differences for the earlier versions, RCS saves you a lot of disk space at a price of slower access times for earlier versions.

The **ci** command also removes the file from the current directory, which can be disconcerting. The -u command-line parameter takes care of this and checks out the file again in unreserved mode. An *unreserved file* has read-only permission.

Only one user at a time can check out a file for *editing* (read-write). Such a file is said to be *reserved* or *locked* in RCS terminology. But more than one user can check out a file unreserved (read-only) mode.

To check out a file for editing, use the **co** command with the -l (for *lock*) command-line parameter:

```
$  co -l filename.c
RCS/filename.c,v  ->  filename.c
revision 1.1 (locked)
done
```

The **co** command checks out the file from RCS. **co** generates an error if someone already has the file checked out in reserved mode. The -l command-line parameter creates a lock on the file. This ensures that no one else can check out the file while you have it locked, and it gives you a read-write version of the file in the current directory.

When you're finished editing the file and want to store the current version of the file in RCS, check the file back in with the **ci** command:

```
$ ci -u filename.c
RCS/filename.c,v  <- filename.c
new revision: 1.2; previous revision: 1.1
enter log message, terminated with single '.' or end of file:
>> Latest version.
>> .
done
```

Again, you're prompted for a log message, ending with a period on a line of its own. (Normally, you'll want a more descriptive message than the one shown here.) The –u command-line parameter keeps a read-only copy of the file in the current directory. This is the same as using **co -u** to check out a file unreserved.

ci and **co** are the most-used RCS commands. There are more commands, though, to help you work with file revisions.

More RCS Commands

RCS offers more than the simple check-in and check-out commands. RCS extends the **ci** and **co** commands with a number of command-line parameters. In addition, RCS offers other useful commands for controlling your source code. Table 9.1 lists the most important RCS commands and their command-line parameters.

Table 9.1 RCS Commands

Command	Meaning
ci -l *filename*	Check in *filename*, then check out again and lock.
ci -u *filename*	Check in *filename*, then check out again unlocked (read-only).

ci -i *filename*	Initial check in for *filename*; won't work if already checked in.
ci -m*Message filename*	Check in *filename*; uses *Message* as the log message.
co -r *filename*	Check out a file for read-only use.
co -l *filename*	Check out a file for modification.
rcs -u *filename.c*	Abandon changes and uncheck out *filename.c*.
rcs -l *filename.c*	Check out without overwriting *filename.c*.
$ co -r3.5 -l *filename.c*	Check out a particular version, 3.5 in this case.
rlog *filename.c*	View RCS log for *filename.c*.
$ rlog -R -L -l*username* RCS/*	Lists all files locked by user *username*.

For beginners, the only commands you need to worry about are **ci -u**, which checks a file in and then retrieves a read-only copy of the file, and **co -l**, which checks out a file, locking the file from modification by other users.

The RCS Directory

Each directory you keep source code in needs an **RCS** subdirectory. Inside each **RCS** subdirectory, RCS keeps all its version information for the source files in the parent directory. Each **RCS** subdirectory is independent of all other **RCS** subdirectories. The total collection of **RCS** subdirectories holds all your precious source code. This makes it extremely important for you to back up the contents of all the **RCS** directories. Remember, these directories contain the crown jewels of your source code.

Inside each **RCS** directory, you'll see a **,v** file for each file in the source code control system, for example:

```
$ ls RCS
Makefile,v        khdata.h,v       khevent.h,v      khstring.h,v
kh.h,v            khdebug.cxx,v    khiter.cxx,v     khtest.cxx,v
khcompos.cxx,v    khdebug.h,v      khrect.cxx,v     khtypes.h,v
khdata.cxx,v      khdraw.h,v       khstring.cxx,v   khwidget.cxx,v
```

Working in Groups with RCS

If you work alone, you normally create an **RCS** subdirectory in each source code directory. If you work in a group, you need to share the **RCS** directories, because that's where RCS stores all the version and locking information.

The usual procedure is to create source code directories on a shared disk, usually a network-mounted disk. Inside each of these source code directories, you place the crucial **RCS** subdirectories.

When working, though, you do *not* work in the shared directories. Instead, you make your own directory hierarchy—without the **RCS** directories—somewhere within your own account. This is called creating a *local work area*. Despite the fancy name, all you're doing is mirroring the main set of directories. When you do this, you need to use slightly more complicated RCS commands to check out files and check them back in.

You need to refer to the exact file name in the **RCS** directory, in the shared location. For example, to check out a file from a shared RCS location and place the checked-out file into the current directory—called your *local work area*—you can use a command like the following:

```
$ co -l /shared_source/RCS/khiter.cxx,v
/shared_source/RCS/khiter.cxx,v  ->  khiter.cxx
revision 1.2 (locked)
done
```

Note the **,v** at the end of the file name in the preceding command. You need to refer to the exact name in the shared **RCS** directory, called **/shared_source/RCS** for this example. You're free to place your source code anywhere you want.

When you check the current directory, you should see the file you checked out:

```
$ ls
khiter.cxx
```

To work in this mode, you usually need to check out all files unreserved, using the **co -u** command. This is how you get a starting set of files into your local work area.

To check the file back in, you need to use a command like the following:

```
$ ci -u /shared_source/RCS/khiter.cxx,v
new revision: 1.3; previous revision: 1.2
enter log message, terminated with single '.' or end of file:
>> Fix bug # 7089
>> .
done
```

All your RCS commands need to refer to the source files in the proper shared directories. Because this makes for more complicated RCS commands for all users, most people create utility shell scripts for working with RCS. These shell scripts hide the location of the shared source code RCS repositories and make for much easier commands. For example, here's a shell script, called **mycheckin**, to check in files into the shared source code base:

```
#!/bin/sh
ci -u /shared_source/RCS/$1,v
```

The $1 is replaced with the file name you pass on the command line. To mark this file as executable, you need to run the **chmod** command. For example:

```
$ chmod +x mycheckin
```

Then, to check in a file, all you need to do is pass the name of the file to the **mycheckin** shell script:

```
$ mycheckin khiter.cxx
new revision: 1.3; previous revision: 1.2
enter log message, terminated with single '.' or end of file:
>> Fix bug # 7089
>> .
done
```

The shell script to check out files is also quite simple. The **mycheckout** script follows:

```
#!/bin/sh
co -l /shared_source/RCS/$1,v
```

216

You can use these scripts by changing the **/shared_source** directory to the name of the directory where you keep the **RCS** subdirectory. If you use multiple **RCS** directories, perhaps one for each source code library, you'll need to change the shell scripts to reflect your directory organization. This makes for more complicated shell scripts, but it is relatively easy to accomplish.

Checking the RCS Log

Whenever you check a file into RCS, the **ci** command prompts you for a log message. You can view these messages with the **rlog** command:

```
$ rlog khwidget.cxx
RCS file: RCS/khwidget.cxx,v
Working file: khwidget.cxx
head: 1.2
branch:
locks: strict
access list:
symbolic names:
keyword substitution: kv
total revisions: 2;     selected revisions: 2
description:
Initial RCS version
----------------------
revision 1.2
date: 1996/10/05 09:48:02;   author: erc;   state: Exp;   lines: +2 -1
Call khData constructor.
----------------------
revision 1.1
date: 1996/09/22 13:59:31;   author: erc;   state: Exp;
Initial revision
```

The **rlog** command supports some command-line parameters to get different information about the files managed by RCS. The -L command-line parameter forces **rlog** to only look at files that are checked out. The -l command-line parameter allows you to specify only files locked by a particular user. The -R command-line parameter tells **rlog** to merely list the RCS file name.

You can combine these command-line parameters as follows:

```
$ rlog -R -L -lerc RCS/*
RCS/khstring.cxx,v
RCS/khstring.h,v
RCS/khtest.cxx,v
```

This command lists all files locked by user erc.

Abandoning Changes

If you've made changes to a file and things haven't worked out, you can abandon changes made to a checked-out file with the **rcs -u** command:

```
$ rcs -u filename.c
```

The -u command-line parameter to **rcs** unchecks out a file.

Locking without Overwriting

When you check out a file with the **co** command, RCS generates a version of the file from the data stored in the RCS directory and writes this new file into the current directory. This can be a problem if you have modified the file without checking it out. You shouldn't do this, but you may get into a situation where you need to apply changes already made to a file that hasn't been properly checked out.

To get around this problem, you can use the **rcs -l** command:

```
$ rcs -l filename.c
```

The -l command-line parameter to **rcs** locks the file but does not overwrite it with the latest version from the **RCS** directory.

Breaking Locks

If someone else has a file reserved, RCS prevents you from checking out that file in reserved (read-write) mode. You can always check out a file unreserved to get a read-only copy.

Sometimes, though, you need to edit a file checked out by someone else. For example, you may discover a critical bug and need to fix it *now*. In this case, you need to break the lock on the file held by the other user. To do this, you use the same **rcs -u** command to uncheck out a file, but you uncheck out a file checked out by someone else. For example:

```
$ rcs -u khtest.cxx
RCS file: RCS/khtest.cxx,v
Revision 1.3 is already locked by erc.
Do you want to break the lock? [ny](n): y
State the reason for breaking the lock:
(terminate with single '.' or end of file)
>> Sorry, I need to fix Bug # 7076 NOW
>> .
1.3 unlocked
done
```

When you break the lock on a file held by someone else, that person gets an email message containing the reason you gave for breaking the lock. For example:

```
From: Eric Foster-Johnson <efj@yonsen.com>
Subject: Broken lock on khtest.cxx,v
Your lock on revision 1.3 of file /home/erc/src/toolkit/kh/RCS/khtest.cxx,v
has been broken by efj for the following reason:

Sorry, I need to fix Bug # 7076 NOW
```

Version Numbers

RCS applies a version number to each revision of a file you check in, starting with version 1.1. After version 1.1, the next revision is 1.2, then 1.3, and so on. If these version numbers are fine, you need do nothing, as RCS automatically updates version numbers when you check files out.

To start the next major revision, such as 2.1, you can use the following command-line parameters when checking a file in:

```
$ ci -r2.1 filename.c
```

You can also use the following shortcut:

```
$ ci -r2 filename.c
```

When you later check in the file, it will have a version number of 2.1.

Extracting Particular Versions

To check out a particular version, such as 3.5, you can use the following command:

```
$ co -r3.5 -l filename.c
```

If you want to check out the latest 3.n version, you can use the following command:

```
$ co -r3 -l filename.c
```

By default, **co** always checks out the highest regular version, i.e., 3.6. If you want to check out a different version, you need to use the -r command-line parameter.

Branching

You can use RCS to create a branch in the source code tree. Much like on a tree, a *branch* diverges from the main source code trunk. For example, if you're still finishing version 1.0 of your software but another team has already started long-term projects on version 2.0, chances are you need to branch the source code tree. You still need to be able to fix bugs on the version 1.0 branch and the other team needs to be able to check in files on their version 2.0 branch.

To create a branch in RCS, you add an extra digit to the revision number when checking a file out. For example, to create a branch off of revision 1.6, you'd use a command like the following:

```
$ co -l -r1.6.1 filename.c
```

This command actually creates revision number 1.6.1.1. Revision numbers nested this deep tell you you're working on a branch.

In general, branching is an advanced topic; you should become familiar with RCS before attempting to create a branch. Look at the online manual entries for **co**, **rcs**, **rcsdiff**, **rcsfile**, **rcsmerge**, and **rcsintro** for more information on branching. Appendix A also lists a book on RCS that may help.

Placing RCS IDs in Your Code

You can use RCS to automatically update your source code files with information from the RCS log. By convention, RCS looks for specially formatted text strings in your code using the format of *$string$*. The most common such string is Id. If you place Id in your source code files, RCS expands the *Id* part to include the RCS file name, revision number, date, time, username of the person making the changes and the RCS state (usually *Exp*) of the file.

In most cases, place the Id into a comment. For example:

```
/* $Id$ */
```

When you check in a file with a $string$ message that RCS understands, RCS expands the message. For example:

```
/* $Id: khwidget.h,v 1.3 1996/10/05 13:22:20 erc Exp $ */
```

This allows you to keep RCS information up to date inside your files.

If you place the Id string inside a comment, this won't get compiled into the executable program (unless you use Tcl or another interpreted language). Sometimes, you want to place RCS version information into your binary executable files. To do this, you can add code like the following to your source files:

```
static char rcsid[] = "$Id$";
```

The name of the variable, `rcsid`, is a convention.

The static character array will get compiled into your C and C++ programs.

To see the RCS Id strings in files, you can use the **ident** program. **ident** searches for *$string$* constructs in files and prints them. For example:

```
$ ident khwidget.h
khwidget.h:
     $Id: khwidget.h,v 1.3 1996/10/05 13:22:20 erc Exp $
```

ident also works on binary files, for example:

```
$ ident khtest
```

```
khtest:
     $Id: khtest.cxx,v 1.4 1996/10/05 13:31:51 erc Exp $
```

The Id string first gets expanded when you next check in the file.

NOTE

Other *$string$* keywords include $Author$, $Date$, $Header$, $Locker$, Log, $Name$, $RCSfile$, $Revision$, $Source$, and $State$.

Checking the Differences between Versions

To compare the differences between versions of the same file, you can use **rcsdiff**. In its simplest form, **rcsdiff** displays the differences between the current file and the last version checked in. The syntax follows:

```
$ rcsdiff filename.c
```

For example:

```
$ rcsdiff khstring.h
===================
RCS file: RCS/khstring.h,v
retrieving revision 1.1
diff -r1.1 khstring.h
48c48
<         khString(const char* cstring);
—
>         khString(char* cstring);
67a68
>                   // Returns 0 if there are problems.
70,71c71,73
<                   // Convert string value to double
<         operator double() const;
—
>                   // Convert string value to float
>                   // Returns NAN (not a number) if there are problems.
>         operator float() const;
```

You can also explicitly name the revisions you want to compare:

```
$ rcsdiff -r1.4 -r1.2 khtest.cxx
```

This example compares revision 1.4 with revision 1.2 of the file **khtest.cxx**. The ability to specify a revision number is very handy when you need to merge changes created on two RCS branches.

Merging Versions

rcsdiff helps show you differences between versions. **rcsmerge** tries to combine the differences of three versions together.

The basic syntax follows:

rcsmerge -r*Ancestor* -r*Descendent* -p *filename.c* > *combined_file*

The -r command-line parameters tell **rcsmerge** which versions to use when merging. The basic task of **rcsmerge** is to merge the current checked-out file with another version of the file on a different branch. The *Ancestor* version names the revision number for an ancestor version. This ancestor must be common to both the current version of the file—the one you've checked out—and the *Descendent* version.

For example, if your current **filename.c** is at version 1.8 and you need to merge the changes made on the 1.7.1 branch into this file, you can use a command like the following:

```
$ rcsmerge -r1.7 -r1.7.1.5 -p filename.c > combined_file
```

This command tries to merge all the changes made on the 1.7.1 branch—through revision 1.7.1.5—with the changes in the current file.

The -p command-line parameter tells **rcsmerge** to send the combined changes to standard output (the screen) instead of overwriting **filename.c**. In most cases, you redirect the output to a new file.

rcsmerge is rather tricky. I strongly suggest you use the -p command-line parameter to output all changes to another file instead of overwriting your working file. The merging algorithms always worry me—I just don't trust a program to ran rampant through my source code.

rcsmerge does its best at merging the changes between the files. There's no perfect way to combine files like this, so you need to carefully examine the **combined_file** output. Sometimes, the merger goes perfectly. Other times you'll see results that don't make sense, which you'll need to correct.

rcsmerge is the trickiest part of the whole RCS system. Be very careful with it.

Graphical Views

To get a graphical view of the differences between versions, you can use the Tcl script **rcsview**. **rcsview** shows the changes made in different versions of a file using color to identify the sections that changed.

CD-ROM

rcsview is located in the **src_cntrl** directory. It requires Tcl/Tk.

To launch **rcsview**, you just need to pass the file name:

```
$ rcsview filename.c
```

rcsview displays two windows, as shown in Figure 9.1.

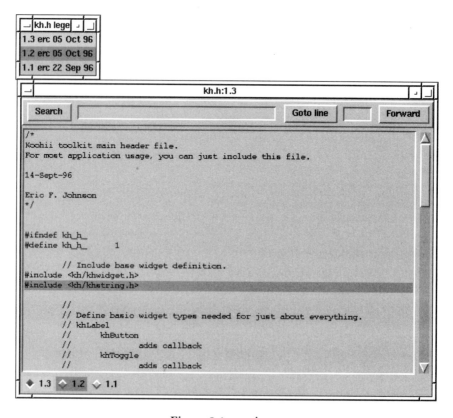

Figure 9.1 rcsview.

The small window describes the colors used to identify changes made in a particular version; the larger window shows the file.

Using RCS from emacs

emacs, that all-singing, all-dancing text editor, provides a special RCS mode called vc, allowing you to check out files, check them back in, and perform other RCS commands from within **emacs**.

In most cases, **C-x v v** will do the next right thing. If a given file is read-only, **C-x v v** will check it out. If you have the file already checked out, **C-x v v** will check the file in. This is the closest to do-what-I-mean that I've ever seen in software.

Table 9.2 lists the major version control commands in **emacs**.

Table 9.2 RCS Commands in **emacs**

Command	Action
C-x v v	Do next logical thing: check out, check in, etc.
C-x v l	Show version log.
C-x v u	Uncheck out; revert to the previous version.
C-x v h	Insert RCS Id header at cursor.
C-x v d	Run the **dired** directory mode, with RCS extensions.

You can see part of how version control integrates RCS into the **emacs** environment in Figure 9.2.

```
                          emacs@yonsen.com
 Buffers Files Tools Edit Search Help
     subclassing.
*/
class khLabel : public khWidget {
public:
        ///////////////////////
        // Constructor.
    khLabel();

        ///////////////////////
        // Destructor.
-----Emacs: kh.h          (C RCS:1.3)--L66--58%-----------------------
description:
Initial RCS version
-----------------------
revision 1.3    locked by: erc;
date: 1996/10/05 17:52:17;  author: erc;  state: Exp;  lines: +1 -0
*** empty log message ***
-----------------------
revision 1.2
date: 1996/10/05 09:32:51;  author: erc;  state: Exp;  lines: +13 -3
Latest version.
-----------------------
revision 1.1
--**-Emacs: *vc*          (Fundamental from kh.h)--L11--33%------------
```

Figure 9.2 emacs in RCS mode.

RCS versus SCCS

RCS now dominates mainstream UNIX usage, but an older package called *SCCS* appears on some versions of UNIX. SCCS, short for Source Code Control System, acts very much like RCS.

Both SCCS and RCS only store the differences in versions of the same file. Neither keeps a full copy of each version of a file. Version control policy wonks still debate whether the RCS or SCCS method is more efficient for performance and disk space. In the end, RCS is available on more UNIX systems and has had more active development, so I stick with RCS.

CD-ROM

The **src_contrl/sccs2rcs** directory on the CD-ROM contains a shell script that helps you migrate from SCCS to RCS. It copies files into RCS and tries to maintain the SCCS revision history information.

For more information on RCS, you can check the following online manuals entries: **ci, co, rcs, rcsclean, rcsdiff, rcsintro, rcsmerge**, and **rcsfile**.

Going Beyond RCS

RCS scales fairly well for most software projects, but if you are involved in the creation of very large applications with multiple versions, many branches, and a large staff of developers, you'll soon find some problems with it. To help with this, there are several freeware systems that go beyond RCS. Some are built on top of RCS; others follow completely different paradigms.

The most common of these is CVS, the Concurrent Version System.

CVS: The Concurrent Version System

CVS was designed for working on very large software projects, with code coming from other teams and perhaps even third-party vendors.

CVS is optimized for the following cases:

- Over the course of your product's lifetime, you get multiple versions of third-party libraries, perhaps for licensing or user interfaces, and you sometimes need to edit the code coming from the third parties and you need to apply your changes to each new release coming from the vendor.

- You have a number of files that it seems are always checked out, sometimes for long periods of time, and you have a lot of conflicts over breaking RCS locks on files.

- With a large source code base, you need to apply RCS commands to many files all at once, going from directory to directory.

CVS acts as a front end for RCS commands. One of the best additional features added by CVS is called lazy locking. *Lazy locking* allows you to check out a file without having RCS lock that file. Any conflicts are resolved when you try to check the file in. Because of this, you can check out a file and make modifications for a long time, and others can check out the same file without breaking your locks.

Of course, you still have to merge the files when you're finished, but lazy locking means you only need to merge files one version at a time.

A Graphic Interface to CVS

tkCVS provides a graphical front end to the CVS set of commands. Within tkCVS you can check in and check out CVS-controlled modules.

tkCVS also comes with a graphical difference program, **tkdiff**, as shown in Figure 9.3.

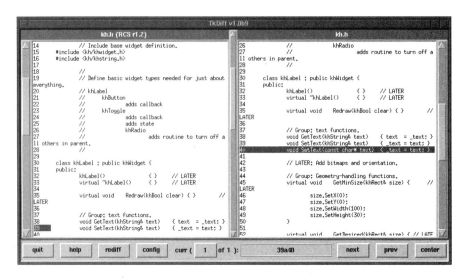

Figure 9.3 Using **tkdiff** to compare versions.

You can launch **tkdiff** to compare two files with the following command:

```
$ tkdiff file1 file2
```

You can also use **tkdiff** with either RCS or CVS to compare a file with previous versions.

With CVS, to compare a file with its immediate previous version, you can use the following command:

```
$ tkdiff -c filename
```

You can also place a version ID after the -c command-line parameter to compare with a particular version.

With RCS, to compare a file with its immediate previous version, you can use the following command:

```
$ tkdiff -r filename
```

As with CVS, you can pass a version number on the command line to compare against that particular version:

```
$ tkdiff -r1.2 filename
```

Chapter 8 covers other graphical comparison programs such as **gdiff** and **mgdiff**.

CVS and tkCVS appear in the **src_cntrl/cvs** directory on the CD-ROM.

CD-ROM

PRCS: Project Revision Control System

PRCS, the Project Revision Control System, provides a different front end to RCS. The main feature of PRCS lies in its claim that it is much easier to use than either RCS or CVS.

PRCS also allows you to treat a set of files as a unit. This makes sense, in that fixing one bug or adding a new feature may result in changes to several files. With PRCS, you can treat all the files that make up one modification to the product as a unit.

PRCS appears in the **src_cntrl/prcs** directory on the CD-ROM.

CD-ROM

Aegis

Aegis is a transaction-based version control system that differs greatly from RCS. Like CVS, Aegis is designed for large programming teams and helps to coordinate merging files into the main source code base with the least disruption possible.

Unlike CVS, though, Aegis applies a formal method to working on software projects. If you don't like this formal method, Aegis isn't the tool for you.

230

One of the major goals of Aegis is to constantly maintain a working version of the software. Thus, before you can check in any code with Aegis, you must provide a test program that proves that the new code passes the test. By enforcing this, Aegis makes it much more likely that your software will always work.

Aegis enforces reviews of all software checked in. Unless it passes the review (and the test program), Aegis won't let you check in files.

Aegis also restricts you from making any changes unless you have a proper change request. If you like this kind of formal development style, Aegis may be the tool for you. (I'm not such a person.)

You'll find Aegis on the CD-ROM in the **src_cntrl/aegis** directory.

CD-ROM

Summary

All version control systems maintain a form of database for each file you want to control. RCS, the main tool on UNIX, maintains revision information within subdirectories named **RCS**.

You check in files with the **ci** command and check files out with the **co** command. The **co -u** and **co -l** commands are the main RCS commands you'll use.

rcsdiff shows the differences between RCS versions, and **ident** prints the RCS header information stored in your files.

UNIX Commands Introduced in This Chapter

ci

co

ident

rcs

rcsdiff

rcsmerge

rlog

## CHAPTER 10

Developing for Multiple Platforms

This chapter covers:

- Differences in UNIX flavors
- Compiling and linking on different platforms
- Configuring your Makefiles with the GNU Autoconf package
- User interface libraries
- Graphics
- Cross-platform scripting
- Working with Windows NT

Different Flavors of UNIX and Other Platforms

The UNIX world is not a monolith. Historically, each UNIX vendor developed its own version of UNIX. Some of these versions, like SunOS, came from the Berkeley UNIX tree. Others, such as Hewlett-Packard's HP-UX, came from the AT&T branch of the UNIX tree. Each version of UNIX appeared similar, but unfortunately left subtle differences that haunt programmers to this day.

If you develop software for UNIX systems (you wouldn't be reading this book if you don't), chances are that you need to support more than one version of UNIX. This means, unfortunately, that you need to pay attention to these differences between UNIX systems from the major vendors.

Three developments eliminated many differences between these flavors of UNIX for programmers: POSIX , System V Release 4 UNIX, and ANSI C. *POSIX* is an international standard that defines how many UNIX commands work and what programming libraries should be available. *System V Release 4* UNIX merged the main branches of UNIX history: AT&T's System V UNIX and Berkeley UNIX. *ANSI C* defined an American and then an international standard for the C programming language, upon which UNIX was built. ANSI C defines the standard C programming library, cleaning up many differences.

Two more recent developments have continued this standardization effort: the Common Desktop Environment and the Spec 1170. The *Common Desktop Environment* aims to create a common graphical user interface for most versions of UNIX. While still in development, the main factor for programming is that as part of these efforts, Sun dropped the Open Look interface and programming libraries it had been championing and jumped over to endorsing Motif. This made Motif the de facto X programmer's toolkit on all commercial versions of UNIX. As an offshoot of the Common Desktop Environment, the major UNIX vendors such as Sun, IBM, and Hewlett-Packard agreed on approximately 1170 programming functions that all versions of UNIX should provide. This helps even more than POSIX in providing a standard set of programming libraries for use on UNIX.

Even with all this standardization effort, though, there are still differences among UNIX systems that you must deal with when programming, compiling, and linking. This chapter covers some of the main differences, flagging the ones that have hit me the hardest; delves into ways to handle multisystem configurations; and shows how to program defensively around these differences.

Compiling and Linking on Different Platforms

One of the main differences between UNIX systems lies in the options you pass to **cc** and **CC** to compile and link programs.

The one thing that hits me the most is the requirement to use the -Aa command-line parameter to **cc** on Hewlett-Packard systems if your C code uses ANSI C function prototypes. Just about every C programmer has been using such prototypes for years, but HP's C compiler defaults to old-style C that did not support function prototypes.

Another major difference that effects the compilation command is the location of X Window include files and libraries. The default location for X Window include files is in **/usr/include/X11**. When your C or C++ programs include these files, the convention is to refer to the files relative to the **X11** subdirectory in **/usr/include**:

```
#include <X11/Xlib.h>
#include <X11/Xutil.h>
```

Because every X file gets included relative to the **X11** subdirectory, you normally don't require any special options to **cc** or **CC** when compiling X programs. Both compilers look by default in **/usr/include**. Unfortunately, some UNIX system vendors decided to place the X Window include files in non-default locations. This requires you to use special -I command-line parameters when compiling code. For example, when compiling on Hewlett-Packard systems, you need to use a **-I/usr/include/X11R5** parameter to **cc**:

233

```
$ cc -Aa -I/usr/include/X11R5 -c foo.c
```

Hewlett-Packard isn't the only major vendor to place the X Window include files in odd locations. Table 10.1 lists the location of X Window include files on major versions of UNIX.

Table 10.1 Where X Window Include Files Reside

System	Location
default UNIX	/usr/include
Hewlett-Packard	/usr/include/X11R5
IBM	/usr/include (symbolic link)
Linux	/usr/X11R6/include and /usr/openwin/include
Sun	/usr/openwin/include

CROSS-PLATFORM

IBM places the X include files in an odd location but sets up a symbolic link to the default location. This means you don't need special options when compiling.

UNIX vendors also place the X Window libraries in odd locations, as shown in Table 10.2.

Table 10.2 Where X Window Library Files Reside

System	Location
default UNIX	/usr/lib
Hewlett-Packard	/usr/lib/X11R5
IBM	/usr/lib (symbolic link)
Linux	/usr/X11R6/lib and /usr/openwin/lib
Sun	/usr/openwin/lib

File Names

Most C programs use a **.c** file name extension. Most C and C++ include files use a *.h* extension. The most common extensions appear in Table 10.3.

Table 10.3 UNIX File Name Extensions

File Suffix	Meaning
.c	C source file
.C	C++ source file (note the uppercase *C*)
.cc	C++ source file
.cpp	C++ source file
.cxx	C++ source file
.c++	C++ source file
.h	C or C++ include file
.hxx	C++ include file

The extensions you use are largely a matter of personal choice, but there are a few things to consider. The Windows NT file system does not differentiate between upper- and lowercase file names on reading. (NT does differentiate on writing.) Therefore, when compiling, there's no difference between **foo.C** and **foo.c**. These names refer to two distinct files on UNIX, though, so I avoid using a **.C** uppercase file name extension for my C++ programs.

WARNING

Never use **.cpp** as the extension for your C++ program files. The Silicon Graphics compiler uses the **.cpp** extension for temporary files created by the compiler. This means that if you use **.cpp** as the file extension for your source code, code that you know works well won't compile and the compiler will issue very strange errors when you try to compile on an SGI system. This is because the compiler has overwritten your file and is trying to compile something else—the temporary file.

One way to handle compiling and linking problems is to configure your environment on each platform to handle system differences.

Solving Configuration Issues

When you try to compile code on another UNIX system, you need to reconfigure all Makefiles and build scripts to handle the differences on that platform. Few substantial applications require no configuration, so you need to find a way to deal with this problem.

The three main methods for solving configuration issues are:

- Creating scripts and Makefile variables manually to encapsulate the differences between UNIX systems.
- Using **imake** to generate platform-specific Makefiles from a generic Imakefile.
- Using the GNU Autoconf package to automatically create Makefiles from a shell script that investigates a given system to find the necessary information.

If your software is a relatively small program that makes little use of graphics or the operating system libraries, you can probably get away with editing all Makefiles and other configuration files manually.

If you use X Window graphics, **imake**, as described in Chapter 3, may be the tool for you. If your program reads disk directories or delves into other areas of the operating system, you may find the GNU Autoconf package useful.

The GNU Autoconf Package

The GNU Autoconf package is a set of **m4** macros that can create a shell script to investigate a UNIX system and create a Makefile (or other configuration files) from the shell script. Sound complicated? The idea is to make the task of configuring your software on another platform as easy as possible, at the price of work you need to do up front.

On the other platforms, all you do is run a shell script called **configure**. The **configure** script checks for the system services your program requires and builds up a Makefile tuned to that system. The main problem lies in creating the **configure** script in the first place.

To do this, the GNU Autoconf package uses the **m4** preprocessor and a number of files you need to create. **m4** is a UNIX utility that acts like the C preprocessor, **cpp**. **m4** accepts macro commands such as #define and #include, much like **cpp** does.

 To use the GNU Autoconf package, you must have the GNU version of **m4**. Both Autoconf and GNU **m4** appear on the CD-ROM in the **config** directory.

NOTE

How GNU Autoconf Works for the End User

The whole idea of Autoconf is to make things easy on the user on other platforms. This user may well be you, so that's a good thing. In general, the user runs a shell script called **configure** in the current directory. **configure** attempts to guess the value of system-dependent variables and then creates a **Makefile**. configure may also create a **config.h** file that gets used in the program code. After that, all the user should need to do is compile the code with **make** and then install the resulting program with **make install**. For example, the following commands should build just about any program that was set up with the GNU Autoconf package:

```
$ ./configure
$ make
$ make install
```

Pretty easy, huh? Usually, the configure step involves a lot of data being printed and sometimes questions for the user to answer. For example:

```
$ ./configure
creating cache ./config.cache
checking for gm4... no
checking for gnum4... no
checking for m4... /usr/bin/m4
checking for mawk... no
checking for gawk... gawk
checking for perl... /usr/bin/perl
checking for a BSD compatible install... /usr/bin/ginstall -c
```

```
updating cache ./config.cache
creating ./config.status
creating Makefile
```

The user usually has the option of modifying the values determined by the configure script, for example, the directory location to install the program. In most cases, **configure** sets up the program to be installed into **/usr/local/bin**, with manual entries in **/usr/local/man** and support files in **/usr/local/lib**. The user can change this with the **--prefix=*PATH*** command-line parameter to **configure**. For example:

```
$ ./configure --prefix=/mylocal
```

The **configure** script itself is merely a Bourne (**/bin/sh**) shell script. This script is entirely independent of the GNU Autoconf package, so the end user does not need to install special software. The user just needs the Bourne shell.

This is very handy because other tools, such as **imake**, depend on both your UNIX system supplying **imake** and a proper set of **imake** configuration files. Some vendors, such as Hewlett-Packard, don't include **imake** as a standard part of their operating systems.

Setting Up GNU Autoconf Scripts

Autoconf is very confusing to use for the first time, but you'll soon get the hang of it. The basic idea is that you need to develop input files—usually with a *.in* file name extension—that list the system dependencies and services used by your program. These dependencies are listed in special **m4** macros in the **.in** files. Autoconf then expands the macros into the tests it needs to perform.

By default, the product of your work with Autoconf will be a shell script called **configure**. When run, **configure** should create a Makefile and perhaps a header file for inclusion in your code. The Makefile should be properly targeted to the user's system.

The main thing you need to do is create a file named **configure.in**, which Autoconf uses to create the configure shell script. You also need to create a **Makefile.in** file, which defines the basic layout of your Makefile. The **configure** script will generate the actual Makefile.

Creating the configure.in File

The **configure.in** file contains a number of **m4** macros, which Autoconf expands when run. You must start your **configure.in** file with an AC_INIT(*file-name*) and end your **configure.in** file with an AC_OUTPUT(*filename*) macro.

When you first get started, Autoconf can be a bit daunting. To help you get going, I'll use a sample C++ program and show how to build a **configure** script for the program. You'll see how to place Autoconf variables into a Makefile and how to get the whole thing going.

To start your **configure.in** file, you need to first call the AC_INIT macro with the name of any file in your source directory. **configure** uses this file to test whether it is being run in the proper directory. So use the name of any file in the directory that seems like a unique name.

The basic syntax follows:

AC_INIT(*filename*)

For example, if you have a header file named **kh.h**, you can use the following AC_INIT macro in your **configure.in** file:

```
AC_INIT(kh.h)
```

The next step is to check for a C or C++ compiler—whichever your program requires. To check for a C++ compiler, place the following line in your **configure.in** file:

```
AC_PROG_CXX
```

AC_PROG_CXX will define the variable CXX, which will contain the name of the C++ compiler, such as **CC** or **c++**. Most of what Autoconf does is set variables based on the system setup. AC_PROG_CXX also defines the standard flags to pass to the C++ compiler in the variable CXXFLAGS. We'll use both of these variables in the **Makefile.in** file.

To check for a C compiler, use the following line in your **configure.in** file:

```
AC_PROG_CC
```

AC_PROG_CC defines the CC variable with the name of the C compiler, such as **cc** or **gcc**. AC_PROG_CC also defines the basic flags in CFLAGS.

If you need to build a library, you should check for the **ranlib** program, mentioned in Chapter 2. Some flavors of UNIX require that you run **ranlib** on library **.a** files to properly build up the library's table of contents. With Autoconf, you can use the AC_PROG_RANLIB macro to test for **ranlib**. If **ranlib** is needed, the RANLIB variable gets set to the name of the program, usually **ranlib**. If not, the RANLIB variable gets set to a colon, :.

To use the AC_PROG_RANLIB, add the following line to your **configure.in** file:

```
AC_PROG_RANLIB
```

AC_CANONICAL_SYSTEM sets build, host and target with information on the name of the system you're building on and the target architecture.

If you have a number of source code directories and want to run **configure** in each subdirectory, you can include an AC_CONFIG_SUBDIRS macro, naming a subdirectory in which to run **configure**. The syntax follows:

AC_CONFIG_SUBDIRS(*directoryname*)

At the end of your **configure.in** file, you need to call AC_OUTPUT to create the Makefile and any other file that you find necessary, such as a header file. To create a Makefile, you can use an AC_OUTPUT line like the following:

```
AC_OUTPUT(Makefile)
```

To show these macros in use, a complete **configure.in** file follows:

```
AC_INIT(kh.h)

AC_PROG_CC
AC_PROG_CXX

AC_PROG_RANLIB

AC_OUTPUT(Makefile)
```

To create the **configure** script from this **configure.in** file, simply run the **autoconf** command in the current directory:

```
$ autoconf
```

autoconf creates a **configure** file from the **configure.in** file. To use the **configure** file, you also need a **Makefile.in** file. You need to ship both the **configure** and the **Makefile.in** file to your users on other platforms. You do not need to ship the **configure.in** file, because it is no longer needed, except to regenerate the **configure** script file.

In addition to the **configure.in** file, you need a **Makefile.in** file to create a Makefile.

Creating the Makefile.in File

The **Makefile.in** file contains a valid Makefile (see Chapter 3) with some extra Autoconf variables. Any new variable uses the following syntax:

@VARIABLE@

configure will fill in any such variables with the value set in the **configure** script.

The main use of the *@VARIABLE@* syntax is inside your **Makefile.in** file. The **configure** script will output a Makefile, given the AC_OUTPUT(Makefile) macro.

In the preceding example **configure.in** file, we used Autoconf macros to set the CC, CXX, CFLAGS, CXXFLAGS, and RANLIB variables. You can then use these variables to generate a Makefile called **Makefile.in**. The **configure** script will use **Makefile.in** as a base and fill in all the *@VARIABLE@* items defined in the **Makefile.in** with appropriate values for the current platform and then output a valid Makefile (assuming you have things set up properly).

For example, you can use the following **Makefile.in** file as a guide:

```
#
# Makefile for showing configure.

# Define programs for building libraries.
AR= ar
RANLIB=@RANLIB@

# C compiler.
CC = @CC@

# C++ compiler.
CXX= @CXX@
```

```
# Flags for C compiler.
CFLAGS = @CFLAGS@

# Flags for C compiler.
CXXFLAGS = @CXXFLAGS@

OBJS=   khdata.o khrect.o

# Build a library.
libkh.a:        $(OBJS)
    /bin/rm -rf libkh.a
    $(AR) rv libkh.a $(OBJS)
    $(RANLIB) libkh.a

# Compile a C++ program.
khdata.o:       khdata.cxx
    $(CXX) $(CXXFLAGS) -c khdata.cxx

# Compile a C program.
khrect.o:       khrect.c
    $(CC) $(CFLAGS) -c khrect.c
```

When you run the **configure** script, you should see a system-specific **Makefile**. For example, on a Sun Solaris system, you'll see a **Makefile** like the following:

```
# Generated automatically from Makefile.in by configure.
#
# Makefile for showing configure.

# Define programs for building libraries.
AR= ar
RANLIB=:

# C compiler.
CC = cc

# C++ compiler.
CXX= CC
```

```
# Flags for C compiler.
CFLAGS = -g


# Flags for C compiler.
CXXFLAGS = -g


OBJS=   khdata.o khrect.o


# Build a library.
libkh.a:        $(OBJS)
        /bin/rm -rf libkh.a
        $(AR) rv libkh.a $(OBJS)
        $(RANLIB) libkh.a


# Compile a C++ program.
khdata.o:       khdata.cxx
        $(CXX) $(CXXFLAGS) -c khdata.cxx


# Compile a C program.
khrect.o:       khrect.c
        $(CC) $(CFLAGS) -c khrect.c
```

Note how the *@VARIABLE@* items from the **Makefile.in** file are now filled in with values appropriate for Solaris.

As another example, on a Linux system using the GNU C and C++ compilers, you'll see a Makefile that looks different:

```
# Generated automatically from Makefile.in by configure.
#
# Makefile for showing configure.


# Define programs for building libraries.
AR= ar
RANLIB=ranlib


# C compiler.
CC = gcc
```

```
# C++ compiler.
CXX= c++

# Flags for C compiler.
CFLAGS = -g -O

# Flags for C compiler.
CXXFLAGS = -g -O

OBJS=   khdata.o khrect.o

# Build a library.
libkh.a:        $(OBJS)
        /bin/rm -rf libkh.a
        $(AR) rv libkh.a $(OBJS)
        $(RANLIB) libkh.a

# Compile a C++ program.
khdata.o:       khdata.cxx
        $(CXX) $(CXXFLAGS) -c khdata.cxx

# Compile a C program.
khrect.o:       khrect.c
        $(CC) $(CFLAGS) -c khrect.c
```

Note how two variables got filled in with the GNU compiler values. (GNU C and C++ allow for mixing the -g debugging and -o optimization flags.)

That should be more than enough to get going with Autoconf. Even so, there's a lot more to learn. Luckily, the program comes with scads of documentation in the form of info files. Look in all the files that end in **.info** for documentation on the Autoconf family of utilities.

Two other scripts of note are **autoscan**, which tries—not very well—to create the **configure.in** file for you, based on the source code in the current directory, and **autoheader**, which creates a **config.h.in** file, used as a base to create a **config.h** file. Look in the **.info** files for more on these utilities.

When choosing among Autoconf, **imake**, and configuring things by hand, choose the tool that you think will work best for you—there's no one best tool.

Creating User Interfaces

The X Window System, discussed in Chapter 2, provides graphics routines for two-dimensional graphics and most user interface needs. While a few other windowing systems exist, X is by far the de facto graphics standard on UNIX. To maintain maximum portability among UNIX systems, your graphical programs should use the X libraries.

Programming with the low-level X library involves a lot of work. Luckily, a number of toolkits provide easier programming for X Window applications. The main X toolkit for C and C++ programs is called Motif. The Motif programming libraries are available on just about every version of UNIX.

 Freeware versions of UNIX, such as Linux and NetBSD, don't come with Motif. For those systems, you need to purchase the Motif libraries from a vendor such as MetroX.

NOTE

 The CD-ROM comes with LessTif, a freeware clone of the Motif API. While you can compile and link many Motif programs with LessTif, LessTif is still far from ready for serious use, unfortunately.

CD-ROM

User Interfaces for Java Programs

When creating Java programs, you should use Java's windowing toolkit, the Abstract Window Toolkit, or AWT. You can create new user interface widgets from AWT's basic set, but you shouldn't use system-specific widgets, such as ActiveX controls on Windows. If you stick to the basic AWT, your Java programs should run fine on all supported platforms.

Cross-Platform User Interface Libraries

Motif runs fine on just about every UNIX system that supports X. So if you program to the Motif APIs and you only need to support UNIX, you should be fine for cross-platform portability as far as the user interface goes. Once you start porting to other operating systems, such as Windows NT or MacOS, though, you're in a bind.

Motif does not work on the Macintosh, although you can purchase Motif on Windows NT through Hummingbird. (This uses an X server on NT to display your programs.) If you also need to support multiple non-UNIX operating systems, you might want to look into some cross-platform user interface toolkits.

Three commercial toolkits are Galaxy from Visix, XVT from XVT Software, and zApp from Rogue Wave. If you're starting from the Windows world, Brisotol and Mainsoft both sell a Win32 API on UNIX, which comes with the Microsoft Foundation Classes, or MFC C++ framework. This is a great help if you're already locked into the Microsoft C++ compiler on Windows and coded to the MFC.

For freeware toolkits, wxWindows works on UNIX and Windows platforms.

wxWindows is a freeware toolkit that uses native XView, Motif, or Win32 widgets. wxWindows is a C++ application framework library, on a par with Microsoft's MFC (although nowhere near as extensive). wxWindows contains approximately 60 classes, with 650 public functions.

You can find more information about wxWindows on the Internet at:

```
http://www.aiai.ed.ac.uk/~jacs/wxwin.html
```

In general, Windows NT programs don't free graphic resources, like Windows and device contexts (GCs in the X Window world). If you have a cross-platform application, you may need special code on exiting to avoid using up all the Windows resources.

NOTE

Graphics

For high-performance graphics under the X Window System, you're left with two main choices: PEX and OpenGL.

PEX is an X Consortium standard, albeit a somewhat dormant standard, for three-dimensional graphics under X. PEX is available from several of UNIX vendors, including Hewlett-Packard and Sun. In addition, the source code for PEX and the entire X Window System is free and available on the Internet. The main problem with PEX is that in recent years it has fallen behind its main rival OpenGL.

OpenGL is a three-dimensional graphics library based on an earlier library called GL developed by Silicon Graphics. OpenGL provides two key advantages over the older GL: OpenGL provides just 3D graphics, it does not specify the windowing system and OpenGL is available on many non-UNIX platforms, including Windows NT.

With GL, the windowing system and three dimensional graphics system were tightly linked, detracting from cross-platform compatibility. With OpenGL, all windowing functions are removed from the main specification and pulled into a separate auxiliary library with function names starting with *glX*. This development frees OpenGL from the X Window System, allowing OpenGL to work on other systems, most notably Windows NT.

To work with OpenGL on either UNIX or Windows NT, you first create a graphics window using the native windowing APIs, X or Win32, respectively. You then set OpenGL to use your new window for rendering. OpenGL has no input functions, leaving these to the underlying windowing system.

For systems that don't support OpenGL, you can use a freeware library called Mesa. Mesa is not a full replacement for OpenGL, but it works adequately for many applications.

Mesa appears in the **graphics** directory on the CD-ROM.

CD-ROM

Cross-Platform Scripts

Many software developers use shell scripts to help compile, build, and distribute software. If you need to port your scripts to other operating systems, you're in for another shock. The batch language on Windows is laughable compared to the Korn, C, or even Bourne shells on UNIX. To help get around this problem, you can write your scripts in Perl or Tcl—both covered in Chapter 2.

Perl excels at system-level tasks like launching the compiler, comparing output, or copying files. Tcl works best as a glue language; you write your functions in C or C++ and then user Tcl as a scripting language to tie things together. Tcl also provides a graphical toolkit called Tk, which you can use to quickly create graphical applications. Perl/Tk provides this same ability to Perl.

Developing for Windows NT and UNIX

Windows NT claims to support the POSIX standard API, which most UNIX versions conform to. This *should* mean that porting UNIX code is easy. Unfortunately, while Microsoft does support POSIX, you cannot access any functions in the POSIX subsystem from applications that use the Win32 subsystem. The practical effect of this is that if your application has a graphical interface, you're all but locked out of the POSIX functions in the POSIX subsystem. This brain-dead implementation of POSIX seems designed to mollify government contract administrators and not much else.

NT does include most ANSI C functions, so as long as you stick to standards other than POSIX, you should be fine. The Microsoft Visual C++ compiler, as well as C++ compilers from other vendors such as Symantec, often exceed UNIX C++ compilers at conforming to the latest standards.

You'll find many—if not most—UNIX tools missing from Windows NT, but key tools like **vi** and **emacs** are readily available in the freeware community. Vendors such as MKS have ported many UNIX utilities, including the Korn shell, to Windows NT.

If you program graphics on NT, you'll need to use the Win32 API, or one of the cross-platform toolkits mentioned above. For three dimensional graphics, Windows NT supports OpenGL.

Networking Issues

The most common way to share disk space on UNIX comes from NFS, the Network File System. Virtually every UNIX system supports NFS, as do a great many other operating systems, including Windows 95 and Windows NT with the proper add-on software.

One of the odd problems with the Windows environment, though, lies in file names. On the old DOS FAT file system, file names could only have eight characters, a single period, and a three-character extension. (This is often called an *8.3 file name*.) File names could not mix upper- and lower-case, as DOS treated them all as the same case. The Windows 95 file system allows for mixed-case and longer file names but hides the new name within an older 8.3 file name. (This is the price of backward compatibility.)

Windows NT supports the DOS FAT file system and NTFS, the NT File System. With NTFS, you can have long file names with multiple periods, and you can even store files using mixed upper- and lowercase letters. But, when you read files, NT ignores the case of the file name.

This led to many PC NFS packages mapping UNIX file names into the DOS conventions. In most cases, you'll find your UNIX files mapped to single-case DOS file names. This creates a problem when you start copying files. You'll often need to map the resulting file names to upper- or lower case to undo the effects of the PC NFS package.

To get around this, you need tools to quickly map file names to upper- or lowercase. I've had good luck with the following Perl scripts. To convert a file name to uppercase, you can use the following script:

```perl
#!/usr/bin/perl
# Convert all file names passed in to
# uppercase.
#
foreach $filename (@ARGV) {

    $newname = $filename;

    # Convert lowercase to upper.
    $newname =~ tr/[a-z]/[A-Z]/;

    #
    # Only rename if different and
    # the $newname doesn't already exist.
    #
    if ($newname ne $filename) {

        #
        # If the new name already exists,
        # don't clobber this file.
        #
        if ( -e $newname ) {

            print "ERROR: Won't clobber existing $newname.\n";
```

```
        } else {

            print "Renaming $filename to $newname.\n";
            rename($filename, $newname);
        }
    }
}
```

```
# toupper.pl
```

You can mark this script as an executable (which the **chmod a+x** command) and then pass any number of file names to it. All the file names will get changed to uppercase. To convert to lowercase, you can use the following script:

```
#!/usr/bin/perl
# Convert all file names passed in to
# lowercase.
#
foreach $filename (@ARGV) {

    $newname = $filename;

    # Convert uppercase to lower.
    $newname =~ tr/[A-Z]/[a-z]/;

    #
    # Only rename if different and
    # the $newname doesn't already exist.
    #
    if ($newname ne $filename) {

        #
        # If the new name already exists,
        # don't clobber this file.
        #
        if ( -e $newname ) {
```

```
            print "ERROR: Won't clobber existing $newname.\n";

        } else {

            print "Renaming $filename to $newname.\n";
            rename($filename, $newname);
        }
    }
}
# tolower.pl
```

Summary

This chapter covers a plethora of issues dealing with cross-platform development.

The UNIX world is not a monolith. Historically, each UNIX vendor developed its own version of UNIX. Due to these platform differences, you need to plan ahead and code defensively to create portable code.

One of the main differences in UNIX platforms lies in the way you compile and link programs, especially X Window applications. On different UNIX flavors you may require different libraries, compile options, and determine the location of header files. One tool that can help with this is the GNU Autoconf package, which helps create configuration files tuned to a particular system.

For the most portable user interfaces, the Motif library comes with just about every commercial version of UNIX, but, alas, not with freeware Unices, where Motif is a separate, extra-cost product. For three-dimensional graphics, OpenGL has surged ahead of PEX, the ostensible standard.

If you need to port to Windows NT, you need to be aware of a number of issues, especially if your code uses POSIX functions.

UNIX Commands Introduced in This Chapter

autoconf

autoheader

configure

## CHAPTER 11

Analyzing Performance

This chapter covers:

- Techniques for optimizing your programs
- The **prof** utility for analyzing performance in your applications
- **gprof**, another tool for analyzing performance in your applications

It's All in the Performance

In the highly competitive software arena, no program is fast enough. We'd all like our software to run faster. The problem is that optimization takes time—a lot of time if you have to redesign the application.

Because of the potentially massive amounts of programmer time needed to speed up applications, a common approach is to measure the performance of the application. The goal is to find those areas of the program that have the greatest impact on overall performance and concentrate on optimizing those areas.

This is very important. If you just start looking at the code and recoding to make things faster, you may end up with a section of code that is really fast but doesn't improve the overall performance of the application. If you could find the areas of the application that require the most time to execute—the bottlenecks—you could concentrate your efforts on those sections of the code. This will provide the largest overall performance increase for the least effort.

Remember, if you don't check for areas of the code that require the most time to execute, then you may optimize something that has no real effect on the performance of your whole application.

So, analyze for bottlenecks first, then optimize. You want to find the main, or most-used, path in your code. You then want to determine which functions have the greatest impact on performance. Once you've discovered the most-used path and which functions have the greatest impact on performance, the next step is to optimize those areas that most effect performance.

To help optimizing, here are some tips from Raj Jain's excellent *The Art of Computer Systems Performance Analysis*:

- Optimize the common case. The most-used path must operate efficiently. Question each statement in the main path.

- Arrange a series of `if` statements so that the most likely value is tested first.

- Arrange a series of and conditions in an `if` statement so that the condition most likely to fail gets tested first.

- Arrange tables of data so the most frequently used value gets checked first.

- Avoid file input and output as much as possible. Batch file operations together. For example, read in a file as one unit and process the data from memory rather than reading in the file line by line from disk and processing each line in turn.

- Try to pull out as many operations as possible from within loops. If a value doesn't change within a loop, avoid computing it each time through the loop.

See Appendix A for more on this book.

Analyzing Performance

UNIX provides two main tools for performance analysis: **prof** and **gprof**, both short for *profiling*.

Both systems insert instrumentation into your code. Then, when you run the application, both packages keep track of how many times each function gets called and the total time spent on each routine. From this information, you get a good idea about which functions take a long time to execute and which may require a short time to execute but get called over and over again, making these functions important for overall performance.

 Unfortunately not all UNIX systems offer these utilities. In addition, some systems support **prof** and **gprof** only for C programs, not C++.

N O T E

The **prof** and **gprof** packages operate similarly. First, you compile your code with a special command-line option that tells the compiler to insert code to count the number of times each function gets called and to keep track of the total time spent in the function.

You then need to run the application. It's a good idea to run the application in a real-life setting so that the performance numbers generated apply to real-world usage.

256

It takes time to check the time. That may sound weird, but one of the first things you'll notice when working with **prof** and **gprof** is that your applications become a lot slower when compiled with the **prof** or **gprof** options. In fact, you'll regularly see the routine that keeps track of the time each function executes, called mcount, at the top of the list for functions that take up time. Remember to compile your program normally before release and none of this will be an issue.

gprof provides more and more detailed output, but in the end **prof** and **gprof** are very similar. In the next sections, I'll show how to use both on the same application, starting with **prof**.

Working with prof

To work with **prof**, you need to recompile (and link) all your code with the –p command-line parameter. For example, the following command works for a simple program:

```
$ cc -o foo -p foo.c
```

Every file must be recompiled with the –p option to fully test your program.

After recompiling all your code, run the application. I usually try to run a set of tests in the application. The goal is to try to run the application as the user would. Otherwise, you may be tracking data on parts of the software that don't matter for performance.

If possible, you want to be able to repeat the tests for multiple runs of the program. If you can't repeat the tests, you'll have a hard time determining if you really improved performance. As you quit the application, the instrumented code will output a data file, usually **mon.out**. This file contains data in a special format that can be read by the **prof** command.

The data stored in the **mon.out** file contains information about each function called when you ran the program, how many times, and how long—in total. The time figure tells you how much of your program was spent in the function.

For example, with a Motif application named **xmkana**, the following command displays the profiling data:

```
$ prof xmkana | more
%Time Seconds Cumsecs  #Calls   msec/call  Name
 21.3   0.10    0.10                       _mcount
 14.9   0.07    0.17    2585       0.03    _write_sys
 10.6   0.05    0.22   50054       0.00    memcpy
  6.4   0.03    0.25   35743       0.00    _strcmp
  4.3   0.02    0.27    8535       0.00    free
  4.3   0.02    0.29    3494       0.01    _ioctl_sys
  3.7   0.02    0.31    1323       0.01    _memcmp
  2.1   0.01    0.32   30649       0.00    memmove
  2.1   0.01    0.33   10638       0.00    malloc
  2.1   0.01    0.34   10413       0.00    _strlen
  2.1   0.01    0.35    9984       0.00    _strncmp
  2.1   0.01    0.36    3494       0.00    _ioctl
  2.1   0.01    0.38      26       0.38    SwitchWidgets
  0.0   0.00    0.41    2430       0.00    CreateKanaXmString
  0.0   0.00    0.41     298       0.00    gettimeofday
  0.0   0.00    0.41      58       0.00    XtVaSetValues
  0.0   0.00    0.41      57       0.00    strncpy
  0.0   0.00    0.41      50       0.00    switchWidgetsCB
  0.0   0.00    0.41      26       0.00    build_romanji
  0.0   0.00    0.41      26       0.00    display_kana
```

For each function, **prof** prints the total time spent in the function (Time), the number of times the function was called (#Calls), and the average milliseconds per call (msec/call).

The two main situations **prof** helps with are functions that take a large amount of time with each call and may be called only a few times, such as SwitchWidgets in the example, and functions that may take only a short period of time to execute but get called many, many times, such as memcpy, also in the example.

NOTE The _mcount function looks odd. You'll almost never call this function in your code. (It was not in the code example I used.) Instead, _mcount is the main function used by **prof** to keep track of how many times each function is called and how long it takes. Thus, in the example, the most expensive operation timewise was to profile the program. Ignore any references to _mcount when looking for bottlenecks in your code.

From the looks of things, this program allocates a lot of memory, as shown by the large amounts of time used by the `malloc` and `free` routines. In addition, this program uses a lot of text strings, as shown by the results for the `memcpy`, `_strcmp`, `_memcmp`, `memmove`, `_strlen`, `_strncmp` and `strncpy` functions.

`malloc` and other memory allocation functions, such as `new` and `realloc`, tend to be expensive operating system calls. If possible, try to collect memory requirements and call `malloc` to allocate a larger block of memory in one call. This is more efficient than calling `malloc` multiple times for small blocks of memory.

N O T E   The C++ `new` operator makes this harder, unless you override `new` with your own function.

For text strings, if you can avoid copying strings from one array to another, you'll save time. In addition, many text-handling programs repeatedly test the length of the string with `strlen` and then operate on the string. C stores text strings in an array of bytes, with a NULL byte terminating the string.

The `strlen` function then iterates over every character in the array, returning the index of the first NULL character found. In many cases, your text processing code will check the length of a string and then go through the string byte by byte. Thus, the code has gone through each element in the array twice. You can often avoid this by simply checking for the NULL byte, terminating the string as you go through the string. This avoids two iterations over every character in the array. For large text strings, this can save a lot of time.

Finally, some architectures have optimized instructions for moving blocks of memory, notably the Intel architecture used for most personal computers and quite a few UNIX systems. On these systems, it is more efficient to call `memcpy` and `strcpy` than to copy each byte yourself, presuming the compiler vendor's standard C library takes advantage of these special machine instructions.

Performance Monitoring with gprof

The **gprof** utility works very much like **prof**. Like with **prof**, you need to recompile your program, but this time using the `-pg` command-line parameter.

Sun Solaris systems use a -xpg command-line parameter rather than -pg.

CROSS-PLATFORM

On Hewlett-Packard systems, you compile with -G instead of -pg. You also need to link with the -ldld command-line parameter because **grof** profiling requires dynamic loading.

CROSS-PLATFORM

Like **prof**, when you run your program, the mcount routine will output a data file, named **gmon.out** for **gprof** (instead of the **mon.out** used by **prof**). Then, after running the tests on your program, you can use the **gprof** utility to format the data in the **gmon.out** file.

When you run **gprof** on the output data, you'll see results like the following:

```
$ gprof xmkana | more

%time cumsecs seconds    calls  msec/call name
 22.5    0.09    0.09                      _mcount
 20.0    0.17    0.08    1865      0.04 _write_sys
 12.5    0.22    0.05   39475      0.00 _memcpy
  7.5    0.25    0.03    8099      0.00 malloc
  5.0    0.27    0.02    8806      0.00 tree_insert
  5.0    0.29    0.02    8680      0.00 tree_cut
  2.5    0.30    0.01   24583      0.00 strcmp
  2.5    0.31    0.01   23403      0.00 _memmove
  2.5    0.32    0.01    6648      0.00 _strncmp
  2.5    0.33    0.01    2480      0.00 ioctl
  2.5    0.34    0.01    1865      0.01 _write
  2.5    0.35    0.01    1736      0.01 _abs
  0.0    0.40    0.00    1620      0.00 CreateKanaXmString
  0.0    0.40    0.00      40      0.00 sbrk
  0.0    0.40    0.00      39      0.00 strcat
  0.0    0.40    0.00      38      0.00 isupper
  0.0    0.40    0.00      37      0.00 find_in_kana_array
  0.0    0.40    0.00      34      0.00 SetLabel
  0.0    0.40    0.00      34      0.00 switchWidgetsCB
```

N O T E The results between **gprof** and **prof** are indeed different. The main reason is that with a GUI-based application, it's hard to exactly reproduce the same test each time. Don't depend on the exact results. What you're looking for are trends. You want to find out which routines take up the most time, so you can direct your efforts for optimization.

gprof first outputs a chart like that used by **prof**. Then **gprof** tries to find cycles in the graph of how functions were called. This data gets shown in the call graph profile chart, which comes after the first chart, as shown here in abbreviated format:

```
           0.00      0.00     14/14          MakeWidgets [59]
[58]   0.0  0.00      0.00     14           CreateKanaXmString [58]
           0.00      0.00     14/65           _strncat [473]


           0.00      0.00      7/14          SwitchWidgets [123]
           0.00      0.00      7/14          print_multibyte [44]
[59]   0.0  0.00      0.00     14          MakeWidgets [59]
           0.00      0.00     37/51           clearCB [47]
           0.00      0.00     37/37           strchr [53]
           0.00      0.00     14/14           CreateKanaXmString [58]
           0.00      0.00     14/65           _strncat [473]
           0.00      0.00     14/34           delete_mora [54]


                             6964            _strncat [473]
           0.00      0.00      7/65           deleteCB [60]
           0.00      0.00      7/65           SwitchWidgets [123]
           0.00      0.00      9/65           scanf [26]
           0.00      0.00     14/65           clearCB [47]
           0.00      0.00     14/65           CreateKanaXmString [58]
           0.00      0.00     14/65           MakeWidgets [59]
[473]  0.0  0.00      0.00     65+6964     _strncat [473]
                             6964             _strncat [473]
```

Note how the routine CreateKanaXmString gets called in separate cycles in the call graph.

After the graph profile chart, **gprof** prints an index, which looks like the following:

58	CreateKanaXmString		625	_getpid
	1	_res_setvalue		
59	MakeWidgets		37	_getrlimit
	482	_sbrk		
123	SwitchWidgets		57	getuidfromyellow
	26	scanf		
133	append_multibyte		50	getwc_unlocked
	67	search		
475	_atexit		646	_kill
	20	_select		
12	build_romanji		21	__lc_load
	477	_select_sys		

gprof provides more data than **prof**, but both are effective at tracking down what parts of your programs are the worst bottlenecks for performance.

Summary

Because of the potentially massive amounts of programmer time needed to speed up applications, the most effective approach is to analyze the performance of your applications looking for the areas that have the most effect on performance and speeding up those areas. Two UNIX tools to help with this are **prof** and **gprof**.

These tools act similarly. First, you compile your code with a special command-line option (-p and -pg, respectively) that tells the compiler to insert code to count the number of times each function gets called and to keep track of the total time spent in the function.

Then run your program. It's best to follow a predefined script so you can reproduce the tests. After the program quits, the data on each function gets printed.

Depending on the system you use, the **prof** or **gprof** command will display the performance data from the run of your program.

UNIX Commands Introduced in this Chapter

gprof

prof

SECTION 3

Documenting Your Work

In addition to building and maintaining your programs, you need to document your work, for both yourself (for use later) and others. This short section covers UNIX tools for the documentation process.

Every UNIX command comes with an online manual entry; the same goes for all the functions in the C library and all operating system calls. Users expect these online manual entries, so you need to provide the same for the functions and applications *you* deliver. Chapter 12 covers the **man** command, where manual files are stored, and delves into how to create your own online manual entries using **nroff** formatting commands, as all manual pages do.

In addition to online manuals, the World Wide Web proves an effective means for distributing documentation, especially to users at locations other than your own. Chapter 13 covers a variety of tools to help create HTML Web documents from your program code, including C, C++, Java, and Perl programs.

## CHAPTER 12

Creating Online Manual Pages

This chapter covers:

- How UNIX manuals work
- Where manual files reside
- Viewing online manuals
- Conventions followed in manual files
- Creating manual files
- Installing and testing manual files

UNIX Online Manuals

The best and worst of UNIX lies in the online manuals. UNIX comes with a huge set of reference information, and all of it is online. That's also the main problem: the only documentation you get is what's online.

UNIX documentation is justly famous for its terseness. The manuals do describe the available commands, but there's little to guide you in selecting which command to use. For programmers, the situation is worse. UNIX supports a huge number of functions, such as `fopen`, `select`, and `bind`, each with its own manual entry. But you'll find very little information online to help you determine which functions to call or how to put functions together to get your job done.

Each UNIX command comes with its own online manual entry, often called a *manual page* (the original manuals fit each entry on a page, though only a few UNIX command entries fit on a page now).

The online manuals are terse and provide no real clues as to how to fit things together.

For all that, though, you should still create online manual files for all new commands and functions you create. This is simply expected in the UNIX community. Standards do have merit, even old standards.

That's why it's important to know how the UNIX online manual system works. This chapter discusses the UNIX **man** command, how **man** works, and how to create your own online manual files.

Historically, the UNIX online manuals have been divided into sections, with each section devoted to a single topic of UNIX usage or programming. Table 12.1 lists the major online manual sections.

Table 12.1 Major Sections in the UNIX Manuals

Section	Usage
1	User commands
2	System calls (functions)
3	Subroutines
4	Devices
5	File formats
6	Games
7	Miscellaneous
8	System administration
n	New (usually commands in **/usr/local**)

NOTE   Many UNIX variants place system administration commands in section 1M, such as Hewlett-Packard's HP-UX. Some UNIX systems place new commands in section l (*ell*, not one), short for local. Some systems divide section 3 on subroutines into subsections such as 3b, 3s, and 3v. Looking in **/usr/man** will generally show you your system's layout.

The most important sections for programmers include section 1 on UNIX commands, sections 2 and 3 on functions callable from your C and C++ programs, and the new section—the place where most of your new programs should get documented. Descriptions for new functions you create should go into section 3.

When referencing other online manual entries, you'll note that most references take the form of `cc(1)` or `fopen(3)`. The number in parenthesis refers to the section of the online manuals.

N O T E The section number is very important if there are more than one entry with the same name in different sections. For example, open(2) refers to a system function that opens a file. open(n) refers to the Tcl command open (for those who have installed Tcl/Tk.)

The new section usually includes software you added to the system rather than software that comes with UNIX. For example, if you install Tcl/Tk, the manuals for the Tcl commands usually go in section n.

If you create a suite of related applications, such as **ci**, **co**, **rcs**, **rcsdiff**, and **rlog** (described in Chapter 9), you may want to provide an introduction manual entry. The **rcsintro** entry, for example, provides a good introduction to the RCS Revision Control System. Many UNIX systems, such as Linux, provide brief introductions to each section in the form of an entry named **intro**.

Where the Online Manuals Appear on Disk

Most of the UNIX online manuals reside in subdirectories under **/usr/man**. Each online manual entry appears in the subdirectory for the major section in which it resides. For example, the entry for the open function appears in section 2, as listed in Table 12.1, and so it goes into the section 2 subdirectory, **man2**.

Each section has a subdirectory starting with *man* and ending with the section number (or *n* for the new section). You should see the following directories under **/usr/man**:

```
man1/
man2/
man3/
man4/
man5/
man6/
man7/
man8/
man9/
mann/
```

Inside each section's subdirectory, each manual entry has a file. The file name is the name of the entry, such as **open**, with an extension of the section number, such as **.2**, making a file name of **open.2**.

To save disk space, online manual files are often compressed, so you'll see names like **open.2.Z** or **open.2.gz**.

You may also see a number of subdirectories under **/usr/man** with names such as **cat1**, **cat2**, with a **cat** subdirectory for each manual section. These directories hold preformatted online manual files.

The online manuals are formatted documents that use **nroff** formatting commands. The **man** program formats a manual file when you ask for the entry corresponding to the file. Because this formatting takes time, many systems cache the results in these **cat** subdirectories.

Some systems don't ship **nroff** so the **man** program cannot format any online manual entries. This is because **nroff** is often part of a package called the Documenter's Workbench, an add-on package that costs extra for many commercial versions of UNIX. These systems tend to ship only the preformatted manual files.

In addition to **/usr/man**, you'll often find online manual files in **/usr/openwin/man**, for Open Windows online manuals (popular on Sun and Linux systems), and **/usr/local/man**, for commands you've added to your system that were not part of the UNIX distribution.

The MANPATH Environment Variable

The **man** command uses the MANPATH environment variable to list the directories it should search for a given online manual entry. Each directory in the MANPATH is separated by a colon. For example, the default MANPATH for many systems follows:

```
MANPATH=/usr/local/man:/usr/man:/usr/openwin/man
```

270

Add-on packages, such as Perl, often extend the MANPATH to add new directories.

You can add a directory to the MANPATH by merely extending the environment variable. Usually the MANPATH is set in your **.login** or **.profile** file in your home directory. (The C shell uses **.login**; the Korn and Bash shells use **.profile**.) The easiest way to extend the MANPATH is to add another directory to the MANPATH setting in **.login** or **.profile**. Remember to put in the colon to separate the directories, as shown here from a **.login** file (for C shell users):

```
setenv MANPATH /usr/local/man:/usr/man:/usr/openwin/man:/usr/lib/perl5/man
```

Viewing Online Manuals

The main program for viewing online manuals is the **man** command. You can view any of the online manual files in any of the directories in your MANPATH from the **man** command.

To view a manual entry for a C function such as fopen, you can use the following command:

```
$ man fopen
```

You'll see a manual entry a page at a time. The **more** program is the default pager. The PAGER environment variable often determines which pager to use. Some really yucky systems hard-code the pager to the **pg** command, which is sort of a brain-dead **more** command.

If your manual entry appears in more than one section, the wrong manual may be displayed. For example, if you need to mount a hard disk onto your system and you don't remember the exact syntax, you'll usually issue the following command:

```
$ man mount
```

On most UNIX systems, you'll be surprised, as the mount C function from section 2 is listed. To get the **mount** command, you need to reference section 8 (system administration):

```
$ man 8 mount
```

On Hewlett-Packard systems, you need to specify section *1m* instead of *8*. You can call up any manual entry using its section number first.

NOTE Some versions of the **man** command require a different syntax for listing the desired section. If the preceding command fails, try **man man** to verify what command-line parameter your system's version of **man** requires.

In addition to the ubiquitous **man**, there's **xman**, an X Window graphical interface to online manuals. The best part of **xman** is that is displays a list of the available manual entries in each section. This is very handy if you don't know the actual command. You can get **xman** to show both the listing of available entries and an entry by selecting **Show Both Screens** from the Options menu, as shown in Figure 12.1.

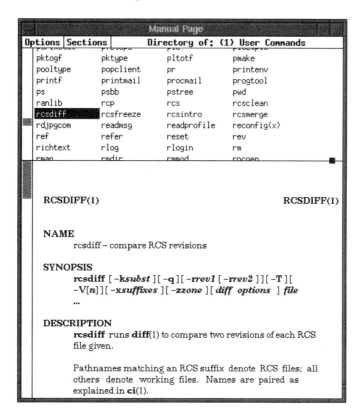

Figure 12.1 xman showing both a listing and a manual entry.

272

Another manual entry viewing program is called **olxvman**. Written with the XView toolkit using the Open Look interface, **olxvman** presents two windows: one listing all the sections and entries, the other showing a single manual entry, as shown in Figure 12.2.

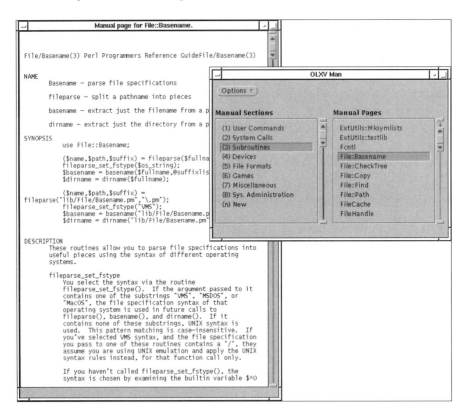

Figure 12.2 Viewing online manuals with **olxvman**.

You can also search for entries with **olxvman**.

olxvman resides in the **man** directory on the CD-ROM. It requires the XView library to compile and link. XView is most common on Sun and Linux systems.

CD-ROM

You should now have a good idea where manual entry files reside and how to view the manuals. The next step is to create online manuals for all your programs and functions.

Creating Your Own Manuals

As you can tell from viewing the online manuals, each manual entry follows a fairly rigid format. Because this is what users expect, it's good to follow this same format. To start, you need to provide the expected sections within a manual entry, in the expected order. Table 12.2 lists these sections, in order, for manual entries on commands.

Table 12.2 Sections within Each Manual Entry for a Command

Section	Usage
NAME	Name of program with one-line description.
SYNOPSIS	List all command-line parameters.
DESCRIPTION	Describe program.
OPTIONS	Go over each command-line parameter in depth.
EXAMPLE	It's always good to provide an example.
ENVIRONMENT	Describe any environment variables that affect the program.
SEE ALSO	List other manual pages related to the same subject.
BUGS	List any known bugs.
AUTHOR	Your name in lights.

You can omit any section that isn't appropriate. Even so, every manual entry must have the NAME, SYNOPSIS, and DESCRIPTION sections.

When you document functions, there are a few more sections to include in your entries. Table 12.3 lists these sections.

Table 12.3 Sections within Each Manual Entry for a Function

Section	Usage
NAME	Name of function with one-line description.
SYNOPSIS	List all parameters to function.
DESCRIPTION	Describe function and use of parameters.
RETURN VALUES	List the values returned by the function.
ERRORS	What happens on errors.
EXAMPLE	It's always good to provide an example.
ENVIRONMENT	Describe any environment variables that effect the function; very rare.
SEE ALSO	List other manual pages related to the same subject.
BUGS	List any known bugs.
STANDARDS	List standards the function conforms to, for example, IEEE Std1003.1-1988 (POSIX).
AUTHOR	Your name in lights.

To create the online manual entries, you need to edit text files and learn the **nroff** and **troff** formatting commands.

Document Formatting with nroff and troff

Online manual files get formatted with the **nroff/troff** system, an ancient text-formatting system (and ironically, part of the reason UNIX got early funding at Bell Labs). **nroff** typically formats documents for the screen, while **troff** uses drivers for different output systems, including PostScript and other typesetting systems.

The original idea behind **nroff** and **troff** is that the source code for the document can be run through a formatting program such as **nroff** or **troff** and properly formatted for any of a number of output devices, from dumb ASCII terminals to fancy typesetting systems. In all cases, the document source remains the same. You just use different commands and command-line options to format the document from the **nroff/troff** source.

Manual Files

Each manual entry resides in its own file. All the manual files are ASCII text files with **nroff/troff** formatting commands. These commands, commonly called *dot commands*, because most begin with a period (.) in the first column of the line, permeate the manual file. For example, to specify the title of the document, you use the .TH command:

```
.TH WUNDERWORD 1 "17 Oct, 1996"  "Eric's Software"
```

The title will appear as WUNDERWORD(1) and each new page will get Eric's Software, 17 Oct, 1996 and the page number. All this comes from the .TH command, one of many **man** macros used by **nroff** and **troff**.

The man Macros for nroff

nroff and **troff** support a set of dot commands. There are also several add-on packages of combined commands, called *macros*, aimed at a particular task. The **ms** macros help you write letters. The **man** macros help you write manual entries.

To format a document using the **man** macros, you can use the following command:

```
$ nroff -e -man filename | more -s
```

This is nearly the same as how the **man** command works for formatting the manual file. Usually, the **man** command is smarter and automatically detects compressed files and checks the **cat** directories to see if the document was already formatted.

Inside your manual files, you'll make extensive use of **nroff/troff** commands and the **man** macro commands. Table 12.4 lists the key **man** macros and **nroff** commands that you'll need to use when creating your manual files.

Table 12.4 Formatting Commands for Manual Files

Command	Usage
.B	Bold.
.br	Line break, needed between sections.
.I	Italic.
.LP	Use between paragraphs within a section.
.PP	Paragraph line break.
.RI	Roman (normal) then italic.
.SH *section*	Starts *section*.
.TH title	Title of manual entry; necessary at beginning.
.TP	Starts each command-line parameter in OPTIONS section.
\-	Em-dash, rather than just a hyphen.
.\"	Comment, ignored.

Some of these commands are quite complicated. Because of this, the best way to create an online manual file is to copy an existing one and edit the file, filling in the description of your program or function. I also make extensive use of trial and error, using the **nroff** command to test each step in creating a manual file.

Creating a Manual Entry

To show how to create an online manual file, I'll lead you through a manual entry for a fictional word processor, WunderWord, the most wonderful program in existence. The UNIX command to call up WunderWord is **wunderword**. Because this is a command, it would logically go in section 1. Thus, our file name should be **wunderword.1**.

The full manual file follows:

```
.\" This is a comment.
.TH WUNDERWORD 1 "17 Oct, 1996"  "Eric's Software"
.SH NAME
wunderword \- The most wonderful thing in the universe
.SH SYNOPSIS
.B wunderword
.RI [ filename ]
.PP
.B wunderword
.RI -c " filename "
.br
.SH DESCRIPTION
.I wunderword
is the most wonderful word processor ever
invented. Copious online help is available
from the Help menu.
.br

.SH OPTIONS
.TP
.B filename
If you pass a file name on the command line,
.IR wunderword
will load up that file.

.TP The
.B \-c filename
command-line parameter tells
.IR wunderword
to convert
the file, from any other word processor format.
.br
.SH BUGS
Are you kidding?
.br
.SH AUTHOR
Eric Foster-Johnson <erc@bigfun.com>
```

Don't expect to understand all the formatting commands yet. I'll explain each section soon.

If you type in the preceding file and save it under the name **wunder-word.1**, you can see the formatting with the following command:

```
$ nroff -e -man wunderword.1 | more -s
WUNDERWORD(1)                                    WUNDERWORD(1)


NAME
       wunderword - The most wonderful thing in the universe

SYNOPSIS
       wunderword [filename]


       wunderword -c filename


DESCRIPTION
       wunderword  is  the  most  wonderful  word  processor ever
       invented. Copious online help is available from  the  Help
       menu.


OPTIONS
       filename
              If  you  pass a file name on the command line, wun-
              derword will load up that file.


       -c filename
              command-line parameter tells wunderword to  convert
              the file, from any other word processor format.

BUGS
       Are you kidding?


AUTHOR
       Eric Foster-Johnson <erc@bigfun.com>


Eric's Software           17 Oct, 1996                          1
```

Starting at the beginning, the first line of the file has a comment. .\" tells **nroff** to ignore the text following:

```
.\" This is a comment.
```

The mandatory title comes next:

```
.TH WUNDERWORD 1 "17 Oct, 1996"  "Eric's Software"
```

You must have a title, as well as a name:

```
.SH NAME
wunderword \- The most wonderful thing in the universe
```

The name must follow this format, as many tools that track online manual files and search for the summary information expect this format.

NOTE
Sometimes you can double up on manual entries. For example, the strcpy manual entry usually also describes strncpy and sometimes the entire set of string functions in the standard C library. You can type in **man strcpy** or **man strncpy** and get the same page.

To tell the **man** command that your file pertains to more than one command or function, you can follow this example:

```
.SH NAME
strcpy, strncpy \- copy a string
.SH SYNOPSIS
```

The synopsis section lists each command-line parameter, without any explanation:

```
.SH SYNOPSIS
.B wunderword
.RI [ filename ]
.PP
.B wunderword
.RI -c " filename "
.br
```

There are only two command-line parameters listed here:

```
wunderword [filename]
wunderword -c filename
```

The .PP separates the lines.

The .B makes the entry bold. The .RI ensures that *filename* is printed in italics or underlined on ASCII terminals. The section ends with a line break command, .br.

N O T E   You can often skip commands like .br at the end of each section. But some versions of the **man** command require the older formatting commands, so it's best to follow a working entry, even if it means more commands.

The description should be easy to follow. Only the word *wunderword* gets formatted, in italics:

```
.SH DESCRIPTION
.I wunderword
is the most wonderful word processor ever
invented. Copious online help is available
from the Help menu.
.br
```

The options are harder to put together. Each command-line parameter starts with a .TP command, which takes care of the hanging indent for the text of the option:

```
OPTIONS
       filename
              If  you  pass a file name on the command line, wun-
              derword will load up that file.

       -c filename
              command-line parameter tells wunderword to  convert
              the file, from any other word processor format.
```

The options section follows:

```
.SH OPTIONS
.TP
.B filename
If you pass a file name on the command line,
.IR wunderword
will load up that file.
.TP The
.B \-c filename
command-line parameter tells
.IR wunderword
to convert
the file, from any other word processor format.
.br
```

Note the em-dash, \- for the -c command-line parameter, as well as the italics for the word *wunderword*.

Finally, the bugs and author sections are trivial after the options:

```
.SH BUGS
Are you kidding?
.br
.SH AUTHOR
Eric Foster-Johnson <erc@bigfun.com>
```

You can copy this example and use it to create your own manual files.

Testing Your Manual Entry

Now that you have an online manual file, the next step is to test the formatting. You can use the following command for the **wunderword.1** file:

```
$ nroff -e -man wunderword.1 | more -s
```

If everything looks OK, its time to install the file in a location that the **man** command will look in.

Installing Your Manual Entry

You're now ready to install your manual file. New manual entries normally go into **/usr/local/man**. Of course, the user should be able to specify a different directory. For a command, you probably want section 1, meaning you should copy the file **wunderword.1** to **/usr/local/man/man1**:

```
$ cp wunderword.1 /usr/local/man/man1
```

 You may not have permission to write into **/usr/local**. You may need to become root user with the **su** command or talk to your system administrator. You can always extend your MANPATH environment variable if you cannot get your files into a location used by the **man** command.

N O T E

You should now be able to test your new online manual entry with the **man** command:

```
$ man wunderword
```

You should see an entry like the one shown earlier.

That's all you really need to know about creating online manual pages. Appendix A lists books on **nroff** and **troff** where you'll find more than you want to know about these ancient formatting systems.

Summary

All commands and functions you create should come with online manual files, formatted as expected by legions of UNIX users.

These manual files are ASCII text files that contain special formatting commands used by the **nroff** and **troff** document-formatting programs. You don't have to know a lot about **nroff** or **troff** to create a manual page. Simply copy an existing page and edit.

The next chapter will show how to create documentation for the new world of the mighty Web. In addition to covering how you can create HTML files automatically from C, C++, or Java source code, the section on the Perl Plain Old Documentation format shows another method for creating online manual pages with the option of HTML output.

UNIX Commands Introduced in This Chapter

man

nroff

olxvman

xman

283

## CHAPTER 13

Delivering Documentation on the Web

This chapter covers:

- Extracting documentation from C++ header files and creating HTML files
- Extracting documentation from C source code
- Converting Java programs into HTML files
- Documenting Perl programs

The World Wide Web

The World Wide Web has proven itself to be the premier method for document distribution. Whether you work entirely on a company network or access the wide-ranging Internet, the World Wide Web and the HyperText Markup Language, or HTML, provide a handy way to get documents into the hands of your audience. Whether your audience uses PCs, Macintosh, or UNIX systems, the Web works for all.

There are many limitations to the HTML format and the World Wide Web, but it provides a great way to distribute programming documentation.

This chapter covers a number of tools that create HTML documents out of your source code, sometimes automatically but usually with a bit of work on your part. That effort is well spent, as you get document distribution, cross-reference links, and formatting all at once.

Converting C and C++ Code to Web Documents

Because the World Wide Web protocols are available from just about every UNIX system and free HTML viewers abound, there are many tools to convert C and C++ code into HTML documents.

The theory behind many of these tools is that any document you write has the chance to become obsolete as you continue to maintain your code. Over time, the code changes but the documentation isn't always updated. (We all know we should update the documentation, but sometimes things fall through the cracks.)

To get around this problem, a number of tools try to extract documentation from the actual code. The code must always be right, because that's what was compiled into the application. The comments in the code may get out of sync with the actual code, but they are less likely to than external documents, because when you change the code, you'll see the comments right there.

Anyway, the theory points to trying to automate as much documentation as possible, with the documents coming from the actual source code, in an attempt to make the documentation stay as close to reality as possible.

One of the best tools in this regard is called Cocoon; it spins a web of documentation from C++ class header files.

Using Cocoon to Create HTML Files from C++ Class Headers

Cocoon is a program that tries to create documentation from C++ header files using special formatting commands you place in the header files. Cocoon outputs a linked set of HTML files, one for each class and one for each library.

By linking the files together, Cocoon creates a set of cross-referenced documentation for libraries of C++ code. Cocoon links classes together in a way that makes browsing the code easier.

Developed by Jeff Kotula, Cocoon is based on two main concepts. First, Cocoon tries to extract as much information as possible from the actual C++ code. Cocoon knows about C++ classes and some other limited aspects of C++ syntax. Second, Cocoon assumes that you fill in your C++ header files with special comments that describe how to use your C++ classes. The theory behind Cocoon is that you'll deliver header files and object modules to other software developers. The header files should contain enough information to help the other developers use your code. Cocoon helps by formatting the documentation and linking the sections.

Some of the best features of Cocoon include:

- Each C++ class gets a complete list of all public and protected member functions, even functions inherited from parent classes. Thus, each class gets defined with its full API.

- Each class lists its ancestors, which provides access via a single click to any parent class.

- Each class lists its descendants, which shows which classes are derived from the current class.

- Each class contains a link to the source code of the actual header file used to generate the Web page. You can always check the real source code.

288

Working with Cocoon

To work with Cocoon, you need to add special comments to your C++ header files. These special comments must follow the syntax Cocoon expects. This involves a bit of work, because Cocoon requires special comments to tell it when the documentation for one function stops and the next function starts. While it may take some time to enter the special sentinel comment before each function, Figure 13.1 shows the result of all this work, a linked set of Web pages automatically created from your C++ header files.

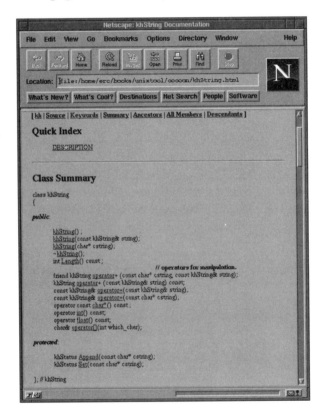

Figure 13.1 A Web page output by Cocoon.

To start with Cocoon, you need to place a special comment block before each class definition. This comment block requires, at a minimum, the word *CLASS* and the name of the class:

```
/*
CLASS
    classname
*/
```

You can also add an optional one-line description:

```
/*
CLASS
    khLabel

    Static text label widget
*/
```

NOTE The word *CLASS* must be all uppercase. It must also appear in the first column of the line. Cocoon requires a number of items to appear in the first column of the line.

NOTE If you have forward declarations for classes, indent them, so that Cocoon isn't fooled into thinking a class definition is beginning. For example, you can indent like this:

```
// Forward declaration
        class    khCompositeWidget;
```

Your class definitions must then follow this format:

```
class  classname
{

public:

protected:
```

```
private:


};
```

You can have as many `public`, `protected`, and `private` sections as you desire. Each must appear in the first column of the line.

Each member function must have the sentinel comment, at least ten slashes, i.e., `//////////`, *before* the function is defined. All comments for the member function should appear after the sentinel comment and before the function definition. For example:

```
class MyClass
{
public:
    ////////////////////////////
    // Constructor
    MyClass();

    /////////////////////
    // Destructor
    virtual ~MyClass();
};
```

You can also document function parameters with Cocoon. To do so, place extra comments after the `//////////` sentinel comment. Each parameter needs to be marked with how it will be used. For read-only parameters, use `[in]`. For parameters that get modified, use `[out]`. Then, after the `[in]` or `[out]`, place the parameter name and its description. For example:

```
class MyClass
{
public:
    ////////////////////////////
    // Constructor
    //
    //    [in] string - name of new object
    //    [out] i - number of elements
    //    [out] j - width of elements
```

```
    //
    MyClass(char* string, int& i, int& j);


};
```

Cocoon transforms these comments into HTML, as shown in Figure 13.2.

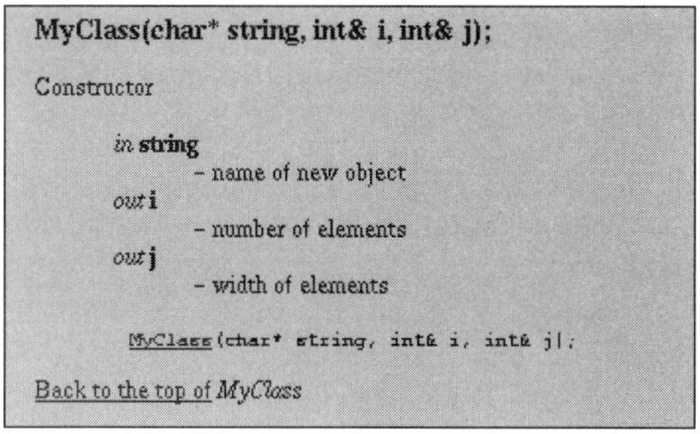

Figure 13.2 Function parameters in Cocoon.

You can group member functions with a comment that starts with //
GROUP:. For example:

```
// GROUP:    Data access members
```

Cocoon will group the functions in the HTML file.

Filling out the Class Header Block

As explained earlier, Cocoon requires that you precede each class definition
with a comment block like the following:

```
/*
CLASS
    classname
*/
```

You can extend this block with more sections, and Cocoon will enhance the
output for the HTML document. Each section in the comment block gets a
section in the output HTML file.

The KEYWORD section lists keywords Cocoon uses to create a cross-referenced list of keywords. Cocoon creates another HTML file with all the keywords linked to the classes referenced.

You can create other sections in the class header block. Cocoon takes any section that begins in the first column and contains all uppercase characters. For example, Cocoon will expand the following sections into the HTML file:

```
/*
CLASS
    classname

    brief description of class.

KEYWORD
    widget, UI, GUI, text

DESCRIPTION
    A longer description of the class and its use.

HOW TO USE
    Information on using the class in your code.

HOW TO SUBCLASS
    Information on how to create your own derived classes.

*/
```

Cocoon converts each of these sections, with all comments underneath, into sections in the output HTML file. Figure 13.3 shows the expanded class header sections as created by Cocoon.

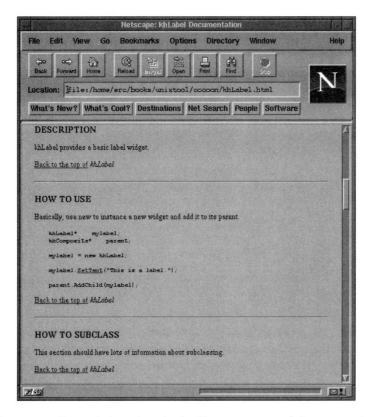

Figure 13.3 Expanded sections in the Cocoon-generated documentation.

The HOW TO sections often contain code examples. To ensure that these sections get bracketed with the proper <pre> and </pre> HTML tags, you can use the EXAMPLE and END directives, which must be indented:

```
/*
CLASS
    classname

    brief description of class.
```

```
KEYWORD
    widget, UI, GUI, text

HOW TO USE
    Information on using the class in your code.

    EXAMPLE
        MyClass    obj("name", 10, 100);


        obj.do_everything(DO_IT_NOW);


    END


*/
```

All the code between the EXAMPLE and END directives will appear in a fixed-width font in the HTML file.

To pull this all together, the following code shows a C++ header file with Cocoon-specific comments:

```
/*
Koohii toolkit main header file.
For most application usage, you can just include this file.
Eric Foster-Johnson
*/


#ifndef kh_h_
#define kh_h_      1


    // Include base widget definition.
#include <kh/khwidget.h>
#include <kh/khstring.h>


/*
CLASS
    khLabel


    Label widget class
```

KEYWORDS

    widget, UI, GUI, text

DESCRIPTION

    khLabel provides a basic label widget.

HOW TO USE

    Basically, use new to instance a new
    widget and add it to its parent.

    EXAMPLE

    khLabel*   mylabel;
    khComposite*   parent;

    mylabel = new khLabel;

    mylabel.SetText("This is a label.");

    parent.AddChild(mylabel);
    END

HOW TO SUBCLASS

    This section should have lots of information about
    subclassing.

```
*/
class khLabel : public khWidget {
public:
        ///////////////////
        // Constructor.
    khLabel();

        ///////////////////
        // Destructor.
    virtual ~khLabel();

        ///////////////////////
        // Redraw widget.
```

```
        //
        // [in] clear - True to clear.
    virtual void     Redraw(khBool clear);

    // GROUP: Text functions.

        /////////////////////
        // Get text from widget.
    void GetText(khString& text)     { text  = _text; }

        //////////////////////
        // Store text in widget.
    void SetText(khString& text)     { _text = text; }

        ///////////////////////
        // Store text in widget.
    void SetText(const char* text)   { _text = text; }

private:
    khString     _text;

};   // khLabel

#endif  // ! kh_h_
// kh.h
```

Cocoon purposely skips all private data end member functions. The idea is to document what users can use from a class.

NOTE

Running Cocoon

Once you've added all the special comments to your C++ class headers, you can run the **cocoon** program to generate a Web page for each class. **cocoon** also creates a master page for the entire library and a keyword page, if you include the KEYWORD section in the header block before each class.

The basic command to launch **cocoon** follows:

```
$ cocoon -l libname
```

Replace *libname* with the name of your library. For example, to have **cocoon** examine all the **.h** files in the current directory and output HTML files for each class for a library named **kh**, you can use the following command:

```
$ cocoon -l kh
```

You'll see a lot of output, like the following:

```
cocoon Utilities, Version 2.5
Starting generation of document set.
Writing out customization data...
Done.
Generating basic and partial files...
     Library kh
         kh.h...
                   khLabel...
Done.
Generating lineage partial files...
         khLabel...
Done.
Cleaning up...

Done cleaning up...
COMPLETELY DONE!
```

N O T E By default, Cocoon places a reference to an image on each class HTML file. The image is listed as the following URL:
`http://www.cs.umn.edu/~kotula/cocoon/coclogo.gif`
You can change this with a customization file.

Customizing Cocoon

The way you customize Cocoon is by creating a customization file. You'll find you need to do this because Cocoon always tries to include its logo image from `http://www.cs.umn.edu/~kotula/cocoon/coclogo.gif`. If you're not connected to the Internet, you won't be able to acquire this image.

To get around this problem, you can create a Cocoon customization file. To specify a new image file, the syntax follows:

customize

  logo *image_file_name*

end_customize

Replace the *image_file_name* with the name of your image file, for example:

```
customize
    logo        ../images/green-ball.gif
end_customize
```

You can add these lines to a text file. The name doesn't matter; you need to pass the name to **cocoon** as a command-line parameter.

One large drawback to using a customization file, though, is that you can no longer use the -1 libraryname command-line parameter. Instead, you must add more data to the configuration file.

At a bare minimum, you need to add two more entries to the configuration file: the webroot and the library.

The webroot specifies the name of a directory to write all the output HTML files. (Some files get output to subdirectories.) This path must be a full path from the root; **cocoon** will overwrite files in the directory, so watch out.

For example, you can use the following as a guide:

```
webroot     /usr/local/doc/
```

The webroot specifies the top-level directory for the output files. The library directive specifies the name of the library to convert and where the source files are located. The syntax follows:

  library *name source_directory web_subdirectory*

This tends to get complicated. The *name* is the name of the library, **kh** in the examples. The *source_directory* is where the library header files are located—these files do *not* have to be in the current directory. The *web_subdirectory* tells **cocoon** where to put the output HTML and header files for the library. This is a subdirectory of the **webroot** directory.

The key concept here is that you can have more than one `library` directive. Thus, you can run **cocoon** on all the libraries you have. **cocoon** will cross-reference all the links.

This is different from the simple **cocoon -l** command, where all files are assumed to be in the current directory.

Once you create a customization file, you must tell **cocoon** about each library with the `library` directive.

For example, a valid `library` directive is:

```
library  kh /usr/local/src/kh cocoon
```

To pull this all together, the following configuration file tells **cocoon** that the source code is located in the **/usr/local/src/kh** directory. **cocoon** will expect to find header files in this directory. The top-level directory to write to is **/usr/local/doc**. The **kh** library HTML and header files will get written to the **/usr/local/doc/kh_docs** subdirectory.

All this is specified by the following configuration file:

```
webroot     /usr/local/doc/

library  kh /usr/local/src/kh kh_docs

customize
    logo        ../images/green-ball.gif
end_customize
```

Note how the **webroot** directory gets combined with the **library** Web subdirectory entry, **kh_docs**, to form **/usr/local/doc/kh_docs**. You can add more `library` directives if you want.

If you save the preceding file under the name **cocoon.opts**, you can execute **cocoon** with the following command-line parameter:

```
$ cocoon cocoon.opts
```

This will document the **kh** library and use a custom image at the top of each HTML document created. This is more difficult to set up than the simple –l library name mode, but you can get **cocoon** to do far more by generating documentation from multiple libraries of C++ code.

300

CD-ROM

Cocoon is not part of any UNIX distribution. It appears on the CD-ROM in the **doc_tool** directory.

When complete, you should have an HTML file for each class, as well as one for the library that references each class, and a list of keywords. The library HTML file should look like Figure 13.4.

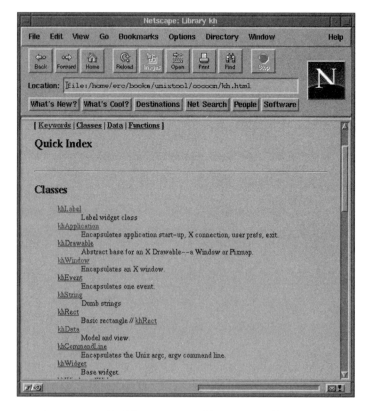

Figure 13.4 The library HTML file generated by **cocoon**.

More information on Cocoon is available on the Internet at the following URL:

```
http://www.cs.umn.edu/~kotula/cocoon/cocoon.htm
```

I've used Cocoon for a number of years and really appreciate how it can generate a lot of documentation with very little work.

Cross-Referencing C Code with cxref

While Cocoon generates documentation from header files, **cxref** cross-references C source code files and C headers.

For each C function, **cxref** generates a list of all functions called by the function and all other functions that call it. This is great for browsing code created by others, because **cxref** provides organization over a potentially large set of functions.

cxref appears in the **doc_tool** directory on the CD-ROM.

CD-ROM

cxref provides many options, including HTML or LaTeX output. The options appear in Table 13.1.

Table 13.1 cxref Command-Line Parameters

Parameter	Usage
-I*directory*	Look in *directory* for include files.
-all-comments	Include all comments in output file, rather than just **cxref**-formatted comments.
-xref-all	Generate all cross-references.
-xref-file	File cross-references.
-xref-func	Function cross-references.
-xref-var	Global variable cross-references.
-xref-type	Type cross-references.
-index-all	Produce all indices.
-index-file	Index of files.
-index-func	Index of functions.
-index-var	Index of global variables.
-index-type	Index of types.
-html	Produce HTML output.
-latex	Produce LaTeX output.

To generate cross-references for a set of **.c** files, you can use the following command as a guide:

```
$ cxref -html -xref-all *.c
```

This command tells **cxref** to output HTML files and cross-reference everything it can for all files ending in **.c** in the current directory. When you run this command, you'll see output like Figure 13.5.

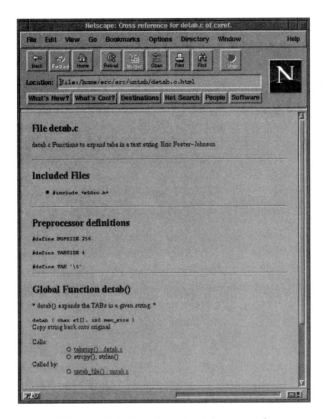

Figure 13.5 Sample output from **cxref**.

cxref creates a **.html** file for each **.c** file it examines. If you ask for an index, **cxref** also creates index files, most notably **cxref.apdx.html**.

NOTE On Linux, I needed to tell **cxref** about the GNU C include files, stored in **/usr/lib/gcc-lib/i486-linux/2.7.2/include**, so I used a **cxref** command like the following:

```
$ cxref -xref-all -html -I/usr/include filename.c \
        -I/usr/lib/gcc-lib/i486-linux/2.7.2/include
```

If you see an error about not finding a file such as **float.h**, chances are this is the problem.

With the `-index-all` command-line parameter, **cxref** creates indices for all files, functions, variables, and types, as shown in Figure 13.6.

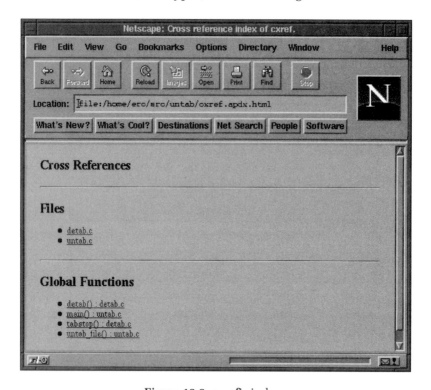

Figure 13.6 cxref's index.

To generate an index and to cross-reference all **.c** files in the current directory, you can use the following command:

```
$ cxref -html -index-all -xref-all *.c
```

cxref normally uses only the specially formatted comments you create. If instead you want a listing of all comments, you can use the `-all-comments` command-line parameter:

```
$ cxref -html -index-all -xref-all -all-comments *.c
```

Unfortunately, **cxref** just concatenates all the comments in one block together, usually resulting in poor output.

cxref Comments

Like Cocoon, **cxref** requires you to use a special format for the comments you want listed in the documentation. **cxref** recognizes two kinds of comments: file comments, which go at the top of the HTML document, and data comments, which go with the current statement in the C code. A file comment requires an extra asterisk with the standard C comment brackets, thus `/* */` becomes `/** **/`. You can use as many extra asterisks as you'd like, but only one extra is necessary. For example:

```
/**
  detab.c Functions to expand tabs in a text string.
  Eric Foster-Johnson
**/
```

Data comments apply to functions, type definitions, and global variables. These comments use a +, thus `/* */` becomes `/*+ +*/`. Any comment like this gets associated with the C statement before it.

These comment markers are generally easier to add than the ten characters required by Cocoon.

Working with emacs and cxref

cxref also provides a special **emacs** mode to ease the burden of entering these special comments. The **cxref.el** file contains this special mode. You can load this file into **emacs** with the **M-x load-file cxref.el** command.

 Remember that *M* stands for the **emacs** Meta key, usually the **Alt** or **Escape** key on your keyboard. *C* stands for the **Control** key.

N O T E

Once this mode is loaded, **C-c C-f** adds file comments at the top of the file. If the file is a header file, **C-c C-f** places a `#ifndef`, `#ifdef`, and `#endif` surrounding the whole file to prevent multiple inclusions. Because most C pro-

grammers use a scheme similar to this anyway, the **C-c C-f** command provides a handy head start. For example with a file named **foo.h**, **C-c C-f** enters
the following text:

```
/**************************************

   $Header$


   **************************************/

#ifndef FOO_H
#define FOO_H     /*+ To stop multiple inclusions. +*/


#endif /* FOO_H */
```

C-c f adds comments for a function. For this to work, you must have the cursor on the line containing the function name. This comment includes the
names of the function parameters. For example:

```
/*+++++++++++++++++++++++++++++++++++++++

   tabstop

   column

   max_size
   +++++++++++++++++++++++++++++++++++++++*/

tabstop( column, max_size )
int     column, max_size;
```

C-c v adds a comment before the current line. For example, if the cursor is
on a line with an int statement, you'll see the following output:

```
/*+  +*/
   int     i;
```

C-c e adds a trailing comment to the end of the current line. For example:

```
   int     i;          /*+  +*/
```

Finally, **C-c i** adds a normal comment that will be ignored by **cxref**. All this makes working with **cxref** much easier for **emacs** users.

Other C++ Tools

Like Cocoon, **cxx2html** extracts documentation from C++ header files and output HTML files. **C++2html** converts C++ files into HTML documents. Both tools are in the **doc_tool** directory on the CD-ROM.

Documenting Java Programs

You can automatically generate HTML files from Java programs.

The **javadoc** program, which comes with the Java Development Kit from Sun Microsystems, knows enough about the Java syntax to extract a lot of useful documentation without any work on your part. Without any work, **javadoc** parses all classes in all *the* **.java** files you pass to it. If you are willing to do a bit of work, you can add **javadoc**-specific comments, much like the comments required by Cocoon or **cxref**.

A **javadoc** comment starts with /**, which is fairly easy to add to your sources. Because /* starts a comment, /** requires just one extra character. Any text inside a **javadoc** comment gets included in the output HTML file.

You can add HTML tags in the special **javadoc** comments, and these tags will become part of the output HTML file.

NOTE

Don't use HTML headline tags such as <H1> or horizontal rules, <HR>, in your Java comments. These interfere with the way **javadoc** formats HTML files.

In addition to supporting embedded HTML, **javadoc** supplies a number of shortcuts to help you add links and formatting without a lot of extra typing. You need to add these shortcuts inside the special **javadoc** comments.

All these **javadoc** shortcut tags start with an at sign, @. In addition, all tags must start at the beginning of a line inside the comment.

In the comments before the class definition starts, you can include the tags listed in Table 13.2.

Table 13.2 javadoc Class Tags

Tag	Usage
@author	Adds an Author entry.
@see class	Adds a See Also link to class.
@see class#method	Adds a See Also link to the method in the class.
@version text	Adds a Version entry.

There can be more than one @author or @see tag, but you must combine all the @author tags together and all the @see tags together.

N O T E The version and author tags won't work unless you pass the -version and -author command-line parameters to **javadoc**. For example:

```
$ javadoc -author -version UNIXProgTools.java
```

Before each method definition, you can describe the member function parameters and return data with more tags, as listed in Table 13.3.

Table 13.3 javadoc Tags for Method Parameters

Tag	Usage
@exception class description	Method throws an exception.
@param param description	Describes a method parameter.
@return description	Describes the return value.
@see class	Adds a See Also link to the class.
@see class#method	Adds a See Also link to the method in the class.

Putting this all together, the following Java file uses most of the tags listed in Tables 13.2 and 13.3:

```
//
// A simple first Java programming example.
//

/**
This is a javadoc comment.

You can add <b>HTML</b> tags inside a
javadoc comment.

Note: version and author tags only appear
with the -version and -author command-line
parameters, respectively.

@version This is my version.
@author Eric Foster-Johnson
@see        awt.Button

*/

public class UNIXProgTools
{
/**
* @param args    Command-line parameters to program.
* @return    Nothing
*/
    public static void main(String[] args)
    {
        System.out.println( "Java application example." );
    }
}
```

To generate HTML documentation for this program, you can use the following command:

```
$ javadoc UNIXProgTools.java
Generating packages.html
generating documentation for class UNIXProgTools
```

```
Generating index
Sorting 2 items . . . done
Generating tree
```

This command creates the following HTML files:

```
AllNames.html
UNIXProgTools.html
packages.html
tree.html
```

The main file is **UNIXProgTools.html,** the documentation for this small Java class. This documentation appears in Figure 13.7.

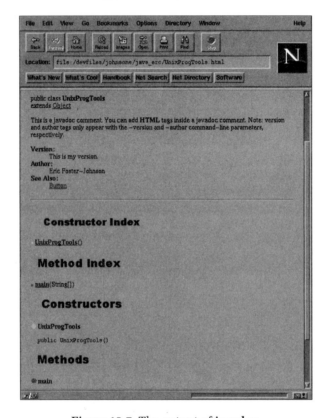

Figure 13.7 The output of **javadoc.**

Images for javadoc Pages

To make effective use of **javadoc**, you'll need the following GIF images, all of which should be stored in a subdirectory named **images**:

```
images/constructors.gif
images/constructor-index.gif
images/methods.gif
images/method-index.gif
images/yellow-ball.gif
images/yellow-ball-small.gif
images/green-ball.gif
images/green-ball-small.gif
```

The HTML files created by **javadoc** reference these images, so you need to have files with these names.

CD-ROM

I've made my own GIF images for the items, which you can find on the CD-ROM in the **java/images** directory.

javadoc is the main documentation tool for Java programs. Sun provides **javadoc**-generated documentation for all the Java classes it provides with the Java Development Kit.

Documenting Perl Scripts

Perl ships with a documentation format that allows you to embed documentation within your Perl scripts. This is not only useful for Perl; you'll find other uses for this handy format.

The Perl documentation comes in a format called *POD*, short for Plain Old Documentation. Developed in the days before the World Wide Web, the POD format is relatively simple, but it becomes powerful when you start using the utility programs that convert documents in the POD format into text, HTML, manual pages, and LaTeX formats.

POD documents, like manual files, are formatted ASCII text. Closer to the GNU info or HTML formats, POD doesn't allow for much formatting—just simple things like italic and bold. You can add lists of elements and section headings, but not much else.

Once you've written an ASCII text file using the POD format, you use a special utility to convert the POD document into another format, such as HTML, plain text, or online manual entry.

The conversion utilities, all Perl scripts, are listed in Table 13.4.

Table 13.4 POD Utility Scripts

Script	Use
pod2html	Convert to HTML Web format.
pod2latex	Convert to LaTeX.
pod2man	Convert to UNIX manual entry format.
pod2text	Convert to ASCII text.

Because these are all Perl scripts, you must install Perl first. See Chapter 2 for more on Perl.

Creating POD Documents

The central idea behind the POD format is that you can use simple formatting commands within the document, and the utility scripts will convert the document into a number of formats. You only have to create the document once; the utilities do the work of converting to other formats. This proves useful when you can create one file and have the POD utilities output different formats.

Perl scripters, for example, usually deliver the documentation—in POD format—within their Perl scripts. One file is all you need to deliver and install. The POD utilities extract the documentation for you.

If you can accept the limitations in the POD format, this will work for you. You can use POD for any purpose. The Perl interpreter provides special support for POD commands, but you don't have to write code in Perl to use the POD format.

The POD format treats a document as being made up of paragraphs—a somewhat looser definition than English paragraphs. Each POD *paragraph* is identified by a type, one of verbatim paragraphs, section commands, and formatted text.

313

Any indented paragraph is considered a *verbatim paragraph* and the POD utilities promise to leave such paragraphs alone. No formatting gets applied to these paragraphs—so long as you indent them with one or more spaces or tabs. This type of paragraph is similar to the <pre> tag in HTML and is useful for short source code examples. Like the <pre> tag in HTML, the POD utilities will attempt to display verbatim paragraphs in a fixed-width font.

The second type of POD paragraph, section commands, identify major sections in the document, allow for formatted lists, and identify special Perl sections for the Perl interpreter.

Each section command paragraph starts with an equals sign, =, and a command. The commands appear in Table 13.5.

Table 13.5 POD Section Commands

Command	Usage
=head1 *heading*	Used for section headings.
=head2 *heading*	Used for section headings, smaller than =head1.
=over 4	Starts a list, indenting four spaces.
=item *text*	Item paragraph, must be in a list.
=item *	Bulleted item paragraph, must be in a list.
=item 1	Numbered item paragraph, must be in a list.
=back	Ends a list.
=pod	Perl ignores all text until next =cut.
=cut	Ends a =pod section in Perl programs.

The POD format supports very few commands. =head1 and =head2 identify section headings. =over, =item, and =back define formatted lists. The =pod and =cut commands can be used within Perl scripts. The Perl interpreter ignores all text starting with a =pod command, until after the next =cut. These commands allow you to embed documentation within a Perl script, as described in the section on documenting Perl scripts.

The third and final POD paragraph type, formatted text, is just plain text. The POD utilities will format this text, for example, justifying text to span from the left to the right margin. Unlike the verbatim paragraph text, you can embed formatting commands inside formatted paragraphs. There are only a few simple formatting commands, listed in Table 13.6.

Table 13.6 POD Text Formatting Commands

Command	Meaning
B<*text*>	Makes *text* bold.
C<*code*>	Literal code, which requires a fixed-width font.
E<*charcode*>	Character code, e.g., E<lt> for less-than sign, <.
F<*filename*>	Highlights a file name, in italics for HTML documents.
I<*text*>	Italicize *text*.
L<*linkname*>	Cross-reference link to a manual page.
L<*linkname/item*>	Cross-reference link to a manual page item.
L<*linkname/"section"*>	Cross-reference link to a manual page section.
L<*"section"*>	Cross-reference link to a section in this document.
L</*"section"*>	Cross-reference link to a section in this document.
S<*text*>	For text containing nonbreaking spaces.
X<*index*>	Marks an index entry.
Z<>	Zero-width character.

Documenting Perl Scripts

The most common usage for the POD format is documenting Perl scripts. The Perl interpreter ignores all text from a =pod command until it encounters a =cut command. Going even further, the Perl 5 interpreter ignores all text from the start of any POD section commands, such as =head1, until the =cut command.

The standard modules that come with Perl make extensive use of this fact. For example, from the **Basename.pm** module, the documentation appears almost at the beginning, as shown here:

```
package File::Basename;

=head1 NAME

Basename - parse file specifications

fileparse - split a pathname into pieces

basename - extract just the filename from a path

dirname - extract just the directory from a path

=head1 SYNOPSIS

    use File::Basename;

    ($name,$path,$suffix) = fileparse($fullname,@suffixlist)

=cut

require 5.002;
require Exporter;
@ISA = qw(Exporter);

$Fileparse_fstype = $^O;


1;
```

Only after the =cut command does the Perl code commence (highly abbreviated here). When the **Basename.pm** gets loaded by the Perl interpreter, all the documentation gets ignored and only the actual code gets executed, as you'd expect.

From the style of the major sections, NAME and SYNOPSIS, this example looks very much like an online manual entry.

You can also use the POD format to output online manual files. Thus, with one document, you can choose to output text, HTML or online manuals, a handy combination for one format.

After reading Chapter 12, you're probably amazed at how primitive the **nroff/troff** formatting commands are. I find the POD format makes for cleaner-looking documents, so long as you accept the POD conventions for online manuals.

To output a proper online manual file, you need to have major sections as required by the online manual conventions (and listed in Table 12.2). This isn't required by the POD format, just by the conventions for online manuals.

The preceding example provides these sections. As a further example, the WunderWord online manual entry from Chapter 12 appears as follows in the POD format:

```
=head1 NAME

wunderword - The most wonderful thing in the universe

=head1 SYNOPSIS

B<wunderword> [I<filename>]

B<wunderword> C<-c> I<filename>

=head1 DESCRIPTION

I<wunderword> is the most wonderful word
processor ever invented. Copious
online help is available from the Help menu.

=head1 OPTIONS

=over 4

=item Z<> [I<filename>]
```

```
If you pass a file name on the command line,
I<wunderword> will load up that file.

=item C<-c> I<filename>
command-line parameter tells I<wunderword> to
convert the file, from any other word
processor format.

=back

=head1 BUGS

Are you kidding?

=head1 AUTHOR

Eric Foster-Johnson F<erc@bigfun.com>,
F<http//:ourworld.compuserve.com/homepages/efjohnson>.
```

I find this format easier to read and create than the cryptic **nroff** commands used for most online manuals. The way you can escape writing these cryptic commands is to execute the **pod2man** script, which converts a POD document into the online manual page format. For example, you can use the following command for the preceding example manual entry:

```
$ pod2man wunderword.pod > wunderword.1
```

To display this file, you can use the following commands:

```
$ pod2man wunderword.pod > wunderword.1
$ nroff -e -man wunderword.1 | more -s

WUNDERWORD(1)  User Contributed Perl Documentation  WUNDERWORD(1)

NAME
        wunderword - The most wonderful thing in the universe

SYNOPSIS
```

```
wunderword [filename]

wunderword -c filename
```

DESCRIPTION

    wunderword is the most wonderful word processor ever
invented. Copious online help is available from the Help
menu.

OPTIONS

    [filename]

        If you pass a file name on the command line,
wunderword will load up that file.

    -c filename command-line parameter tells wunderword to
convert the file, from any other word processor
format.

BUGS

    Are you kidding?

AUTHOR

    Eric Foster-Johnson erc@bigfun.com,
http//:ourworld.compuserve.com/homepages/efjohnson.

```
17/Oct/96              perl 5.003 with                    1
```

As usual for online manual files, you need to copy the output manual file
into one of the directories used by the **man** command (as listed in the MAN-
PATH environment variable), such as **/usr/local/man/man1** for a new command. Remember to copy the output manual file, not the original POD document, because the **man** command won't be able to do much with a
POD-formatted file.

Note the odd-looking *User Contributed Perl Documentation* at the top of
the entry and *perl 5.003* at the bottom. The **pod2man** program automatically
inserts these into the document. To get rid of this, you need to edit the output manual file.

Converting POD Documents to Text

The **pod2text** Perl script converts a POD document to plain ASCII text:

```
$ pod2text wunderword.pod > wunderword.txt
```

The text appears very similar to how an online manual entry appears when you call the **man** command. There are no underlines or other special formatting, though.

Converting POD Documents to HTML

To convert POD documents to HTML, you can use the following command:

```
$ pod2html wunderword.pod > wunderword.html
```

Without any command-line parameters, the **pod2html** Perl script will convert every file in the current directory into an HTML file:

```
$ pod2html
```

Because the POD format was created to document Perl scripts, the **pod2html** script supports some conventions that make for nicer HTML output. The main limitation is that all links, set up using the L<linkname> formatting command, are assumed to be in the same directory.

When converting to HTML, L<linkname> is expanded to the following:

```
<A HREF="linkname.html">the <EM>linkname</EM> manpage</A>.
```

Note also how the link is assumed to connect to a manual page.

The **pod2html** script will also set up other links within the documents to command-line parameters. The short form of the command-line parameters in the SYNOPSIS gets linked to the longer description of the command-line parameters in the OPTIONS section. All you need to do is follow the online manual conventions, and **pod2html** will do the rest.

pod2html is particularly smart in that it can often detect email addresses and automatically create `mailto` Web links. For example, the following line in the POD file:

```
Eric Foster-Johnson F<erc@bigfun.com>
```

gets converted to a `mailto` link in the output HTML file:

```
Eric Foster-Johnson
<EM><A HREF="MAILTO:erc@bigfun.com">erc@bigfun.com</A></EM>,
```

 This is a fake email address.

N O T E

Summary

Cocoon tries to extract documentation from specially formatted comments in your C++ header files and output cross-referenced HTML-based documentation. **cxref** acts similarly for C program files.

Your should follow the **javadoc** conventions in your Java programs so that you can automatically create HTML documentation. In addition, **javadoc** has been promoted as the standard means to document your Java applications.

The POD format was created to document Perl scripts, but you can use it to create documents that can easily be converted into other formats, such as online manual entries or HTML files. If you're used to the **nroff/troff** format for online manuals, the POD format looks a lot easier to use and a lot more open for formatting.

UNIX Commands Introduced in This Chapter

cocoon

cxref

javadoc

pod2html

pod2latex

pod2man

pod2text

For More Information

Learning More

UNIX is a very large and complex system that sports many flavors from many vendors. In general, most UNIX systems work similarly, but subtle differences remain. Because of that, no book can cover all of UNIX or even all the programming tools available. The first place to look for further information is the online documentation that comes with every UNIX system. That's the source of lots of information and examples. In addition, it covers the tools you have already installed.

Internet Resources

There's a lot of material available on the Internet, but, because of the fluid nature of the Internet, links sometimes go out of date. The following sections list some of the most useful Internet resources for programming UNIX applications.

```
http://ourworld.compuserve.com/homepages/efjohnson
http://ourworld.compuserve.com/homepages/efjohnson/motif.htm
```

I try to provide valuable programming resources on my Web pages. You'll find information on programming, particularly for the X Window System and Motif, freeware applications, Linux, Perl, and Tcl (along with a few other unrelated interests of mine). The Motif page covers Motif, the X Window System, and a plethora of X Window programming APIs.

The Open Group/Motif

http://www.opengroup.org/

In 1997, the Open Group is scheduled to take over the X Window System from the X Consortium. The Open Group already develops Motif and the Common Desktop Environment.

LessTif

http://www.hungry.com/products/lesstif

A freeware implementation of Motif that is still in development.

XFree86 Consortium

http://www.XFree86.Org/

Makers of a freeware implementation of the X Window System for PC versions of UNIX, such as Linux and FreeBSD.

Cross-Platform Toolkits

The following links describe a number of toolkits that work on UNIX and other operating systems, most notably Windows.

Fresco

http://www.faslab.com/fresco/HomePage.html

A C++ toolkit based on the earlier InterViews, which also follows the CORBA object distribution architecture.

XForms

http://bragg.phys.uwm.edu/xforms

An easy-to-use simple library for creating user interface applications. XForms sacrifices some flexibility for simplicity but makes X applications very easy to create. Free for noncommercial, nonprofit use.

wxWindows

http://www.aiai.ed.ac.uk/~jacs/wxwin.html

A free cross-platform C++ toolkit. This library requires Motif, XView, or Win32. That's right, your wxWindows applications can run on UNIX and Windows (with a recompile).

V

http://www.cs.unm.edu/~wampler/vgui/vgui.html

A portable C++ GUI framework library that runs on Windows and UNIX.

Wind/U

http://www.bristol.com/Bibliography/mfc.html

Bristol's Wind/U offers the Microsoft Foundation Classes, or MFC, on UNIX.

Galaxy

http://www.visix.com/

A commercial toolkit from Visix.

Open Interface Element

http://www.neurondata.com/products/oie.htm

A commercial toolkit from Neuron Data.

zApp

http://www.roguewave.com/products/zapp/

A commercial toolkit from Rogue Wave.

Java on the Internet

Java works well for creating Internet applications, which is one reason there are many Java-related sites on the Internet.

JavaSoft

http://www.javasoft.com

Main site for JavaSoft division of Sun. You can download the Java Development Kit from this site. In addition, all the official Java documentation is online here.

Blackdown/Java for Linux

http://www.blackdown.org/java-linux.html

You can download the Java Development Kit for Linux from here.

Guavac

http://http.cs.berkeley.edu/~engberg/guavac

Guavac is a freeware Java compiler.

Kaffe

http://www.sarc.city.ac.uk/~tim/kaffe

Kaffe is a freeware Java run-time engine, which executes the Java byte codes.

Perl on the Internet

`http://ourworld.compuserve.com/homepages/efjohnson/perl.htm`

My Perl page contains a number of links to major Perl sites.

Perl Home Page

`http://www.perl.com`

The main Perl home page.

Tcl on the Internet

`http://ourworld.compuserve.com/homepages/efjohnson/tcl.htm`

My Tcl/Tk pages show how to create your own Tcl interpreter, cover cross-platform issues (I maintain the Tcl/Tk on Windows Frequently Asked Questions list), and link to major Tcl sites.

Tcl/Tk at Sun

`http://www.sunlabs.com:80/research/tcl/`

Sun Microsystems employs the Tcl/Tk team, developing new releases and porting Tcl to Windows and Macintosh platforms.

Usenet Newsgroups

In addition to the preceding Web pages, you'll find the following Usenet newsgroups contain a lot of information about UNIX and programming, as listed in Table A.1.

Table A.1 Usenet Newsgroups for Programming Information

Group	Covers
comp.unix.programmer	Programming on UNIX.
comp.lang.c++.moderated	Moderated discussion of C++ issues.
comp.software.international	Internationalization.
comp.std.unix	UNIX standards.
comp.unix.cde	The Common Desktop Environment.
comp.windows.x.motif	Programming Motif applications.
comp.windows.x	General X Window programming.
comp.windows.x.announce	X Window announcements.
comp.lang.java.announce	Java announcements.
comp.lang.java.api	The Java API.
comp.lang.java.programmer	Programming Java.
comp.os.linux.development.apps	Developing Linux applications.
comp.lang.perl.misc	Main Perl newsgroup.
comp.lang.perl.announce	Perl announcements.
comp.lang.perl.tk	Perl/Tk.
comp.lang.perl.modules	Perl add-on modules.
comp.lang.tcl	Main Tcl newsgroup.
comp.lang.tcl.announce	Tcl announcements.

Books

There are many books available on UNIX and programming. You'll see from the following lists that I'm biased on a number of subjects (being responsible for a few books of my own).

Programming Books

I've found the following books the most useful in my work:

- *Advanced Programming in the UNIX Environment*, W. Richard Stevens, Addison-Wesley, 1992. By far the best UNIX programming book.

- *UNIX Network Programming*, W. Richard Stevens, Prentice Hall, 1990. Another great book from Stevens on programming network applications, this book provides a great deal of C source code for network tasks.

- *The Standard C Library*, P. J. Plauger, Prentice Hall, 1992. Very useful for writing portable C code, this book lists the functions and header files in the standard C library.

- *The Annotated C++ Reference Manual*, Margaret A. Ellis and Bjarne Stroustrup, Addison-Wesley, 1990. A daunting book covering the definition of the C++ language. If you want to know why C++ alternatives like Java are so popular, read this book.

- *Design Patterns: Elements of Reusable Object-Oriented Software*, Erich Gamma et al., Addison-Wesley, 1995. A neat book covering object-oriented design in any language. Unlike most such books, this one is full of practical examples.

- *Software Portability with imake*, second edition, Paul DuBois, O'Reilly, 1996. If you intend to use **imake** and have trouble figuring it out, get this book from the creator of **imake**.

Java Books

If you placed all the available Java books one on top of the other, you'd probably have a stack that goes from earth to the moon. Among these books are some real turkeys and a few gems. Two of the best ones I've seen are:

- *Core Java*, Gary Cornell and Cay S. Horstmann, Prentice Hall, 1996. This is probably the best overall introduction to Java for experienced programmers.

- *Graphic Java: Mastering the AWT*, David M. Geary and Alan L. McClellan, Prentice Hall, 1997. Just about every application these days requires a graphic user interface, and this book covers Java's means to that end: the Abstract Window Toolkit, or AWT.

UNIX Books

If you're brand new to UNIX, you may need to brush up on some UNIX commands. If the concepts of `chmod` and file permissions are new to you, you should check out an introductory UNIX book, such as *Teach Yourself UNIX*, third edition, Kevin Reichard and Eric F. Johnson, MIS:Press, 1995.

For a UNIX command reference, you may be interested in *UNIX in Plain English*, Kevin Reichard and Eric F. Johnson, MIS:Press, 1994.

X Window and Motif Books

The X Window System provides the standard windowing system on UNIX, but programming X applications is by no means a trivial task. The following books should help:

- *Power Programming Motif*, second edition, Eric F. Johnson and Kevin Reichard, MIS:Press, 1993. Thick enough to stun an ox, this book covers how to create complete Motif applications and how to integrate Motif code with low-level X library calls and the PEX 3D graphics extension.
- *Advanced X Window Applications Programming*, second edition, Eric F. Johnson and Kevin Reichard, M&T Books, 1994. This book covers the low-level X library.
- *UNIX System Administrator's Guide to X*, Eric F. Johnson and Kevin Reichard, M&T Books, 1994. The X Window System is great at providing a common graphical windowing system on UNIX (and other) platforms, but it's difficult to figure out how to configure your environment. This book shows the where's and how's for configuring X.
- *About Face: The Essentials of User Interface Design*, Alan Cooper, IDG Books, 1995. The best user interface book I've seen in a long time.
- *Visual Design with OSF/Motif*, Shiz Kobara, Addison-Wesley, 1991. This book shows how to make your Motif programs look a lot better than the default resource values shipped with the Motif libraries. This book is essential if you work with Motif.

Perl Books

- *Cross-Platform Perl*, by Eric F. Johnson, M&T Books, 1996, CD-ROM included. I'm biased, but this is the only Perl book I know of that covers Perl on both UNIX and Windows.

- *Perl 5 Desktop Reference*, Johan Vromans, O'Reilly, 1996. By far the tiniest and most useful Perl book, this microscopic text provides a quick reference guide to Perl; it is very useful.

- *Programming Perl*, second edition, Larry Wall, Tom Christiansen, and Randal L. Schwartz, O'Reilly, 1996. This very dense book contains a lot of useful information by the creator of Perl, Larry Wall. Much of this material comes from the online Perl reference material, but it provides many interesting Perl scripts you can use for ideas and examples. The updated version covers Perl 5.

Tcl/Tk

There are only a few books available on Tcl and Tk:

- *Graphical Applications with Tcl and Tk*, Eric F. Johnson, M&T Books, 1996.

- *Tcl and the Tk Toolkit*, John Ousterhout, Addison-Wesley, 1994.

- *Practical Programming with Tcl and Tk*, Brent Welch, Prentice Hall, 1995.

Version Control

Applying RCS and SCCS, by Don Bolinger and Tan Bronson, O'Reilly, 1995. One of the few books on RCS, this tome probably goes into far greater depth that you'll ever need on version control issues.

Performance Analysis

The Art of Computer Systems Performance Analysis, by Raj Jain, Wiley, 1991. This large book has many useful tips for analyzing performance.

Text-Formatting

Text Processing and Typesetting with UNIX, David Barron and Mike Rees, Addison-Wesley, 1987. This book covers **nroff** and **troff**, two UNIX text-formatting packages, along with the **eqn**, **neqn**, and **pic** preprocessors.

INDEX

A

Abstract Window Toolkit, 53, 57, 245

  see also Java

AC_CONFIG_SUBDIRS, 240

AC_CONONICAL_SYSTEM, 240

AC_INIT, 239, 240

AC_OUTPUT, 239, 240, 241

AC_PROG_CXX, 239, 240

AC_PROG_CC, 239, 240

AC_PROG_RANLIB, 240

  see also **ranlib**

Aegis, 229-230

  see Revision Control

aliases, 18

a.out, 46

appletviewer, 55, 57-58

apropos, 13-14

ar, 45-46

ATAC, 183

atacCC, 183

Athena library, 52

autoconf, 236-244

config.in.h file, 244

configure, 236, 237, 238, 241, 242

configure.in file, 239-240

Makefile.in file, 238, 239, 241-244

setting up, 238-244

@VARIABLE@, 241

autoheader, 244

autoscan, 244

awk, 110

AWT (*see* Abstract Window Toolkit)

B

bash, 9

bdiff, 193

C

C,

  ANSI, 232

  compiling C programs 36-38

  linking, 38-40

C++,

  compiling C++ programs 37-38

G

How to Use the CD-ROM

The accompanying CD-ROM uses **Rock Ridge extensions** to the standard ISO-9660 format. This allows for longer file names than the old-fashion DOS eight-character names with three-character extension limits. This was necessary because many UNIX packages use long file and directory names. In addition, just about every package comes with a Makefile (see Chapter 3 on **make**), and the name Makefile itself already violates the straight ISO-9960 conventions. So, if you see file names such as **INTEGER-;1**, your system does not support the CD's Rock Ridge extended file names. All the files are still available. It will just require more work to correct the names when you copy files to your hard disk.

You'll find these main subdirectories on the CD-ROM:

- **archive**, file archiving and compression tools like **gzip**.
- **compare**, file comparison tools.
- **doc_tool**, documentation tools discussed in Chapter 13.
- **editors**, text editors such as **emacs**.
- **java**, the Java Development Kit.
- **src_cntrl**, source controls tools such as RCS.
- **configure**, GNU Autoconf and m4.
- **debug**, debuggers.
- **install**, installation utilities.
- **make**, GNU **make** and **pmake**, a parallel make.
- **mem_leak**, memory usage test tools.
- **perl**, Perl 5.
- **texttool**, text tools like **ctags** and **less**.